'*The Persistence of Nationalism* convincingly shows a way out of the either/or quandary between nationalism and cosmopolitanism by bringing the city back to the centre of the debate. By investigating how people actually develop elective affinities, affective investments and identifications through quotidian encounters, it shows how people negotiate workable terms of living together. This is the best critical introduction to nationalism from an urban perspective.'

Engin Isin, The Open University, UK

The Persistence of Nationalism

This is a book about the difficulties of thinking and acting politically in ways that refuse the politics of nationalism. It offers a detailed study of how contemporary attempts by theorists of cosmopolitanism, globalism and multiculturalism to go beyond the nation often reproduce key aspects of a nationalist imaginary. It argues that the challenge of resisting nationalism will require more than a shift in the scale of politics – from the national up to the global, or down to the local – and more than a shift in how we count politics – to an emphasis on diversity and multiculturalism. In order to avoid the grip of 'nationalist thinking', the book argues that we need to reopen the question of what it means to imagine community. It does so by way of various encounters with urban life.

Set against the backdrop of the imaginative geographies of the 'War on Terror', the book shows how critical interventions often work in collaboration with nationalist politics. It claims that a nationalist imaginary includes powerful under-standings of freedom, subjectivity, sovereignty and political space/time which must all be placed under question if we want to avoid reproducing ideas about 'us' and 'them'. Drawing on insights from feminist, cultural and postcolonial studies as well as critical approaches to International Relations and Geography, this book presents a unique and refreshing approach to the politics of nationalism.

Angharad Closs Stephens is a Lecturer in the Geography Department at Durham University, UK.

Interventions
Edited by: Jenny Edkins,
Aberystwyth University
and Nick Vaughan-Williams,
University of Warwick

'As Michel Foucault has famously stated, "knowledge is not made for under-standing; it is made for cutting." In this spirit the Edkins–Vaughan-Williams Interventions series solicits cutting edge, critical works that challenge mainstream understandings in international relations. It is the best place to contribute post disciplinary works that think rather than merely recognize and affirm the world recycled in IR's traditional geopolitical imaginary.'

Michael J. Shapiro, University of Hawai'i at Mãnoa, USA

The series aims to advance understanding of the key areas in which scholars work-ing within broad critical post-structural and post-colonial traditions have chosen to make their interventions, and to present innovative analyses of important topics.

Titles in the series engage with critical thinkers in philosophy, sociology, poli-tics and other disciplines and provide situated historical, empirical and textual studies in international politics.

Critical Theorists and International Relations
Edited by Jenny Edkins and Nick Vaughan-Williams

Ethics as Foreign Policy
Britain, the EU and the other
Dan Bulley

Universality, Ethics and International Relations
A grammatical reading
Véronique Pin-Fat

The Time of the City
Politics, philosophy, and genre
Michael J. Shapiro

Governing Sustainable Development
Partnership, protest and power at the world summit
Carl Death

Alternative Accountabilities in Global Politics
The scars of violence
Brent J. Steele

Celebrity Humanitarianism
The ideology of global charity
Ilan Kapoor

Deconstructing International Politics
Michael Dillon

The Politics of Exile
Elizabeth Dauphinee

Democratic Futures
Revisioning democracy promotion
Milja Kurki

Postcolonial Theory
A critical introduction
Edited by Sanjay Seth

More than Just War
Narratives of the just war and military life
Charles A. Jones

Deleuze & Fascism
Security: war: aesthetics
Edited by Brad Evans and Julian Reid

Feminist International Relations
'Exquisite Corpse'
Marysia Zalewski

The Persistence of Nationalism
From imagined communities to urban encounters
Angharad Closs Stephens

Interpretive Approaches to Global Climate Governance
Reconstructing the greenhouse
Edited by Chris Methmann, Delf Rothe and Benjamin Stephan

Postcolonial Encounters with International Relations
The politics of transgression
Alina Sajed

The Persistence of Nationalism

From imagined communities to urban encounters

Angharad Closs Stephens

LONDON AND NEW YORK

First published 2013
by Routledge
2 Park Square, Milton Park, Abingdon, Oxon OX14 4RN

Simultaneously published in the USA and Canada
by Routledge
711 Third Avenue, New York, NY 10017

Routledge is an imprint of the Taylor & Francis Group, an informa business

British Library Cataloguing in Publication Data
A catalogue record for this book is available from the British Library

Library of Congress Cataloging in Publication Data
Stephens, Angharad Closs.
The persistence of nationalism: from imagined communities to urban
encounters / Angharad Closs Stephens.
p. cm. – (Interventions)
Includes bibliographical references and index.
1. Nationalism. 2. Internationalism. I. Title.
JC311.S828 2013
320.54–dc23
2012035802

ISBN: 978-0-415-62345-2 (hbk)
ISBN: 978-0-203-57538-3 (ebk)

Typeset in Times New Roman
by Fish Books Ltd., Enfield

Printed and bound in Great Britain by MPG Printgroup

I mam,
ac er cof am mamgu

Contents

Figures

Acknowledgements

I spent the academic year that followed the events of 11 September 2001 studying for a Masters Degree in Gender Studies at the London School of Economics. My first thanks must go to Clare Hemmings and Anne Phillips for the inspirational teaching I encountered there. Although I knew that there was some connection between the questions I had about nationalism and the literatures I was reading on sex, gender and sexualities, I couldn't articulate them then. I am still grateful that my PhD supervisor Rob Walker appreciated that I had a question even when I had very little idea how to go about formulating it. I owe an enormous debt to him for pointing me to the depths and breadths of the problem and for encouraging me to follow my own path. Special thanks also to Kara Shaw for her hospitality and friendship during my visit to the University of Victoria, British Columbia and to Sanjay Seth, who examined the final thesis, for his critical comments and generosity.

Thanks to the Economic and Social Research Council for funding the PhD and to SPIRE at Keele University for hosting me. There are many more people who have offered advice, support, friendship or paid work at different points and, in doing so, kept me going. Thanks to Ash Amin, Jens Bartelson, David Campbell, Angharad Davies, Mick Dillon, Jenny Edkins, Steve Graham, Branwen Gruffydd Jones, Xavier Guillaume, Jef Huysmans, Kimberly Hutchings, Naeem Inayatullah, Engin Isin, Emily Jackson, Rachel Jones, Debbie Lisle, Sam Opondo, Tim Parkinson, Mustapha Pasha, Matthew Patterson, Chris Rumford, Mike Shapiro, Vicki Squire, Cindy Weber and Maja Zehfuss. Thank you to my good friends Andrew Neal, Nisha Shah and Nick Vaughan-Williams for following the progress of the book from its beginnings, and to Carolyn Pedwell, for her love, generosity and supreme editing skills as well as for all our city walks. I still miss my beautiful friend Catrin Prys Jones (1976–2006) enormously.

Finally, I am grateful to Louise Amoore, Ben Anderson, Rachel Colls, Martin Coward, Paul Harrison, Colin McFarlane and Stuart Elden for helping to make this a better book. They make it a joy to go to work, along with my other colleagues at Durham University Geography Department: Mike Crang, Chris Dunn, Adam Holden, Kathrin Hörschelmann, Antony Long, Gordon MacLeod, Cheryl McEwan, Rachel Pain, Joe Painter, Marcus Power, Jonathan Rigg, Lynn Staeheli, John Thompson and Divya Tolia-Kelly.

My journey of unlearning nationalism has only taken the shape that it has because I've been able to share all the ideas in this book with Rhodri Davies. I thank him for introducing me to so many imaginative worlds and for creating space and time for me to get on with writing. I'm also grateful to my brother Wil Stephens for challenging all my political convictions along the way and to my mother, Elan Closs Stephens, for all she has made possible for me. She was the first to teach me how to read critically and I dedicate this book to her in gratitude and admiration for all the love, strength and courage she has shown. It is also dedicated to the memory of my grandmother, Carol Stephens (1916–2011), who passed away just as my daughter Elliw arrived in the world. *Elliw fach, rwyt ti'n werth y byd i gyd yn grwn.*

Earlier versions of Chapters 4, 5 and 6 were published in *Alternatives: Global, Local, Political*;[1] *Environment and Planning D: Society and Space*;[2] and *Citizenship Studies*,[3] respectively. I'm grateful to all publishers for granting permission to publish some of that material here in revised and extended form.

The cover of this book features the work of photographer Rachel Jones (www.rachelsarahjones.com) on the urban experience of the everyday. This picture is from the Magenta Series, no. 1.

Introduction

The persistence of nationalist imaginaries

> It is a pretty safe bet that criticism of other people's nationalism, in the name of our own capacity to transcend it or the idea that we have already moved beyond it, is only another figure of nationalism.
>
> Étienne Balibar, *We, the People of Europe?*

> S/he is 'outside' the law, but the law maintains this 'outside' within itself. In effect, s/he embodies the law, not as an entitled subject, but as an enacted testimony to the law's uncanny capacity to produce only those rebellions that it can guarantee will – out of fidelity – defeat themselves and those subjects who, utterly subjected, have no choice but to reiterate the law of their genesis.
>
> Judith Butler, *Gender Trouble*

The problem

This is a book about the difficulties of escaping nationalism. It asks, what is it about nationalism that secures its enduring force in contemporary global politics? Or, put another way, why should nationalism appear persistent, despite the many different attempts over the past quarter-century or so at contesting its founding assumptions? A quick glance at some of the most intense political issues of our times would suggest that nationalism continues to be a problem: these include the Israel/Palestine conflict, the aftermath of the most recent wars in Afghanistan (2001–) and Iraq (2003–), the wave of demonstrations that have come to be known as the 'Arab Spring', and the tensions between those at the core of 'Europe' and its peripheries as part of the current global financial crisis. Despite the abundant work from the 1980s onwards on recasting understandings of identity as contingent and performed rather than stable and solid, nationalism remains pervasive and pernicious. What is it about nationalism, then, that secures this capacity to offer a persuasive narrative, and to keep on structuring the terms of political assembly and struggle?[1]

This book engages the concept of nationalism, as both a discourse of power and as a discourse of critique. As such, nationalism is understood as a tool for the state to discriminate between 'insiders' and 'outsiders', and also as a way of expressing critique of the state. This study therefore begins from the premise that nationalism relies on the principle of state sovereignty. As Anthony W. Marx has elaborated, nationalism can either coincide with a state to provide legitimacy and acceptance of the state's monopoly on the use of force, or, when it doesn't coincide with the state, it can delegitimize, potentially threatening that state's coercive power (2003). However, 'whether as a sentiment inspiring state building or justifying existing states, nationalism implies the ideal of a "nation-state" in which mass allegiance and institutional power coincide' (2003: 7). This point is affirmed by the geographer Matthew Sparke, who argues that the hyphen in 'nation-state' indicates more than an etymological convention: it points to 'powerful world-making processes' (2005: xii). This book addresses nationalism as a concept that relies on the idea of the sovereign state and which depends also upon a particular political imagination. Yet, as we will see in forthcoming chapters, nationalism can appear in many different forms. Indeed, one of the central arguments developed in the course of this book is that different attempts at going beyond the nation, by way of the 'global' or the 'cosmopolitan' for example, often contain a residual nationalism. This is because the idea that 'we' belong to a community that can be distinguished clearly from 'theirs' is not easily defeated or overcome. In this sense, nationalism continues to dominate different ways of expressing who we are and how we understand our relationship to others in the world.

The Persistence of Nationalism develops its discussion against the backdrop of the 'Global War on Terror'[2] – a war that was waged by the United States and its allies in response to the plane crashes of 11 September 2001 into the World Trade Center of New York City, the Pentagon in Washington City and in a field in Pennsylvania. This concept was first deployed by the former US President George W. Bush in a speech to a joint session of Congress on 20 September 2001.[3] Used initially to justify a war with Afghanistan in October 2001, it was also used to mobilize public opinion behind the war in Iraq in 2003, despite the fact that there was no evidence of a link between al-Qaeda, who were held responsible for the events of 9/11, and Saddam Hussein, then President of Iraq. By the time of the election of US President Barack Obama in November 2008, the concept of a 'War on Terror' was considered politically invidious and this led to a decline in use of the term by the US administration and also by the UK government.[4] But this does not mean that the policies pursued and passed in the name of the 'War on Terror' have in any way come to an end; indeed, in 2012, it was reported that members of the Obama administration understood the war to be only at its 'midway point'.[5] Many of the counter-terrorism measures passed in the UK and in the US under the claim that we were living in 'exceptional times' now seem to have been made permanent, including the use of Guantanamo Bay as a detention camp, enhanced powers of surveillance, powers to restrict the movement of those suspected of a connection to terrorism and charges related to the 'encouragement' of terrorism.[6]

The political climate of the 'War on Terror' forms an interesting point of departure for this book because of the way in which it presented a 'heightened nationalist discourse' (Butler, 2006: xi). In the US especially, this was expressed in the thousands of American flags that decorated driveways, schools and apartment blocks in the immediate aftermath of 9/11. It is also ingrained in the decision to build the commemorative One World Trade Center to 1,776 feet, marking the year of American Independence. Whilst other countries may have a different relationship to their national flags, what emerged as a common experience across many states in the global north in response to the events of 9/11, was an atmosphere of 'comprehensive suspicion and punitive orientation' towards Muslims – or, to put it more accurately, minority peoples assumed to be 'Muslim' (Grewal, 2005; Puar, 2007; Volpp, 2002). In this sense, the discourses of 'us' and 'them' were described by the geographer Derek Gregory as representing the 'return of the colonial past' (Gregory, 2004: 11). Indeed, Gregory suggests that the 'War on Terror' was *epitomized* in the 'imaginative geographies' of 'us' and 'them', 'civilization' and 'barbarism', 'Good' and 'Evil' and, as such, performed a revitalized form of Orientalism (2004: 11). The feminist philosopher Judith Butler argues further that this climate of heightened nationalism made it especially difficult to express any dissent or critique of the state (in the US specifically). This is because critical positions were routinely portrayed as disloyal to the nation (2006: 1–2). With this point, Butler touches upon the difficulties of developing a critique of nationalist thought, and how nationalism often structures the terms of political debate. This is a point that will become central to this book. It seems that nationalism often appears as something 'we' all have to 'go along with', especially in 'exceptional times'.

This book explicitly addresses this question of how we might go about developing a critique of nationalism. Among the many different expressions of resistance to the heightened nationalism of the 'War on Terror' was a novel called *The Lacuna* (2009) by the multiple-award-winning American author, Barbara Kingsolver, and a short film, titled *11'09"01*, (2002) by the English film director and winner of the Palme d'Or, Ken Loach. Quite deliberately, Kingsolver decides to focus on, among other things, the hunt for communists carried out by the House of Un-American Activities Committee in the 1950s. In doing so, her novel reveals how the imaginative geographies of the 'War on Terror' have a longer history and that the practice of creating an enemy and a sense of suspicion around the 'other' was ready and available long before the attacks on the World Trade Center and the Pentagon took place (a point that is affirmed by Devji, 2005). Similarly, Ken Loach's short film, produced as part of a collection from different parts of the world, includes footage of another 9/11 – in this case, the military coup orchestrated by the United States on 11 September 1973 against the democratically elected President of Chile, Salvador Allende. Loach's film reminds us that the word 'terrorist' is highly ambiguous and historically contingent. Along with Kingsolver's novel, he demonstrates that political life has been cast as a battle between a different 'us' and a different 'them' in other historical contexts and other geographical locations.

Both these interventions serve as cautionary tales in reading the politics of present times. They invite a critique of 'America' and its attempt at policing all forms of dissent. However, whilst Loach's film in particular raises questions about the identification of 'us' and 'them', what is problematic about it is that it nevertheless keeps the terms of this debate in place. Whilst it may be tempting to pin blame on 'America', the problem with this critical response is that it reifies the impression that world politics can be summed up as a battle between self-contained cultures at war with one another. As with Kingsolver's novel, it is structured within the terms of 'us' and 'them'. Such critical interventions present us with a problem, because in criticizing a scene of heightened nationalism, they risk reproducing another form of nationalism (Balibar, 2004). This suggests that a critique of nationalism will need to go further than contest who is identified as 'us' or 'them'; it must also address 'the terms in which the opposition is framed' (Butler, 2006: 2).

The trouble with avoiding an investigation of the terms of critique is that critical work risks performing what has been described as a form of 'Orientalism in the mirror' (Cooper, 2008). What this suggests is that, in appealing to the same set of terms, critical work risks reproducing those discourses and ideas it initially set out to contest. Effectively, then, this forms a questions about political imagination. Indeed, the point is put in exactly these terms by the Indian novelist and activist Arundhati Roy in her response to the political climate that followed the events of 9/11 (2002). In her article, Roy compares the way in which critics of nuclear bombs, big dams, corporate globalization and Hindu fascism in India are regularly branded as 'anti-national' with the way in which those who criticized the actions of the US government in the wake of the events of 9/11 were understood as performing an 'anti-Americanism'. She then argues that the term 'anti-Americanism' represents a 'failure of the imagination' because it forms

> an inability to see the world in terms other than those that the establishment has set out for you . . . If you don't love us, you hate us. If you're not good you're evil. If you're not with us, you're with the terrorists.

Roy's point about the 'failure of imagination' is particularly useful as it indicates how different attempts at thinking beyond the nation risk leading us towards another version of nationalism. As the post-colonial critic Pal Ahluwalia puts it, it is the risk of becoming co-opted by the dominant forms and cultural discourses of Western liberalism (Ahluwalia, 2007). This book aims to examine this problem in greater depth, in order to ask two questions. First, how might we resist nationalist thought and second, how might we understand coexistence differently.

Approaching nationalism

Theorists of nationalism including Benedict Anderson have long argued that nationalism cannot be aligned with other political ideologies – such as conservativism, liberalism or socialism (1991: 12). Similarly, Michael Billig points to the 'banality' of nationalism, arguing that the performance of national identity takes place all around us, at both micro and macro scales (1995). Such interventions are useful insofar as they suggest that nationalism involves more than an exclusive and extreme ideology. Accepting these starting points, this book also goes further to argue that there is much more at stake in the study of nationalism than to reveal the 'constructed' nature of national identities.[7] This book instead seeks to situate nationalism as part of a broader imaginary, one that relies on the assumption of state sovereignty and involves a particular way of seeing the world. This way of seeing is distinctly modern in the sense that this world is understood to be separate from the next, and the whole world is imagined as part of one map and ordered along a continuous scale (Agnew, 1998). As the geographer John Agnew outlines, it forms a way of thinking about the world that emerged alongside capitalism in Europe and was informed by the European encounter with the rest of the world (1998). This book argues that nationalism needs to be approached in the context of this imaginary, and in particular, the idea of political community as spatially bounded and political communities as orderable along a continuous scale.[8] The first part of the book will unpack the different elements that contribute to what I describe as this 'nationalist imaginary' and pay particular attention to ideas of space and time. This is important in order to develop the second part of the book, which argues that the notion of community as bounded, and as involving a promise that unfolds in time, can return in several attempts at going 'beyond' nationalism.

My use of the term 'imagination' draws on the work of others who have developed what might loosely be described as a 'post-structuralist' approach to reading world politics, including Derek Gregory's study of 'imaginative geographies' (2004, 1994), Rob Walker's work on 'the modern political imagination' (2009) and John Agnew's study of 'the modern geopolitical imaginary' (1998).[9] These writers might all be described as sharing an interest in questioning the foundational claims that make particular ways of understanding the world possible and paying attention to ideas of space and time. As such, they are interested in how state-centred, and explicitly modern, ways of seeing the world become ossified, and in what might be done to lessen the grip of these prevailing ways of seeing and understanding the world around us (Agnew, 2007; Shaw, 2004). In short, this book seeks to trace the connections between particular imaginations of the spatial/temporal and the imagination of the political (Massey, 2005). In terms of its focus on nationalism and the politics of identity, the book follows broadly in the approaches undertaken by Campbell (1998a, 1998b), Connolly (1991), Shapiro (2004) and Sparke (2005).

We can explore an example of how ideas of space/time structure particular imaginations of the political by returning to the case of the 'War on Terror'. As Derek Gregory outlines in *The Colonial Present*, the imaginative geographies of 'us' and 'them' were in this particular climate underpinned by an idea of time as homogenous and linear (2004). This understanding of time worked to enable that 'unfortunate Western habit of locating others in the past' (Hindess, 2008: 201) and describing 'others' as 'backward', 'pre-modern' or 'on the wrong side of history'. This practice is not unique to the 'War on Terror' but is, rather, widely prevalent and forms a way of establishing distance between identity groups that are assumed to be bounded, self-contained and separate. The practice draws upon Enlightenment ideas about civilization and progress, which, as Judith Butler notes, 'define themselves over and against a premodern temporality that they produce for the purposes of their own self legitimation' (2008: 1). This would suggest that ideas of time matter in animating particular narratives of world politics. Whilst several other studies have paid careful attention to the spatial politics of the 'War on Terror' (Gregory and Pred, 2007) – in relation to the camp (Razack, 2008), the changing nature of the border (Amoore, 2006; Vaughan-Williams, 2009b) and the politics of territory (Cowen and Gilbert 2008; Elden, 2009) – there have been far fewer discussions of how the 'War on Terror' was also mobilized through particular ideas of time (Jarvis, 2009; Oza, 2007; Puar, 2007). Yet, as will become evident in the course of this book, questions about time and space cannot be neatly separated.

The book therefore develops an approach to nationalism that goes beyond familiar debates about whether the nation is old or new, real or invented, good or bad, ethnic or civic. As Chapter 1 demonstrates in more detail, these binary choices don't necessarily enable a critical approach to nationalism, because the centrality of the debate tends to cast attention away from questions about the force and politics of nationalism.[10] Thus, whilst questions about the anger, passions and rage that form part of nationalism tend to form a recurring undercurrent in studies of nations and nationalism, for example when Benedict Anderson asks how nations might 'command such profound emotional legitimacy' (1991: 4), such questions often get folded into the aim of defining, classifying or explaining nationalism's historical development.[11] Whilst such work is undoubtedly important, attempts at definition, classification or historical explanation can nevertheless leave us still unable to account for the *persistence* of nationalism in the contemporary world. For this reason, the book argues that critical questions about the politics of nationalism cannot adequately be addressed from within the disciplinary confines of studies of nations and nationalism.

The distinction between 'ethnic' and 'civic' forms of nationalism marks a prevailing and especially limiting entry point to debates in this field. This is because ideas about 'ethnicity' hover around even the most self-proclaimed 'civic' accounts of nationalism. As Arjun Appadurai argues, the distinction between civic and ethnic nationalism is misleading as there is an 'inherent ethnicist tendency in all ideologies of nationalism' (2006: 4). He goes on to claim that we can't begin to understand what happened in Rwanda and the Balkans in the 1990s if we suggest that ideas of ethnic purity only form part of some 'exceptional' nations. According to Appadurai, we must appreciate that 'all nations, under some conditions, demand whole-blood transfusions' (2006: 4). Appadurai's provocative remarks that all nationalisms carry an 'ethnicist tendency' will make some people uneasy, especially those who are keen to defend 'progressive' attempts to mobilize in the name of the nation.[12] But Appadurai's point is important because he implies that cases of ethnic nationalism cannot be explained away as 'bad nationalisms' or as examples of nationalism gone wrong. Rather, there are problems that are *inherent* to nationalist thought, and in the assumption that political life is made up of self-sufficient cultures that find their home in a territorial unit.

In this, Appadurai's remarks concur with those of the philosopher Étienne Balibar (1991), who argues that all nations require an ethnic base. Whilst it is well established in studies of nationalism that the idea of the nation is an invention (Gellner, 1983; Hobsbawm and Ranger, 1992) and that it will need to be narrated and performed into existence (Bhabha, 1990; Billig, 1995), the point that Balibar makes is that the idea of a nation will not only have to be invented but also *imposed*. He argues that all nationalisms must establish a 'fictive ethnicity' because, without one, the idea of a nation would simply make no sense. In his words, it 'would appear precisely only as an idea of an arbitrary abstraction; patriotism's appeal would be addressed to no one' (1991: 96). Balibar's argument suggests that, for nationalism to be nationalism, what needs to be secured is 'the effect of unity by virtue of which the people will appear, in everyone's eyes, "as a people", that is, as the basis and origin of political power' (1991: 94). In sum, Balibar's and Appadurai's interventions demonstrate that questions about the civic or ethnic, good or bad, real or imagined basis of nationalism largely miss the point. *All* nationalisms must in the first instance produce a sense of unity.[13] It is this capacity to conjure a sense of unity that a robust critique of nationalism will have to contest.

Nationalism and being political

Whilst the point about the construction of the nation is well established in the social sciences generally, Étienne Balibar and Arjun Appadurai's approaches address the *politics* of this process. As demonstrated, what they help to make clear is that, regardless of how we go about 'imagining' a community, an account of community will *have* to be established in order for nationalist politics to take place. This point begins to suggest how the problem of nationalism extends beyond self-consciously 'nationalistic' positions. Indeed, this book addresses the different ways in which nationalism keeps on offering the terms through which political theorists (and activists) articulate and practise politics. In doing so, it explores how nationalism often forms the terms of *critiques* of nationalist thought. The key point is not to suggest that mobilizing under the category of the nation is always problematic but rather to engage the broader question of 'being political' (Isin, 2002).[14] The book therefore draws on the approaches outlined by post-structural theorists of international relations,[15] feminist theorists[16] and post-colonial theorists[17] by enquiring into how nationalism often forms the conditions that must be met in order to make a claim about equality, rights or justice. To put it another way, this book is interested in how nationalism persistently structures different imaginations of the political.

This is not in any way a 'new' problem; in fact, the problem has a long history. It can be explored through the case of the hundreds of political movements all over the world mobilizing around a national identity in order to resist the homogenizing forces of larger nation-states or of global capital. For example, in the demand for independence presented by nationalist political movements, both the problem and the solution are understood in statist terms. Or, put differently, the principle of correspondence between identity and territory forms both what such movements seek to challenge – for example, in the argument that a particular constituency has been incorporated into the 'wrong' state – and, at the same time, what they desire – a state of one's own. Another of Ken Loach's films, *The Wind that Shakes the Barley* (2006) offers a further example of this problem. This film recounts the struggle for Home Rule in Ireland in the early twentieth century (and was (deliberately) released against the backdrop of the Iraq War in 2003). In the film, one of the leading characters exclaims: 'All we're changing is the accents of the powerful and the colour of the flag.' This line highlights a central dilemma for insurgent nationalist movements. Whilst nationalism may provide the tools for resisting the state, it also works in service of the state, suggesting that only the narrowest forms of change are possible.[18] The problem is that the idea of politics as a battle between 'us' and 'them' remains firmly in place. As Partha Chatterjee once argued in relation to anti-colonial movements in India, this presents us with a question about political imagination. As he puts it, if nationalism forms both the problem and the solution, then 'where in all this is the working of imagination, the intellectual process of creation?' (1993: 21). Why should we assume that nationalism forms the only model for organizing politically?

This problem was also addressed by Edward Said, writing about the politics of the Palestinian liberation movement. In one particular article, Said warns that nationalism often forms the only recognizable language for making a claim heard on behalf of a culture that finds itself under threat of extinction (1990). Yet, as he makes clear, there are high risks in framing a political struggle on such terms. As he puts it, the 'violently dangerous and awful trap' of national-ist politics is that it reinforces 'a kind of native identity which becomes tyrannical in the end and of course dissolves or occludes important questions as well as issues of class, race, gender, and property' (1990: 150). This idea of the 'awful trap' of nationalist politics is useful because it suggests that nationalism relies upon a model of political identity that can also end up being oppressive.[19] As Raymond Williams similarly argues, the problem in appealing to a sense of distinctive identity as a means for *countering* the force of the state is that this very image of identity as stable and continuous relies upon a political discourse that emerged alongside nation-states (2003: 19). As Edward Said and Raymond Williams both suggest, then, there is more at stake than the risk of deploying an 'essentialist' understanding of identity. The problem lies with reproducing this nationalist account of what politics must be about and how 'identities' may be understood.

How, then, are we to understand the persistence of nationalist political struggles for autonomy, recognition and self-determination in the context of simultaneous claims that we are living in post-national or global times? As the sociologist and feminist theorist Vikki Bell has argued, it seems inadequate to dismiss such move-ments as performing a nationalist politics that critical theorists have long learned to deconstruct or leave behind (2007). As she puts it, 'it feels like an abdication to write as if the world were archaic and has yet to catch up with the values espoused in political philosophical tracts – bemoaning "we can write beyond identity, if only the world could live beyond it?"' (2007: 32). She goes on to say that it's imperative to understand 'why living beyond identity is, for many, neither attractive nor conceivable' (2007: 32). Bell's argument is interesting because it touches upon the question of how ideas of time underpin different critical interventions. For example, reflecting on the way in which the critique of essentialism has become 'mainstream' in sociology and cultural studies specifically, she warns that there is a danger in moving too quickly from the desire to avoid 'essentialist' understandings of 'community' or 'identity' towards 'a refusal or denial of the connectedness, the multiplicity of existing' (2007, p. 31–2). Bell is right to warn against the assumption that questions of 'identity' have already been addressed and that 'we' enlightened cosmopolitans can now all 'move on'.[20] This framing of the problem is indebted to a form of nationalist thought, a point that will be further unpacked in the course of the book. This suggests that a critical approach to nationalism needs to be suspicious of claims that we have already 'been there and done that' (Hindess, 2008). For these reasons, it is necessary for critical work to be attuned to the ideas of space and time that underpin different political interventions.

From nation to city

The first part of this book, 'Unpacking nationalist imaginaries', addresses the broad imaginary that enables nationalist thought. It seeks to locate that imaginary within a narrative about the presumed necessity of the state and about modern life as disenchanted. It also pays specific attention to the ways in which the nation is enabled by a homogenous, linear account of time (Anderson, 1991). This discussion of a 'nationalist imaginary' is developed through the work of Ernest Gellner, Max Weber and Jean-Jacques Rousseau, in Chapters 1, 2 and 3 respectively. Subsequently, the second part of the book, 'Contesting nationalist imaginaries', engages with different attempts at thinking beyond nationalism. More specifically, Chapters 4, 5 and 6 of the book stage encounters with urban life as offering another example of what it might mean to live together.[21] Drawing on the work of others that have turned to the city as a site for rethinking the politics of identity and difference (Amin and Thrift, 2002; Coward, 2009a; Isin, 2002; Magnusson, 2012; Massey, 2005, 2007; Mbembe and Nuttall, 2004; Simone, 2004; Young, 1990), this section considers what precisely is involved in this task of thinking politics beyond nationalism.

Of course, there is nothing new in the idea of thinking the political through the site of the city. Although citizenship in its modern sense is intertwined with the concept of nationality, and dependent on membership in a nation-state, for Plato and Aristotle as for Rousseau, it was originally conceived in relation to the political space of the city – of Athens, or Geneva. As Holston and Appadurai remind us (1999), in order to establish a new and modern relationship between nationality and citizenship, cities had to be actively displaced and usurped as the locus of political identity and authority. This book introduces the site of the city through the work of Jean-Jacques Rousseau, and at the end of the first part of this book, as it notes that Rousseau was aware that urban life raises significant questions about what it means to live in common. Whilst Rousseau chooses to avoid the urban conditions of 'continual flux', and to yearn for a life of harmony and stillness, this book asks: what would it mean to take movement, transitoriness, and unpredictability seriously as conditions for thinking what it means to be political? Whereas social and political theory have tended to be more concerned with order, continuity, and stability, this book aims to think politics as something that takes place in time rather than as an attempt to master time, such as through the further unfurling of the nation. The city is thus introduced as a site that prompts ways of imagining community otherwise (see also Ahmed and Fortier, 2003; Corlett, 1989; Derrida, 1997).

Thus, in turning to the site of the city, the aim is not to invite a 'scaling up' or a 'scaling down' of the political. In this sense, it is important to remember that the city is not a mutually distinct political space, and that cities form key sites for imagining the national (Massey, 2007). Similarly, cities have served as central hubs from which twentieth-century attempts at homogenizing populations have been carried out (Coward, 2009b). Whilst cities are routinely presented – in Sociology and Human Geography in particular – as potentially interesting on account of their 'mixture', one of the main contributions of this book lies in arguing that simply celebrating 'mixture' won't be enough. Indeed, as Chapters 4 and 5 in particular argue, multicultural narratives of identity often rely on key elements of a 'nationalist imaginary', and even provide 'new grammars for national identity' (Fortier, 2008: 4). This suggests that it won't be sufficient to replace the image of the nation with the image of the city, or to replace a focus on 'identity' with a focus on 'difference'. What is required is a more careful study of the way in which 'mixture' is conceptualized, and whether it invites an understanding of politics that undoes the space/time of nationalism.

Outline of the book

Overall, the first part of the book develops what is primarily a theoretical engagement with nationalism, whilst the second part is animated by different empirical examples, drawn primarily but not exclusively from the political context of the global 'War on Terror'. The first part of the book thus seeks to expand the question of imagination, by showing that there is more at stake than different subjects 'constructing' an image of the nation. The second part of the book engages with examples of urban cosmopolitanism to open up the question of what it means to be-in-the-world (Mbembe and Nuttall, 2004: 347). Chapter 6 then introduces another way in to the challenge of 'imagining community' by way of the notion of 'urban encounters'.[22] This discussion is developed through reflections on sites of memory in the city of Berlin built in response to the Holocaust and Second World War. This chapter also draws on Jean-Luc Nancy's invocation of the city as 'the site of a melee' (2003) and uses this work to reconceptualize political community *as* encounters. The key point about this reworking of community through a focus on urban encounters is that community does not appear as something that has been lost and must be regained, or as a promise that guides a unifying account of the political. Rather, the heterogeneity of the global city, and everyday encounters between urban strangers, are presented as what are already there and, as such, they don't have to be celebrated, honoured or mourned. The inexhaustible difference, disagreement and melee of urban life is postulated as the very stuff of politics – the stuff that nationalist approaches seek to avoid, distill or suppress.

Chapter 1 begins by turning to studies of nations and nationalism to argue that the dominant approach offered by this literature makes it difficult to ask critical questions of nationalism. It focuses on key figures in the field, including Ernest Gellner, Anthony D. Smith, Rogers Brubaker and Paul James, to argue that theorists of nations and nationalism often rely on nationalist ways of thinking. This is demonstrated in the binaries that animate this field of study, which include the distinction between the real and the imagined. It is also revealed in the way in which a particular experience of time as homogenous and linear is largely assumed and reproduced in the literature. Arguing that such theorists are caught up in a national-ist imaginary, the chapter concludes by seeking to open up the question of how we might imagine community against attempts to impose closure on this question.

Having established in Chapter 1 some of the implications of allowing a nation-alist imaginary to steer engagements with nationalism, Chapters 2 and 3 unpack the broader elements of what I describe as a nationalist imaginary. This work begins in Chapter 2 by turning to the writings of Max Weber. Weber describes how the nation emerges as a necessary response to what he understands as the disenchanted conditions of modern life. For him, the nation appears as a way of providing meaning in a meaningless world, along with a heroic (masculine) indi-vidual who can reshape the world around him. This chapter unpacks the story that Weber tells about modern life as disenchanted and then poses a challenge to it. It does so by borrowing Jane Bennett's question in *The Enchantment of Modern Life* (2001), when she asks what might it mean to understand modern life otherwise, as enchanted, joyous and affirmative? In refusing Weber's account of modern life, the chapter suggests that it might also become possible to refuse the 'answers' that Weber finds in nationalism.

Chapter 3 continues with the examination of narratives about what it means to be modern and another story of disenchantment, in this case offered by Jean-Jacques Rousseau. Rousseau is central to this study because of the way in which he establishes an account of politics as geared towards regaining a community that has been lost. He also forms a significant figure because of the way in which he is fully aware that a state-centred, sovereign account of politics forms a modern invention, yet goes on to argue that we must nevertheless accept this account of citizen-subjects in a sovereign community as what now constitutes the political. As with the reading of Max Weber in Chapter 2, this chapter suggests that we don't have to accept Rousseau's account of how the world is ordered, which means accepting unity as a constitutive political principle. The chapter closes by showing how Rousseau briefly divulges that there may be other ways of understanding what it means to live with others that draw on an urban and cosmopolitan imaginary. These possibilities are only hinted at in the work of Jean-Jacques Rousseau, as he spends most of his time trying to conceal them. Yet the next part of this book seeks to investigate those possibilities further.

Chapter 4 begins the second part of this book, and as such, expands the study towards cosmopolitanism as a well-established attempt at offering an alternative to nationalism. Specifically, it engages with the relationship between nationalism and cosmopolitanism in the context of political responses to the bombings in London on 7 July 2005. The chapter attends to an example of a poster campaign that ran in the aftermath of the bombings, which called on Londoners to remember their cosmopolitan ethos. The chapter demonstrates that well-intentioned attempts to embrace a politics of difference often reproduce unifying and nationalist accounts of the political. As a result, cosmopolitan narratives can travel alongside a heightened nationalism. Whilst it is argued that this example of urban cosmopolitanism fails to offer an alternative to nationalism, the chapter closes by indicating that the site of the city nevertheless offers some openings for thinking coexistence beyond a nationalist imaginary.

Chapter 5 turns to a bestselling novel published in the aftermath of the events of 11 September 2001 called *The Reluctant Fundamentalist* (2007) by the author Mohsin Hamid. This novel is interesting for the way in which it stages a critique of nationalism by pointing to another understanding of coexistence at work in the global city. Yet, in narrating a story about a post-colonial subject on a journey towards freedom, autonomy and enlightenment in time, this novel also reproduces a familiar nationalist story and, thus, its critical thrust is undermined. Nevertheless, the novel also contains moments that point toward ways of undoing a nationalist imaginary, especially in the brief reflections on loss it presents and in the images of the city. In gesturing towards different ways of conceptualizing the relationship between loss and community, the novel offers an alternative to the works of Max Weber and Jean-Jacques Rousseau. This chapter closes by turning to the work of the feminist political philosopher Judith Butler in response to the events of 11 September 2001 (2006) in order to develop this material further and to ask how we might reorient understandings of loss beyond a nationalist imaginary.

Chapter 6 takes forward the idea of the city as a site that prompts another imaginary of coexistence. It departs from the political context of the 'War on Terror' to address sites of memory in the city of Berlin. Such sites are interesting because they indicate approaches to loss that refuse to reproduce a homogenous and linear understanding of time. They invoke instead the 'time of the city' (Shapiro, 2010). In doing so, these architectural and artistic designs suggest possibilities for contesting a nationalist imaginary. This chapter also brings in the work of philosopher Jean-Luc Nancy who reads the city as the locus of a melee (2003). This concept of the melee works with another grammar of difference to that addressed in Chapters 4 and 5 and as a result, offers the possibility of disrupting a nationalist imaginary. The chapter concludes by recasting the very idea of imagining community by way of the concept of urban encounters. Such encounters can be understood as temporal and unpredictable and as productive of subject positions that are contingent and multiple. This approach suggests the possibility of a future politics beyond what we are already able to imagine and, thereby, forms this book's response to the challenge of 'imagining community'.

Part I

Unpacking nationalist imaginaries

1 Beyond 'imagined communities'

Nationalism and the politics of knowledge

There has never been a scholar who, as such, does not believe in the sharp distinction between the real and unreal, the actual and the inactual, the living and the non-living, being and non-being ('to be or not to be' in the conventional reading), in the opposition between what is present and what is not, for example in the form of objectivity. Beyond this opposition, there is, for the scholar, only the hypothesis of a school of thought, theatrical fiction, literature, and speculation.

Jacques Derrida, *Specters of Marx:*
The State of the Debt, the Work of Mourning and the New International

Imagination has a history. There are changing and conflicting interpretations of what it is and of its value. Imagination also has a structure, at once grammatical and historical, in the tenses of past, present and future.

Raymond Williams, 'The Tenses of Imagination'

Introduction

The idea that a nation forms an 'imagined community' continues to dominate critical entry points to the study of nations and nationalism. In coining the concept, Benedict Anderson could not have anticipated the extent to which this concept would continue to resonate (1991). This is a testament to the argument presented in his book, which encourages us to analyse the conditions that enable us to imagine nations rather than treat nations as solid organisms that are inevitably present in the world. But the impact of Anderson's work and of this concept must also be explained in relation to a wave of writings that emerged across the social sciences in the 1980s and 1990s arguing for an understanding of key concepts as social constructions.[1] *Imagined Communities* was published and became well established against this backdrop – a backdrop that largely dominated late twentieth-century understandings of what it means to do critical work in the social sciences.[2]

This chapter addresses key texts in Anglo-American studies of nations and nationalism[3] in order to show how a social constructivist standpoint dominates critical approaches in the field. Whilst elements of this approach have undoubtedly been progressive, in helping to expand the questions to be asked of nationalism, this chapter argues that the social constructivist approach, captured by the concept of the nation as an 'imagined community', keeps us caught within a nationalist imaginary and ultimately thwarts attempts at resisting it. This claim is developed by engaging with a contradiction in the established literatures on nations and nationalism which dictates that, even when we begin from an under-standing that nations are historical constructions, we are nevertheless led to the conclusion that this was either historically inevitable, politically necessary or something that, today, we can't risk dispensing with.[4] This chapter contends that we encounter this paradoxical claim regularly in some of the most influential texts in the field and that it tends to play out by way of an ongoing debate between the 'real' and 'imagined' aspect of nations. The challenge lies with being able to think the possibilities of political life as open to many different futures, none of which is inevitable, all of which invite contestation, and some of which might go 'beyond' the particular model of political community offered by the nation-state.[5]

The chapter turns to the work of two of the most influential names in studies of nations and nationalism: Ernest Gellner and Anthony D. Smith, in order to show how the real–imagined debate forms a structural starting point for this sub-discipline. The chapter then turns to the writings of critical theorists of nationalism Rogers Brubaker and Paul James in order to show that this real–imagined debate continues to frame and govern the way in which we can ask questions in the discipline, often despite the fact that this is said to form an uncon-structive starting point. The chapter therefore argues that the standard argument that the nation is imagined, invented and a construction is haunted by a sugges-tion that nations are nevertheless somehow quite 'real'.[6] That nations are made and remade is a given, but this acceptance is accompanied by a sense of disquiet among contemporary theorists that the emphasis on imagination, invention and construction has either 'gone too far' (Smith, 1991) or that it leaves us unable to account for how national attachments can become so powerful (James, 2006). Even when the real–imagined question is ostensibly put to one side, what we find is that the idea that such a distinction *can be made* recurs. This matters because it enables a circular set of debates that ultimately make it difficult to enquire into the possibility of *resisting* nationalism. It also makes it difficult to raise the possi-bility that social ties may be organized on non-nationalistic terms.

Time and the politics of knowledge

As Benedict Anderson explains in *Imagined Communities*, the idea of a nation is made possible by way of a linear and continuous experience of time and a bounded understanding of space. This is what secures the appearance of the nation as contained and as a 'solid community moving steadily down (or up) history' (1991: 26). This point about how a particular idea of time enables the image of a nation is important, because it *also* forms a way of 'knowing' concepts in the modern age. Michael Shapiro (2000) has described this linear, horrogenous expe-rience of time as 'national time' because of the way in which it is central to the possibility of the nation. Indeed, Michel Foucault (2002) argues that the shift towards a modern age can be understood by way of the shift in our understanding of entities, and specifically how entities come to be known and assume their presence because of their History. History forms 'the fundamental mode of being of empiricities' (2002: 237) in that objects and things appear to have a past, a present and a future.[7] This temporal dimension is crucial to the process of securing our understanding of the modern nation. It makes it possible to understand how nations *seem* to have been around 'forever' despite the fact that they are a modern invention. Nations appear to have solidity because they give the impression of having a deep history. This relationship between time and knowledge is not incidental; rather, as Michel Foucault put it, this way of understanding beings and things 'bears the stamp of our age and our geography' (2002: xvi).

The discussion that follows addresses the ways in which key theorists of nations and nationalism tend to assume the homogenous, linear time that enables the idea of a nation as the only experience of time available and as *the* way of making sense of the past and future. This experience of time is therefore taken to form the ground of knowledge, that can take us towards a better understanding of nations and nationalism, as opposed to an experience of time that is *informed* by nationalism and therefore forms anything but a 'neutral' starting point. Drawing on Kimberly Hutchings's work on how a particular understanding of time as linear informs so many canonical texts on world politics (2008), the chapter argues that theorists of nations and nationalism similarly tend to assume this linear, temporal experience of Western modernity to be universal and as the only way of making sense of the past, present and future. Borrowing from Hutchings's formulation of the problem, this chapter seeks to outline how theorists of nations and nationalism implicitly position themselves as both 'architects' and 'prophets' in their theoretical investigations of nationalism (2008). This is because, in the process of going about the study of nations and nationalism, they actively draw the lines that determine where and when politics can take place.[8] As a result, many theories of nationalism implicitly or explicitly suggest that, if the future is not understood to unfold within the political space of the nation, then we may not have a political future. The point that will be developed is that there is a 'double connection' between the way in which the idea of the nation is made possible by a linear understanding of time, and the way in which this experience of time forms a condition of knowledge for the discipline (2001).

The question of ideas of time is important because it reveals that the problem is greater than what is captured by the concept of 'methodological nationalism'. This term names the problem of assuming the nation to be a necessary or 'natural' part of the world's furniture. As Paul James puts it, the 1980s saw a profusion of debates about the way in which the nation-state had previously been taken for granted as a foundational and unifying category of analysis. This led to 'the tendency to assume that the nation was a society and that society was the nation' (2006: 18). Whilst this problem has been widely discussed in Anglo-American studies of nations and nationalism, it still leaves many theorists, including James, uneasy. As he argues, this 'overriding interpretative trend' has led to an overemphasis on 'the invented and modernist nature of the nation' (2006: 18). Rather than get caught in this closed debate about the extent to which the nation is constructed or not, a focus on time enables a closer analysis of the relationship between nationlism and the politics of knowledge. For example, one question to ask is whether the argument about 'constructedness' can lead to the possibility of imagining political space otherwise. Commenting on a similar set of debates in the context of the study of gender as a 'construction', Judith Butler says that the idea that gender is constructed only becomes a radical argument when it can appreciate the contingency (and, therefore, the changeability) of possible gender configurations (1999: 49). Paraphrasing Butler, we might say that only when we can appreciate the contingency of the nation-form does 'constructedness' per se become useful to the aim of challenging the persistence of nationalism.

The historical inevitability of nationalism

Ernest Gellner (1925–1995) represents a central figure in studies of nations and nationalism. His most influential work, *Nations and Nationalism* (1983) remains a canonical text in the discipline. His work is significant because it continues to structure the key terms of debate – including the argument over whether the nation is 'real' or 'imagined'. As we will see later in this chapter, even when contemporary theorists reject Ernest Gellner's modernization theory, the real–imagined debate continues to haunt their interventions.

Gellner is well known for having insisted upon the *invention* of the idea of the nation, and locates that invention as part of the trajectory of modernization. For Gellner, nationalism only becomes possible following the Westphalian principle of a state system and represents the marriage of culture and state. Drawing extensively on Max Weber's understanding of what it means to be modern, Gellner argues that the combination of a mass education system and a standardized method of communication across a state's territory enables the nationalist principle which holds that 'the political and the national unit should be congruent' (1983: 2). Nationalism is understood as an integral feature of the transition to an industrial society committed to large-scale productive systems, the centralization of production and cumulative economic, scientific and technological growth. For Gellner, as for Weber before him, modernization involves the unfurling of a rationalizing spirit which enables a 'conception of the world as homogenous, subject to systematic, indiscriminate laws, and as open to interminable exploration' (1983: 22). But whereas Max Weber was deeply ambivalent about the processes of rationalization (Brubaker, 1984), Gellner understands them as overwhelmingly positive. Gellner's understanding of modernization is important because it is directly linked to his view of nationalism: in assuming the former as a sweep of overwhelmingly encouraging advances, he also takes nationalism to be a largely welcome development.

It is not only the case that Gellner understands both modernization and nationalization as 'good things'; he also understands modernization as a force that is propelled by an 'inescapable imperative' (1983: 39). 'Mankind is irreversibly committed to industrial society', he tells us, and by extension, then, given that nationalism forms one of industrial society's essential features, nationalism turns out to be historically inevitable (1983: 39). In locating the imperative for nationalism in the process of modernization, Gellner cleverly rejects the idea that people are *naturally* organized according to culturally homogenous units. In Gellner's approach, the 'origin' of the nation is displaced from an essentialist kin-based core to the process of modernization which serves as a useful 'cause' that secures the development of nations. The problem with this framing, however, is that even when the idea of the nation is put forward as a historical *construction*, the idea of modern nations, 'based on deeply internalized, education-dependent high cultures, each protected by their own state' (1983: 48) is presented as historically inevitable and politically necessary.

What Gellner offers is an account of history that secures the inevitable development of nationalism. This point can be gleaned further by studying Gellner's understanding of culture. On the one hand, Gellner argues that nationalism works by inventing cultures. As he puts it: 'The cultures [that a nation] claims to defend and revive are often its own inventions, or are modified out of all recognition' (1983: 56). Yet, on the other hand, Gellner contradicts this understanding by suggesting that cultures transform and evolve all by themselves. Culture is therefore understood both as a nationalist invention and as an organism that travels straightforwardly through history. Consider, for example, this quotation in which Gellner describes the fate of culture in the age of nationalism:

> Most cultures or potential national groups enter the age of nationalism without even the feeblest effort to benefit from it themselves...most of them go meekly to their doom, to see their culture...slowly disappear...Most cultures are led to the dustheap of history by industrial civilization without offering any resistance.
>
> (1983: 47)

What is interesting is the way in which this account of culture relies on a nationalist imaginary. In using the passive tense to describe the way in which 'cultures are led' along the current of modernization, Gellner succeeds in portraying cultures as having a life of their own, travelling steadily through time, whilst obfuscating the politics involved in determining *which* cultures succeed in becoming dominant cultures. Similarly, in suggesting that some cultures disappear 'without... any resistance', he erases the effort that goes into ensuring that some cultural traditions thrive whilst others are maginalized or castigated to the 'dustheap of history'. According to Gellner's framing, history can now only take place within a nation-state, or else there is no possibility of any history.

In determining the historical origins of nations and nationalism, Ernest Gellner argues that the invention of the nation followed the invention of the state.[9] That order of things would suggest that nations had to be *made*. But in order to support his analysis that the process of nationalization was largely inevitable, Gellner also needs to find a way of displacing the *force* that must accompany any attempt to organize people into standardized cultural units. Thus, in response to the criticism that nationalism – and homogenization – will involve force, Gellner argues that it isn't *nationalism* that imposes homogeneity but, rather, it's the 'inescapable imperative' of modernization that requires the homogenization of cultures. By displacing the causal factor from nationalism, he succeeds in rescuing nationalism from one of its most problematic elements. Yet, in connecting such measures to an 'inescapable imperative', Gellner also brushes over the political practices that will have to be carried out to ensure homogeneity. Of course Gellner is fully aware that such processes, decisions and actions will involve force: this is not a 'blind spot' on his part so much as an attempt to rescue nationalism from its dark side. The force is therefore explained away as the '*objective* need for homogeneity which is reflected in nationalism' (1983: 46, my emphasis). Yet, such homogenizing measures are not in any way 'objective' in that they will privilege certain cultural practices whilst undermining or eradicating others.[10] Homogenizing measures can also be taken to different extremes, as the histories of ethnic nationalism remind us (Coward, 2009a). Yet Gellner tells us that this is an inescapable feature of modern life that will have to be accepted:

> The kind of cultural homogeneity demanded by nationalism is one of them, and *we had better make our peace with it*. It is not the case…that nationalism imposes homogeneity; it is rather that a homogeneity imposed by objective, *inescapable imperative* eventually appears on the surface in the form of nationalism.
>
> (1983: 39, my emphasis)

Assuming that nations must form the final principle, Gellner's version of history is steered into a linear narrative that serves to affirm the inevitability of nations. The nation thus appears as a necessary essence that is gradually revealed by History. Gellner's theoretical stance casts aside any evidence that this smooth, unruffled account of 'history' will have been contested. And, as Paul James argues, Gellner's account of modernization also allows him to assert his right-wing liberalism as a fact, as he describes that 'we all move towards the freedom of civil society and the egalitarianism of market-democracy' (2006: 50). Gellner's study therefore vacillates between offering a critical analysis of the conditions that enable the possibility of nationalism and providing a story of origins that accounts for why cultures *had* to become standardized and organized according to the principle of nationalism. Gellner succeeds in accounting for the necessity of nations, but his historiography serves to establish a much broader political ontology which includes the idea that cultures *must* be ordered into sovereign statist units. The challenge is to recover the political feat that underpins Gellner's presentation of nationalism, rationalization and modernization as *apolitical* achievements.

In the course of studying the history of the nation, Gellner places himself in the position of both 'architect' and 'prophet' (Hutchings, 2008). This is because he provides a powerful account of what it must now mean to form part of a proper, legitimate and 'mature' political community. Before he can unpack his analysis of the development of nations, he must first determine the architecture that will contain – and govern – political life. Gellner therefore offers much more than a 'biased' understanding of history in that he establishes the terms upon which history can be made. Gellner acts as an architect in drawing and then insisting upon a historically contingent way of organizing cultures. This point becomes clear when we look in more detail at the way in which Gellner describes the shift from a pre-modern agrarian society to a society that is organized according to the principle of nationalism (1983: 8–52). In recounting this story of how a shift from one age to the other came about, Gellner portrays the agrarian age as an age of numerous and complex patterns of culture, where relations of kinship, caste, clan and language belonged to diverse and overlapping units. In this age, Gellner tells us a person might have felt an attachment to many different cultures, and not to one distinct identity. Furthermore, the boundaries of culture in the agrarian age were distinct from those determining political affiliation. Gellner then describes the shift from the agrarian to the industrial, nationalist age as a process that involved the standardization of cultures. In doing so, he offers a story about a shift from a time of assorted and overlapping cultures to a time of clearly distinct cultures, where we live side by side for the first time, rather than interwoven. Gellner's account of the history of nationalization is familiar, but it also presents us with a puzzle: if we were so disorganized and jumbled up in the agrarian age, how did we manage to organize ourselves into unified nation-states? The force of the process of establishing order out of disorder is smoothed over in Gellner's analysis. But this is not a straightforward account of an unavoidable process: he is responsible for producing this rent from which the time of nationalism can begin, and Gellner the prophet presents us with an account of what history and politics must now involve – that is, a struggle between nation-states.

Gellner subscribes to a view that modernity involves the necessary organization of individuals and communities into standardized national units and thereby reproduces the dominant ontology that persons and communities must be understood as autonomous and absolute entities. But, in taking this ontology as our point of departure, we are necessarily led to some familiar problems under nationalism. For example, there will always be many more claims to nationhood than there can be potential states. As Gellner points out, 'On any reasonable calculation, the former number (of potential nations) is probably much, much larger than that of possible viable states' (1983: 2). Furthermore, any struggle to decide which nations become viable states and which do not will involve force and resistance.[11] Some states will go to greater extents to subscribe to the principle of nationalism and to the desire for homogeneity, and some will have greater weapons and armoury at their disposal to be used in imposing this principle. Gellner is quite matter-of-fact on the political implications of this process:

> the satisfaction of some [nations] spells the frustration of others . . . It follows that a territorial political unit can only become ethnically homogenous, in such cases, if it either kills, or expels, or assimilates all non-nationals. Their unwillingness to suffer such fates may make the peaceful implementation of the nationalist principle difficult.

> (1983: 2)

Here we get a glimpse of what is at stake under nationalism: the idea of a 'peaceful implementation' of the nationalist principle remains 'difficult' – to say the least. With this revelation, Gellner sets up a specific understanding of political life as the quest to secure a culture within a statist unit. He also (briefly) divulges the problem that will keep on haunting defenders of nationalism: that not all cultures will be able to secure such a state and that the world will have to deal with the implications of frustrated national movements.

Consolidating nationalism

Anthony D. Smith is a former student of Ernest Gellner's and a prolific author of several key texts that have defined this field of study (2001, 1998, 1995, 1991, 1986). Following Gellner, Smith understands nationalism to be a modern development, but departs from him by suggesting that some nations have a much older history. He disagrees with what he terms the 'modernist' account represented by Gellner for overemphasizing the invented element of nations, arguing that some nations reveal elements of a much older common culture and are related to earlier ethnic communities, or what he calls *ethnies*. Smith forms another important figure in this field of study because of the way in which he consolidates the architecture of political space outlined by Gellner and, in doing so, cements particular terms within which debates in the study of nations and nationalism can take place. For example, he frames the debate on nations and nationalism as one between two sides: there is the modernist standpoint that emphasizes the constructed nature of nations and there is the perennialist or primordialist standpoint, which argues that the nation is a natural phenomenon. His favoured 'ethno-symbolist' approach is proposed as a halfway house that, in Smith's view, accepts the better aspects of each side of the debate and which is able to establish a relationship between the modern nation and pre-modern ethnic components. This may seem a sensible compromise, as it is surely intended to seem. However, in framing the debate in this way, Smith also succeeds in managing and limiting the kind of debate we can have about the politics of nationalism. As he admits, hardly any scholars take seriously the view that nations are perennial (1995: 35), yet he still chooses to posit this view as a serious option in this twofold debate. Smith plays a central role in upholding the real–imagined debate as a useful entry point to the study of nationalism. But this starting point is informed by a nationalist imaginary which ultimately leads us to a similar conclusion to Gellner's: the idea that social attachments should be organized according to a nationalist principle remains necessary and must be defended.

Smith agrees with what is by now a general consensus in this sub-discipline that the nation is not a fixed reality and that national myths, memories and symbols must be constantly performed. Nevertheless, picking an argument with Hobsbawm and Ranger (1992), Smith suggests that they overemphasize the element of 'invention' (2001, 1991). Although national elites may select and spin national traditions, symbols and myths, Smith argues that they perform that work by drawing on a storehouse of pre-existing cultural artefacts. For Smith, it is not a matter of inventing from scratch but of selecting motifs from earlier ethnic communities, or *ethnies*. These *ethnies* provide 'the cultural frameworks and parameters within and through which the needs and understandings of the present are formed and articulated' (2001: 83). There are several problems with Smith's postulation of *ethnies* as forming the origins of the nation-form. The first is a historical problem, in that it is difficult to find much evidence of this particular form of community outside ethno-symbolist studies of nationalism. Smith describes it as 'a named human community connected to a homeland, possessing common myths of ancestry, shared memories, one or more elements of shared culture, and a measure of solidarity, at least among the elites' (2001: 13). It sounds very similar to a nation, suggesting that Smith's idea of *ethnies* does more to support an argument about the *enduring history* of nations than it does to explain pre-modern forms of political community. The second problem is that, even if we were to accept that *ethnies* represent a pre-modern form of community, Smith can only engage them by way of a nationalist imaginary that understands history to unfold within the time of the nation. For example, in being able to trace elements of national symbols, traditions and cultural practices all the way back to these *ethnies*, Smith suggests that history seemed destined to morph into nationalist-statist units. Smith is aware of the critique and argues that the relationship between a nation and an *ethnie* remains complex and is not defined by linear progression. But we find little suggestion that *ethnies* could have developed in any other way or into another formation of community. In the same way that the nation must have a point of origin from which a national history and identity can spring, Smith's theoretical approach to nationalism partakes in the same practice of identifying a 'real' national kernel that always already existed and which provides a foundation for the nation's development in time.

What we find is that Anthony D. Smith's study of nations and nationalism slides between offering an analysis of the practices that create the image of a nation existing as a solid community in time and partaking in a similar practice himself, helping to shore up an image of the nation's essence. This is because of the way in which Smith wavers between offering an understanding of how the nation is produced through a linear account of time and reproducing that account of time as the only experience available. For example, in explaining the way in which intellectuals rediscover their 'authentic' histories and 'golden ages', he tells us that they set about reinterpreting for each generation the meanings of the past within the parameters of that particular ethnic culture, sifting the genuine elements from the inauthentic, the intrinsic from the extraneous (2001: 84–5). Smith's use of inverted commas in referring to the idea of 'authenticity' and a 'golden age' suggests something about the way in which he understands that these are not innocuous concepts. Indeed, they form part of the discourse of nationalism. But what we find is that this activity of 'sifting the genuine elements from the inauthentic' is nevertheless presented as almost a compulsory exercise. As with Gellner, there is little consideration of the force and the violence at stake in the process of determining which cultural practices survive, thrive or can afford to die away.[12] This is not only a question of narrating history from the position of the victors. This account also smoothes over Smith's complicity in establishing the contours within which history can take place.

Smith's ethno-symbolist approach to nationalism has already been accused of serving as a way of defending Smith's beloved nation in that it forms 'more an attempt to resuscitate nationalism than to explain it' (Özkirimli, 2003: 340). Özkirimli's characterization is correct, but the problem is more complex than he anticipates. For Özkirimli, the ethno-symbolist position is problematic because Smith refuses to be open about his political investment in nationalism and his *normative* analysis (2003: 352). But Smith is in fact largely upfront about his political allegiances. For example, in one of the final chapters of *Nations and Nationalism in a Global Era* (1995), he lays his cards on the table and presents his argument 'In Defence of the Nation'. In responding to those who pronounce 'the end of the nation', Smith insists that the nation will endure because it is 'historically embedded' (1995: 157). As he puts it, 'the nation remains embedded in a past that shapes its future as much as any present global trends' (1995: 158). He defends the nation as a form of political community that *must* continue. This represents more than a 'normative' standpoint. Smith's approach is already compromised by the nationalist imaginary that informs his attempt at understanding nationalism. This is because Smith's postulation of 'ethnic cores' offers a story of origins that neatly leads us to the unavoidable existence of nations in the present and future. His understanding of the past governs his imagination of the future in that all the possibilities of political life are condensed into the continuation of the nation. His understanding of time therefore represents what the feminist theorist Elizabeth Grosz describes as deterministic, in so far as 'determinism is the annulling of any concept of temporality other than the one structured by the terms and conditions of the past and present' (1999a: 4). As with Gellner, this has serious political implications. Smith warns us that: 'despite the capacity of nationalism to generate widespread terror and destruction, nations and nationalism provide the only realistic socio-cultural framework for a modern world order. *They have no rivals today*' (1995: 159, my emphasis). But it is precisely the capacity of nationalism to 'generate widespread terror and destruction' that makes the task of imagining alternatives to nationalism so vital.

Questioning nationalism

Contemporary theorists of nations and nationalism including Rogers Brubaker and Paul James are more attuned to the violent, problematic and dark sides of nationalism. They are also more attuned to the question of a theorist's complicity in assuming the inevitability of nationalism. For example, Rogers Brubaker presents a persuasive argument against the overwhelming trend to *postulate* nations in the process of studying nationalism, arguing that 'nationalism can and should be understood without invoking "nations" as substantial entities' (1996: 7). As he puts it, it is problematic when the nation is taken as a category of analysis rather than as a category of practice. It is necessary to be attentive to the ways in which nationalism works to 'structure perception, to inform thought and experience, to organize discourse and political action' (1996: 7). Brubaker offers an eloquent understanding of the problems faced in the study of nations and nationalism. Yet his social constructivist standpoint performs a closure that makes it difficult to enquire into the possibility of imagining community beyond the nation. Despite offering a series of important openings, constructivist approaches avoid putting the 'very mode and models of knowledge production into question' (Shaw, 2004: 17). A residual nationalism continues to colour these approaches and enforces limits on what we are able to imagine politically. Thus, whilst the social constructivist position suggests that nationalism is not historically inevitable, it nevertheless succeeds in making nationalism appear so. This is because these approaches continue to rely on the possibility of being able to draw a distinction between the real and the imagined, what is present and what is not. This becomes especially evident in debates around nationalism's affective capacities and the question of imagining a future beyond nationalism.

Rogers Brubaker rightly argues that the signature question, *'What is a nation?'*[13] is problematic. This is because the question invites us to imagine an essential national substance (1996: 14). But this formulation of the question must also be understood as intimately related to how the concept of the nation works, because both the question and the concept send us off in search of an origin that will reveal the *substance* of national community. In understanding this as a sociological argument about the way it enables the idea of the nation, the *political* point about how it also anchors a particular approach to knowledge and affirms the *presence* of a nation is brushed to one side.[14] If the nation forms both the *object* of study *and* the condition of knowledge for this minor discipline, analyses of how the idea of a 'national organism' was made possible risk suggesting that there *are* such national organisms that can guide our way through time. Take, for example this short passage where Benedict Anderson discusses the relationship between a national community and 'mother tongues':

> What the eye is to the lover – that particular, ordinary eye he or she is born with – language – whatever language history has made his or her mother-tongue – is to the patriot. Through that language, encountered at a mother's knee and parted with only at the grave, pasts are restored, fellowships are imagined, and futures dreamed.
>
> (1991: 154)

This description resounds with the idea of a 'lost' origin that is recovered through the community. It isn't necessarily clear whether Anderson reproduces this homogenous empty understanding of time as a *rhetorical* device, to demonstrate its command in forming 'imagined communities', or whether he briefly becomes drawn by its promise. Either way, it would seem that Anderson never fully appreciates the *critique* of this experience of time implicit in Walter Benjamin's use of the concept of 'homogenous-empty time' (Kelly, 1998: 846).

This tendency to assume a national experience of time, which in turn enables the idea of a national organism, nevertheless extends much further than Anderson's intervention. For example, it occurs in particular questions that continue to animate studies of nations and nationalism, including: how do national associations and identifications lead people to harm others? For example, in his extensive study, *Globalism, Nationalism, Tribalism*, Paul James asks:

> How could such abstract associations generate such powerful embodied personal and social identities as nationalism and tribalism? How do those often-positive identifications intensify to the point that a person is willing to kill a known 'other' for that identification?
>
> (2006: 34)

The problem with this question lies with the way in which it invites us to conjure up the image of a national organism that '*intensifies*' to the point of directing ugly passions. It thereby places the focus on this 'national thing' rather than on how the idea of a national community may be mobilized. James's question (inadvertently perhaps) directs our attention away from the governmental and non-governmental organizations and national and transnational institutions that may all have an interest in framing particular political and economic struggles as battles between 'ethnic groups'. Despite James's concerns about nationalism's relationship with force and violence, this particular framing of the question recalls Smith's assumption that there must be *some* essential core that explains the power of national identities, and why nationalism is perhaps *more powerful* than other affiliations and associations. James is especially aware of the problem of 'methodological nationalism'. In response, he attempts to find a 'middle ground' between the idea 'that social life can be understood either in terms of an essentialized ground or a series of discursive formations' (2006: 17). However, rather than displace the 'real' and 'imagined' binary, what we find with James's question is that it keeps these limit points in place. His question ultimately hinges on the suggestion that 'imagined' identities can produce 'real' political tensions.

Rogers Brubaker offers a potentially useful way of breaking this deadlock by suggesting that we need to find ways of understanding 'ethnic conflict' in terms other than as a conflict between groups (2004a). He goes on to say that we need to be able to frame questions about nationalism in a way that displaces our everyday understanding of 'nations as substantial entities, collectivities or communities' (1996: 16). Brubaker offers another way into the study of nationalism, but he also, on occasion, reproduces this ontology of substance. Take, for example, an article written in response to the increasing popularity of constructivist debates at the turn of the twenty-first century, co-authored by Rogers Brubaker and Frederic Cooper (2000). Echoing Paul James's concern about how an 'abstract' concept such as a nation can potentially direct violence, and also Anthony D. Smith's concern that the emphasis on 'construction' has been taken too far, Brubaker and Cooper ask:

If [identity] is fluid, how can we understand the ways in which self-understandings may harden, congeal and crystallize? If it is constructed, how can we understand the sometimes coercive force of external identifications?... How can we understand the power and pathos of identity politics?

(2000: 1)

The rhythm of this passage suggests a fear that identities have the potential to 'wither away' and that 'social constructivist' positions fail to take national attachments seriously. But what is most striking about this article is the way in which the real–imagined debate continues to frame the terms upon which we can have any debate in the study of nations and nationalism. The questions they ask recall the prevailing assumption in studies of nations and nationalism that there must be *something* about national identities that makes them more real and substantial than other identity categories. As such, the questions risk conforming to the problem that Brubaker outlines in other work (2004a): that we postulate the idea of an 'ethnic group' in the process of trying to understand it. It is worth emphasizing that Rogers Brubaker and Paul James represent very different approaches and a different politics to that offered by Ernest Gellner and Anthony D. Smith. But, ultimately, Brubaker also seems concerned to *defend* nationalism and to prove that a national community represents more than an 'abstract association'.

This point can be gleaned in an article where Brubaker seeks to distinguish between nationalism and patriotism. Written in 2004, in the wake of the invasion of Iraq and the heightened nationalism represented by the political climate of the 'War on Terror', Brubaker presents a defence of the American nation by arguing that:

on the whole, the American nation has been imagined – by existing and prospective members – as relatively open and joinable, certainly as much more joinable than most other nations... Given that 'nation' is prevailingly imagined as joinable in time (indeed in a relatively short time), nationalism can indeed serve as a valuable resource for the integration of immigrants.

(2004b: 122)

Unlike figures such as Anthony D. Smith and Ernest Gellner, who offer much more explicit and unapologetic defences of the nation, Rogers Brubaker is aware of the ways in which the nation can be used to 'include or exclude in particular settings' (2004b: 122). He reminds us that 'nations are imagined in different ways, and are therefore differentially joinable' (ibid). Nevertheless, it's possible to list many examples of the way in which the American nation does not seem 'open and joinable' to many thousands of people from day to day. For example, between 2005 and 2009, it is reported that some US \$2.4 billion was spent on the new virtual fence designed to further bolster the border between the US and Mexico, which would track and catch border-crossers using cameras, radar and ground sensors (Tomasky, 2010). Brubaker is of course very conscious of the exclusionary histories of nationalism, as his book on the resurgence of nationalism in the

'New Europe' testifies (1996). He wants to remind us, however, of the ways in which nations can also foster a sense of civic engagement, establish a sense of responsibility for the actions of government and provide support for redistributive social policies (2004b: 121). But the question to ask in response is, why should political engagement, accountability and redistributive social politics be accomplished within a national framework? Does the nation continue to offer the most appropriate model of political space for instituting these fine ambitions? How might political life be arranged in ways that can be more responsive to issues such as climate change, the management of nuclear energy and poverty? Brubaker is right that the point is not to argue over whether the nation is 'good' or 'bad'. Yet we can also question the energies expended by critical theorists of nationalism in defending a 'good' account of the nation.

The future of nationalism

It is not only the case that the point about 'methodological nationalism' has become widely accepted in studies of nations and nationalism; the point about assuming a linear, developmental understanding of time is also appreciated by critical theorists of nationalism including Paul James. For example, in discussing the form of the relationship between tribal, national and global formations, James argues that these cannot be understood as following one another in progressive succession. As he tells us, we cannot reproduce the tendency of modernist theorists of nationalism who 'looked back' to tribal formations 'as the grounding conditions of their own formations' (James, 2006: 31). James therefore argues that we cannot understand nationalism and globalism as temporary stations on a homogenous empty journey through time. Rather, developing a critique of the modernization theory underpinning Ernest Gellner's approach, James claims that globalism cannot be conceived as a stage that *advances* upon nationalism.[15] Rather, he argues that we need to understand global, national and tribal social formations as coexisting in time. Drawing on the works of Michael Mann, Pierre Bourdieu, Anthony Giddens and Michel Foucault, Paul James presents a much richer analysis of nationalism's manifestations than that offered by either Gellner or Smith, which insists on the importance of acknowledging different understandings of time and space in varying cultural contexts. Yet this is what makes it surprising when a linear, homogenous empty understanding of time recurs to animate James's analysis as he considers the possibilities of a 'post-national' future.

For example, James is critical of the tendency to posit the nation-state as something that belongs to the *past*. As he puts it: 'polities and communities alike are being *swept up* in the case to *leave behind* the modern nation-state and to accommodate what has been described as the processes of "deterritorialization"' (2006: 296, my emphasis). Whilst James offers a robust critique of the idea that the national and the global follow one another in progressive succession, in this extract, he seems to assume that 'we' are indeed on our way towards other arrangements of political space that risk the *loss* of community. In this sense, James wavers between offering an analysis of the way in which nationalism has largely been analysed through a modernist, developmental framework and invoking a similar account of time as progressive and unifying. As a result, the possibilities of the future are condensed into a choice between the continuing presence, or the loss of nations. As he goes on to argue, this 'sudden disjunctive loss of community' can often lead to 'reactionary violence' (2006: 296) and a 'misplaced faith in postnationalism and cosmopolitanism' (2006: 297). Whilst there are many good reasons for James to be suspicious of cosmopolitan and post-national literatures, and in particular their capacity to take questions of cultural and affective attachments seriously, the problem here lies with the way in which that suspicion collapses into a defence of the nation. What needs to be resisted is neither 'cosmopolitanism' nor 'post-nationalism', but the persistence of this linear and unifying understanding of time and of the political.

What is striking about James's analysis is that it offers both a critique of Ernest Gellner's modernist approach to reading nationalism and yet remains indebted to Gellner's framing of the problem. The real–imagined debate weighs on James's analysis, as evidenced in his fear that the 'invented' nature of the nation has been over-emphasized (2006: 18). Whilst, for Gellner, the risk of infinite plurality makes the continuation of the nation necessary, James insists that the counter-position to post-nationalism cannot be 'an uncritical political defence of territorial place or integral community' (2006: 295) Indeed, his analysis of nationalism is not uncritical. Nevertheless, it does conjure a similar sense of nostalgia to that which animates Anthony D. Smith's account of nationalism. The challenge that remains is to ask how we can conceptualize coexistence in terms that refuse a return to nationalism.

Conclusion

This chapter has argued that a residual nationalism informs many Anglo-American studies of nations and nationalism, and the constructionist approach favoured by this sub-discipline. This manifests itself in two underlying assumptions: that there is something about a national identity that is more powerful than other identity categories and that the comforts, security and guidance offered by the idea that we should organize ourselves by nations ultimately outweighs the risks presented by nationalist politics. Such anxieties are ultimately informed by a nationalist imaginary which has been unpacked by way of the binary between the real–imagined and how this continues to frame the terms of debate in studies of nations and nationalism. This suggests that the argument about 'methodological nationalism' rarely goes far enough. This is because of the way in which theorists of nations and nationalism place themselves as 'architects' in determining the proper spatial framework for the political and as 'prophets' in declaring that the nation is still important and remains a valuable resource for the present and future. This argument therefore has implications beyond the study of nations and nationalism, as it represents a broader critique of constructionist approaches. The challenge lies with reopening the question of *imagining* community against efforts by theorists of nations and nationalism to impose closure on this question.

The second chapter will now expand on this question of imagination by unpacking the way in which nationalism emerges against the backdrop of a particularly modern way of seeing and understanding the world around us. It will discuss this in relation to the writings of Max Weber (1864–1920), who, in writing at the turn of the twentieth century, paints a picture of modern life as disenchanted and insists on nationalism as an unavoidable response to these desolate conditions. The second chapter therefore leads on from this one by showing how Ernest Gellner's account of modern life as involving a rationalizing ethic draws to a large extent from Max Weber's work. Whilst this chapter has argued that Gellner sought to avoid some of the darker undercurrents of nationalism, Max Weber's work offers an unambiguous account of nationalism's violent aspects.

2 Weberian tales

Disenchantment, mastery and meaning

He was sitting on his bed in the dark, crouching, hugging his knees and thinking, holding his breath from the strain of it. But the more he strained to think, the clearer it became to him that it was undoubtedly so, and that he had actually forgotten, overlooked in his life one small circumstance – that death would come and everything would end, that it was not worth starting anything and that nothing could possibly be done about it. Yes, it was terrible, but it was so.

'Yet I am still alive. And what am I to do now, what am I to do?' he said in despair.

Leo Tolstoy, *Anna Karenina*

Imagine a place, then, where reason engenders, where faculties play, where nature gives hints, where molecules mutate, where tomatoes morph, where files zoom, where curves spiral and fields buzz, where ants swarm and vertigo reveals, and where thinking unexpectedly shouts out from the dutiful litany of thought. That world is not disenchanted.

Jane Bennett, *The Enchantment of Modern Life*

Introduction

In tending to his dying brother Nikolai, the character of Levin in Leo Tolstoy's *Anna Karenina* finds that just as he had 'partly clarified the question of how to live', he was presented with a new and 'insoluble problem' – that death would come and nothing could possibly be done about it. In his despair, he exclaims: 'it was not worth starting anything' (2003: 349). Echoing Levin's sense of despair, this chapter traces a particular understanding of modern life as disenchanted. More specifically, it seeks to outline the way in which this account of modern life as disenchanted has formed a backdrop to the proposition that we *must* have nations and nationalism. Max Weber offers a paradigmatic example of such a story. This chapter discusses some of his work in order to show how the nation emerges to provide *meaning* in the context of a rationalizing, nihilistic world. The chapter unpacks this account of modern life as disenchanted in order to show the way in which it forms part of a nationalist imaginary. The aim of the chapter is to argue that any attempt at thinking beyond the nation will also need to be able to contest this account of modern life.

The last chapter suggested briefly that Ernest Gellner drew to a large extent on Max Weber's understanding of modern life as involving a rationalizing, homogenizing ethos. This chapter seeks to interrogate further that account of modernity and the way in which it led Gellner to postulate the necessity of nations and nationalism. Interestingly, whilst Gellner took modernity's quest for order and rationality to be largely welcome developments, Weber insists that this also makes modern life appear more and more irrational. Thus, whilst Gellner understood disorder as something that was left behind in the era of nationalism, and as an ethos that belonged to the premoderns, Weber argues that order and disorder emerge *together* under modernity. Weber therefore reveals the *ambivalence* of modernity (Bauman, 1991) and this means that we get much more of a sense of the force and violence of nationalism through reading Weber than we do in reading Gellner. Nevertheless, Weber also seeks to suppress that ambivalence in order to assert his account of politics as involving the task of building a great nation-state.

This chapter begins by unpacking Weber's account of modern life as involving a rationalizing ethos. It contends that we need to understand it in order to be able to appreciate it as exactly that – a good story. This forms an important part of an analysis of the persistence of nationalism because of the way in which the story leads to an affirmation of the nation-state as the only noteworthy site of politics. Weber's analysis of the conditions of modern life leads him to set up a powerful political ontology, which includes an understanding of politics as a competition for power among great nation-states as well as a masculinist account of subjectivity as mastery. The point of introducing Jane Bennett's work next to Levin's existential angst in the opening quotations to this chapter is to invoke another way of seeing the world – as enchanted, playful and joyous, rather than as tragic, miserable and without meaning. Jane Bennett's affirmative reading of the world offers a contrasting account of modern life and, thus, it makes clear that there are other ways of understanding the world around us (2001). After unpacking this narrative of disenchantment and the way in which it supports Weber's insistence on the necessity of nationalism, the chapter concludes by asking what happens to nationalism if we take seriously Jane Bennett's provocation that 'the contemporary world is *not* disenchanted' (2001: 34)? In resisting Max Weber's account of the world, it is suggested that we can recover openings for thinking politics (and subjectivity) otherwise.

Weber's world

Max Weber is well known for his analysis that modern life involves systematic and escalating processes of rationalism and rationalization, which form central tenets for any understanding of 'Western civilization'.[1] These processes are expressed in the spirit of modern capitalism, which relies on an ethos of rational calculability and in systems of bureaucratic administration. This ethos of rationality[2] infects the spheres of economic life, law, administration and religious ethics, and leads to a varied set of processes including the depersonalization of social relationships, the refinements of techniques of calculation, the enhancement of social importance of specialized knowledge and the extension of technically rational control over both natural and social processes (Brubaker, 1984: 2). The rationalizing process of capitalism constitutes a particular understanding of how we might conduct ourselves socially. For example, rationality informs a new scientific understanding of the world, which believes everything to be discoverable and mastered by 'technical means of calculation' (Brubaker, 1984: 31). This scientific world view displaces more magical and religious understandings. One of the consequences of this view of the world as calculable and ultimately controllable is the corresponding sense that the world lacks any sense of meaning. There is a sharp tension between 'the deeply rooted demand that life and the world possess a coherent overall meaning and the increasingly evident impossibility of determining this meaning scientifically' (Brubaker, 1984: 31). For Weber, the growing domination of a restricted form of rationality leaves us with a sense of the world as disenchanted. This loss of meaning produces 'a threatening absence of value orientations for individuals' (Frisby, 1987: 429).

This account of modernization as rationalization can be understood in either a negative or a positive vein. As the last chapter discussed, Ernest Gellner accepts Weber's understanding of modern life as a process of increasing rationalization and locates the development of nations and nationalism as part of that process. However, whilst Gellner understands rationalization as a positive thing, Weber is deeply ambivalent about such processes (Brubaker, 1984). Whilst for Gellner, the deleterious effects of nationalism and rationalization are unfortunate consequences that we must nevertheless accept, Weber paints a much grimmer picture of a brutality that is *central* to rationalization. For Weber, modernity doesn't hold any promises and the mounting rationalization of social life threatens to produce the effect of an 'iron cage' (Weber, 2001: 123). Every quest to rationalize paradoxically makes things appear more and more irrational. The irrefutable feature of modern life is that there are no longer any timeless points of authority or constant gods that can ground and guide us. The metaphysical foundations of political life have been swept away. For this reason, 'politics is not a profession with a moral foundation, nor can it ever be' (Weber quoted in Mommsen, 1984: 38). There is no longer a given account of salvation that we can place our faith in, or received moral values that can underpin political order.

It is against this backdrop that we arrive at Max Weber's central problem (Hennis, 1988): what consequences follow for humanity if the rationalization of everyday life, which makes the whole world appear calculable, masterable and controllable, also makes life appear more and more meaningless? It is in the face of this crisis that Weber insists on the importance of a powerful, armed nation-state and a heroic individual that can overcome the banality of everyday life to achieve a meaningful existence. The idea of the meaningful nation and heroic individual[3] both emerge as new value-orientations that can guide us through a world that is now without redemption. Weber insists on the nation-state as the most important form of political community. He also asserts a particular account of freedom as a process of striving for meaning in a meaningless world. Whether we understand the rationalization of modern life as a positive or a negative development matters less than the point that nations and nationalism now appear as *necessary*. Whilst Weber offers us more of a sense of the force required to achieve and maintain a nation-state than Gellner does, what is consistent in both Gellner and Weber's works is the way in which the nation is made foundational to the possibility of *any* politics. This can be gleaned further through a discussion of Max Weber's inaugural address as Professor of Political Economy at the University of Freiburg.

The nation as the highest value principle

Delivered in May 1895, Max Weber's inaugural lecture on the subject of 'The Nation State and Economic Policy' (1994a) argues that the nation must guide and inform all questions of economic policy. Written against the backdrop of the internationalization of capital, as well as a new existentialism, Weber uses the lecture to claim the importance of placing the nation first: 'The economic policy of a German state, and, equally, the criterion of value used by a *German* economic theorist, can ... only be a *German* policy of criterion' (1994a: 15, my emphasis). In his address, Weber discusses the way in which Polish workers were at the close of the nineteenth century displacing German workers in the Eastern marches of the Reich as a result of an internationalizing capitalist economy. The traditional relationship between master and servant was being shattered as workers were hired seasonally and paid directly. In this context, Weber describes how Polish workers were 'willing' to work for less money and adapt to new working conditions. Against this backdrop of changing economic conditions, Weber makes his case for prioritizing the good of the nation – and therefore German workers: 'Policy must not be oriented solely to supposedly objective, purely economic principles, but it must seek the preservation and advancement of nationality as the highest principle' (Weber, 1994a: 40).

In building his case for how to respond to these changing times, Weber declares the nation-state as a superior form of political organization. He then goes on to offer an account of politics as involving a ruthless struggle for power and as an unmitigating battle between nationalities in the economic struggle for existence. Politics is described as a 'bleak', 'dark', activity, from which there is no peace to be had. Although the description of life as a 'struggle' for survival, involving 'the ability to adapt', has Darwinian connotations, Weber rejects a philosophy of history that carries with it a sense of progress. For Weber, there is no developmental imperative built into history and certainly no happiness that awaits us at the end of a political journey. We must prevent ourselves, he exclaims, 'from imagining that peace and happiness lie waiting in the womb of the future' (1994a: 14). As there is no formula for salvation, the only political imperative is to fight for a great and victorious nation. Glory derives from securing a great nation-state. Given that there's no possibility of peace to be had, the nation forms the best gift that one generation can pass to the next. The nation forms the only instance of 'glory' we have available to pass down to our descendants:

> Our successors will hold us answerable to history not primarily for the kind of economic organisation we hand down to them, but for the amount of elbow-room in the world which we conquer and bequeath to them.
>
> (1994a: 16)

Politics should therefore serve 'the enduring power-political interests of the nation' (ibid.). As Wolfgang Mommsen has put it,

> for Weber, who was an unbeliever in the Christian sense, national sentiment clearly took on, to some degree, the form of faith in Germany. It became what once, in his work on the methodology of the social sciences, he had called a 'value concept'.
>
> (1984: 49)

The nation therefore emerges as a solution to the problem of meaning.

The nation and a sense of meaning

Whilst Weber makes it clear that there are no longer any *necessary* grounds for establishing political authority, he nevertheless insists that this void *must* be filled by nations and nationalism. In the absence of any moral foundations, politics now involves the task of raising and preserving the 'national species':

> We do not have peace and human happiness to hand down to our descendants, but rather the eternal struggle to preserve and raise the quality of our national species.
>
> (1994a: 16)

Reading Weber in light of the First and Second World Wars that followed, we can appreciate the horrific implications of this desire to 'raise the quality of our national species'. As William Connolly argues, the price of keeping nihilism at bay is high (1988: 13) and Weber provides us with more of a sense of the violent implications of insisting upon the necessity of the nation-state than what we could read in Ernest Gellner or Anthony D. Smith's work discussed in the last chapter. However, the key point is that there is no necessary reason to respond to 'disenchantment' by opting for nationalism beyond Weber's insistence that things must be so. The nation provides a response to Weber's central problem of how we can establish a sense of meaning under modern conditions. 'If our work is to have any *meaning*', he says, 'it lies, and can only lie, in providing for the future, for our descendants' (1994a: 14, my emphasis). Despite his rejection of a politics guided by a transcendental ideal of happiness, he insists that there must be some overarching *purpose* to political life. Rejecting idealist narratives of a future peace, it is existential questions that lead Weber to insist on the importance of bequeathing a great German nation:

> The question which stirs us as we think beyond the grave of our own generation is not the well-being human beings will enjoy in the future but what kind of people they will be, and it is this same question which underlies all work in political economy.
>
> (1994a: 15)

The 'people' are of course the German people. For Weber, power, 'human greatness' and 'nobility' form the only truly honourable values in politics (ibid.).

The question to ask here is: what is the price of going along with the aim of providing 'meaning' and 'continuity' through a great nation-state? Weber's nationalism suggests that *all* questions of moral purpose should be directed towards the nation and, that any sense of a moral obligation to *others beyond our own nations* can only take second place. It also involves understanding living as a form of 'striving' for higher goals and that being still, immobile, pausing, or going slow can only suggest modes in a life that has not yet 'got going'.[4] This idea of a life lived through striving is deeply gendered, in that the support systems that enable the capacity to strive are mostly obfuscated. It also tends to assume an able-bodied figure that is understood as separate from the world around him and as capable of reordering the world in his vision. The idea of striving to increase the quality of the species also betrays racist, imperialist ambitions, as demonstrated in a letter that Weber wrote to his mother in April 1915, at the height of the First World War:

> We have proved we are a great cultural nation ... People who live in a civilized milieu and are nevertheless able to rise to the horrors of war (no achievement for a black man from Senegal!) and to return as honorably as most of our people do – that is real humanity. We cannot overlook this even in the light of much that is unpleasant.
>
> (Weber quoted in Mommsen, 1984: 191)

The First World War provided an opportunity for Weber to actively aim for a sense of national 'greatness'. Yet, as this quotation demonstrates, this ambition carries with it a pernicious assumption about the greatness of European civilization, a racist understanding of European superiority and a declaration that it is always worth paying a high price for national importance – 'even in the light of much that is unpleasant'. In this sense, Weber's work reveals to us the way in which nationalism has travelled on the back of ideas about Western civilization and European superiority (Chatterjee, 1993). Being a great nation-state represents an overarching value-orientation for Weber and he articulates an idea that continues to be powerful as the means and ends of political life. Weber presents an account of political life as geared towards the good of the nation and as involving a power game where becoming political will involve the struggle to take our place at the table. This represents no less than our 'historical responsibility'. Whilst we may contest this by suggesting that decolonised, newly independent or smaller nations also deserve a place at the table, such an argument ultimately misses what is at stake.[5] The most significant point is the way in which Weber establishes a state-centred architecture as the only valid way of understanding and doing politics.

Nationalism and the urge for mastery

Weber's sense of the necessity of nations emerges in a broader context which includes also an idea of the modern subject as a heroic individual who strives for great things. Significantly, these two points go hand in hand as part of Weber's nationalist imaginary, and they can be discerned in his well-established essay on 'The Profession and Vocation of Politics' (1994c), which puts forward a particular understanding of political subjectivity as involving autonomy, control and self-determination. Based on the lecture, 'Politik als Beruf', delivered in Munich in January 1919, this essay is written at the end of the First World War, but his ideas and understanding of modern conditions nevertheless appear remarkably consistent. In the essay, Weber draws a distinction between the idea of practising politics as a profession and as a vocation. Written in the context of the development of mass elections in liberal democracies and an emerging system of party politics, Weber is concerned with how we might establish a sense of meaning in the context of this evolving statist machine. He asks what are the possibilities for asserting freedom against the backdrop of further rationalization. This essay again affirms that the only way of responding to these rationalizing conditions is to aim for an all-powerful nation-state. It also insists on the need to place our faith in a self-determining individual who can act with a combination of reason, passion and judgement to brighten the nullity of everyday life.

In 'The Nation State and Economic Policy', Weber touched on the problem that an embryonic German nation will require a new political class that can establish 'the nation's sense of political purpose [*Sinn*]' (1994a: 21). This theme of a search for purpose appears again in the context of the 'The Profession and Vocation of Politics' essay, where Weber develops a distinction between people who work *from* politics (ensuring that the bureaucracy of parties, assemblies, elections continue to operate) and those who work *for* politics, and whose main duty it is to 'fight' (recalling the 'struggle' of political life). Into this struggle, Weber introduces the figure of the charismatic individual who devotes himself (*sic*) to politics. The politician who works *for* politics does so from a sense that he is giving his life meaning and purpose (*Sinn*) by devoting it to a 'cause' (1994c: 318). He dismisses politicians who are interested in power for power's own sake. Rather, a politician's actions must serve a greater cause, or else they will lead only to 'emptiness and absurdity' (1994c: 354).[6]

According to Weber, the ideal charismatic leader must possess a combination of three qualities: 'passion, a sense of responsibility, judgement' (1994c: 352). He must understand the need for a deeper meaning to political action and accept that, ultimately, 'The decisive means of politics is the use of violence' (1994c:

360). A leader cannot be a successful political leader on the basis of faith alone. That would represent an idealistic approach to politics, which fails to see that such ideals can no longer be guaranteed. It would also represent an irresponsible attitude to politics – which sometimes calls for violent means and demands taking responsibility for the consequences of one's actions.[7] For example, Weber attacks the revolutionary socialists for believing that politics involves a long wait for a 'flowering of summer' (1994c: 368). Similarly, anyone who turns to politics as a means of saving his soul fails to understand the nature of political struggle and the dark realities of political life. Writing at the end of the First World War, he asks, how many of the revolutionaries will live to see the results of their enthusiasm ten years from now? How many will by then have receded into embitterment, opted for a dull acceptance of the world and one's job or for 'a mystical flight from the world' (ibid.)? In contrast to a political vision based around hope, Weber argues that all that lies ahead is 'a polar night of icy darkness and hardness' (ibid.). In consequence, the only task is to assume responsibility in the face of the *tragedy* of the world. Only a person with the resilience to carry on, to be able to say 'nevertheless' has a true vocation for politics. This is because politics involves 'slow, strong drilling through hard boards, with a combination of passion and a sense of judgement' (1994c: 369). The politician who seeks power for power's sake fails to understand the *tragic* basis of political life under modern conditions: '[he] knows nothing of the tragedy in which all action, but quite particularly political action, is in truth enmeshed' (1994c: 354).

Weber warns us that anyone who gets involved with politics is necessarily getting involved with questions of power and violence, and is effectively therefore 'making a pact with diabolical powers' (1994c: 362). This 'value-creating act of will' must therefore form the foundation of political authority. The rationalization of everyday life leads to the necessity of a 'decisionist ethics' where political action rests simply with a political leader's decision to follow his judgement combined with a sense of faith. Crucially, it doesn't matter what this faith or belief represents: it could be *anything*. The only requirement is that *some* kind of genuine belief is present:

> He can serve a national goal or the whole of humanity, or social and ethical goals, or goals which are cultural, inner-worldly or religious; he may be sustained by a strong faith in 'progress'…or he may coolly reject this kind of faith; he can claim to be the servant of an 'idea' or, rejecting on principle any such aspirations, he may claim to serve external goals of everyday life – *but some kind of belief must always be present. Otherwise (and there can be no denying this) even political achievements which, outwardly, are supremely successful will be cursed with the nullity of all mortal undertakings.*
>
> (1994c: 355, my emphasis)

Weber responds to the loss of firm foundations under modernity by insisting upon a nation-state, a self-determining individual and the need for a sense of purpose.

Unlike Ernest Gellner and Anthony D. Smith, who tend to mask the *politics* involved in insisting on the necessity of the nation, Weber reveals the full force involved in such a claim. He offers a classic account of politics as *RealPolitik*. Nevertheless, this is a historically contingent account of what political life must involve as well as a particularly violent one. Having described that there is no *necessary* moral foundation to political life, Weber concludes that the only way of responding to this abyss is to insist that all social and economic questions should now be subordinated to the 'historical obligation' of building a great nation-state, at whatever cost. But, in the course of making his case, Weber reveals a deep ambivalence around the question of the foundations of political life and offers us a glimpse of the fact that politics could also be organized otherwise.

Modernity and ambivalence

In responding to uncertainty by insisting on the certainty of the nation-state and sovereign subject, Weber seeks a way of overcoming or 'deferring' nihilism (Connolly, 1988). Weber presents an account of the importance of the nation-state and the self-determining individual, and these appear as a way of restoring order and a sense of purpose in response to the rupture at the heart of modernity. However, the problem with such an insistence on order, is that it can only be achieved by dismissing all other forms of organizing political life as less valid, less impressive or plain absurd. As William Connolly puts it:

> Modern denial of the advent of nihilism takes the form of organizing the self and the world to fit into a tightly demarcated order and treating everything that does not fit into it to be matter out of place in need of punishment, reform or destruction.
>
> (1988: 14)

Other forms of being in the world are cast aside as representing weakness or an escape from the world. They don't represent 'real' political heroism or even real politics. Weber's work is interesting because we get a clear sense in it of both the violence and the ambivalence of this account of politics. It is a powerful move to dismiss other ways of being political as immature or not serious, because it determines the conditions for being political – and for making a claim to be heard, seen or counted. Put simply, Max Weber's writings reveal how politics involves the feat of establishing what politics must be about (Walker, 1993; 2009). Yet in the same way that it becomes difficult to imagine what other possibilities might be available, Weber's work also reveals the dangers of insisting upon this singular account of politics.

In order to resist an account of the world as in need of mastery, and of politics as a game of power between nation-states, the task is not to restore metaphysical foundations but to offer a different account of modern life. For example, for Michael Dillon, the impossibility of metaphysical foundations does not leave us at the edge of an abyss but provides an opening through which we can rethink our

relationship to the world around us: 'The impossibility of metaphysical foundations is now the starting point for political thought' (Dillon, 1996: 129). Dillon
offers a very different account of 'tragedy' in order to unfurl another approach to
the political.[8] In doing so, he offers a contrast to a Weberian account of international politics by engaging a different understanding of what it means to be
human. For example, drawing on Hellenic thought, Dillon argues that human life
is profoundly tragic (1996: 138). But this sense of the tragedy of the human
condition should not be understood as something negative, as it is for Weber.
Tragedy is not tragedy because we die, are fated and therefore miserable (Dillon,
1996: 141). Rather, tragedy constitutes the adventure of life itself. Although there
is no avoiding despair, mortality, anger and grief, tragedy offers us the 'fusion of
grief and joy' (1996: 10). Significantly, this understanding of tragedy exposes the
impossibility of mastery because death is taken to be an inescapable condition of
life and not a hindrance that must be overcome. Whilst Weber responds to tragedy
with mastery, which takes the form of an all-powerful nation-state and a self-
directed heroic individual who can differentiate himself from 'lesser mortals',
this understanding of the tragic cannot be surmounted through reason, willpower
or national greatness. This is because tragedy according to this sense involves the
recognition of life as unmasterable.[9]

We may recall that, for Weber, the heroic individual who can appreciate the
tragic conditions of political life is contrasted with those who opt for a 'mystical
flight from the world' – either by opting for an idealist political outlook or by
retreating to a bitter acceptance of the darkness of the world. This alternative
reading of the tragic offered by Dillon by way of Hellenic thought doesn't simply
offer a different *response* to 'darkness' but, rather, challenges this very account of
the world. In this sense, it chimes with Gilles Deleuze's effort (drawing on
Nietzsche) to understand the tragic as affirmative:

> The tragic is not to be found in this anguish or disgust, not in a nostalgia for a
> lost unity. The tragic is only to be found in multiplicity, in the diversity of affir-
> mation *as such*. What defines the tragic is the joy of multiplicity, plural joy.
>
> (1983: 17)

According to Deleuze, joy does not form a way of *overcoming* tragedy. Rather, 'it
is joy that is tragic' (1983: 17). Whilst tragedy poses the question of the meaning
of existence, as suggested by Max Weber, it doesn't understand that question as
something that must be *justified*. As Deleuze explains, 'for a long time the sense
of existence has only been looked for by positing it as something faulty or blame-
worthy, something unjust which ought to be justified. A god was needed to
interpret existence' (1983: 18–19). In contrast to a Christian philosophical heri-
tage which demands that there must be some *meaning* to existence, as affirmed in
the quotation from *Anna Karenina* which opened this chapter, tragedy responds
to the question of the meaning of life with the affirmation of life itself. In this
understanding, 'existence justifies all that it affirms, including suffering, instead
of being itself justified by suffering, or in other words, sanctified and deified'

(1983: 19).[10] This is closer to Michael Dillon's understanding in that tragedy doesn't lead to closure (such as under nationalism), but provides an opening for rethinking the political.

Weber can be read as offering a sense of the *ambivalence* of life, in that we can't easily separate good from bad, the rational from the irrational. But he ultimately seeks to respond to the conditions of modern life by 'filling in' for the lack of meaning. In contrast, in Hellenic accounts of tragedy, Dillon argues that there is nothing to 'fill in': there are only multiple understandings of what it might mean to live, to be in the world and to care for others. This suggests another way of understanding what it means to act politically. According to Dillon, the tragic hero knows that we will never be fully in control of our actions: the demand to act, and to take responsibility, is still important, but articulated differently. This is not a 'moral imperative', arising from a command ethic, or a 'value-creating act of will'. It offers no prescription for a way forward, but it exposes the demand to act, publicly, because this is the unavoidable condition of being human, to respond to the 'terrible movements, demands and responsibilities' of life itself (1996: 145). The tragic hero doesn't take decisions as a way of avoiding nullity and despair, because there is no avoiding despair and tragedy doesn't invite us to reflect on the *lack* of meaning in the world. Tragedy, in the way outlined by Dillon, is 'concerned precisely with the condition in which we do not and cannot know what is correct in advance' (1996: 145) and stages a 'working out' of the agonism that is central to the human condition but without the promise of transcendence (1996: 143).[11]

What does this mean for attempts at resisting nationalist thought? It means that we don't have to accept Weber's options: to embrace willpower and national greatness or retreat into a dull acceptance of the world. It is *this* nihilistic and dualistic view of the world that suggests that, if we don't have nationalism, then we'll be left with nothing. And it is this fear of 'nothing' that ultimately haunts and disturbs the nationalist imagination. This was demonstrated in the last chapter, in the discussion of how theorists of nationalism suggest that it is the risk of 'nothing' – no cultural attachments, no solidarity, no continuity – that prompts the need for nations and nationalism. The point here is not to debate whether the contemporary world offers enough 'solidarity' or not but to reject this binary approach to framing political issues.

This brief excursion into another understanding of the tragic chimes with Jane Bennett's provocation, introduced at the beginning of this chapter. She asks us to consider what happens when we refuse to understand life as disenchanted (2001). As she argues, Weber's account of the modern world as disenchanted is only realized *in opposition* to the sense of an enchanted, cosmological order. A world of magic appears under a 'haze of nostalgia' as an object that is completely other to the modern world and yet is heavily desired (Bennett, 2001: 63). This suggests that Weber is fully aware that there are other understandings available of how to live and organize politically. But rather than accept his ultimatum about the necessity of nationalism, both Bennett and Dillon's works suggest openings for contesting a nationalist imaginary by refusing to understand death as 'meaningless', thereby necessitating arrogant accounts of self-mastery or racist assertions about the contin-uation of the species. They suggest embracing being in the world as a riddle and appreciating that the world does not represent a blank canvas lying in wait for humans to make their mark on it. In this sense, they challenge us to reimagine ideas about what political life must involve.

Conclusion

In recalling Weber's account of modernity, the aim of this chapter has been to show how nationalism, and a particular account of subjectivity as mastery, emerges alongside a story about modern life as disenchanted. In so doing, the chapter has sought to expand on the question of imagination introduced in the last chapter to argue that nationalist thought relies on a broader political ontology. This includes the idea of politics as a power struggle between great nation-states and as a struggle to create meaning in a meaningless world. In situating the idea of the nation in relation to this broader account, the point has been to show that the task of thinking beyond the nation will also need to address this narrative of modern life as disenchanted. The chapter has demonstrated that the quest for order, mastery and meaning appears both in the idea of the nation-state presented as the only proper account of political space and in the idea of a rational, auto-nomous individual. Yet these are neither necessary nor exclusive accounts of how we might organize political life or understand what it means to be in the world. The final part of this chapter turned to different narratives about the 'tragic' nature of existence to demonstrate alternative understandings of what it means to live with others. This involves rejecting a nihilistic account of life that frames options according to a binary logic suggesting that if we don't have nationalism, then we are left with 'nothing', and embracing instead an account of life as *en*chanted, joyful and playful, as well as difficult and occasionally brutal.

This story of modern life as disenchanted will appear again in Chapter 5 of this book, in the case of a bestselling novel published in response to the heightened nationalism of the 'War on Terror' called *The Reluctant Fundamentalist*. That novel offers a critique of nationalism, but it nevertheless reproduces an account of modern life as disenchanted. Chapter 5 argues that critiques of nationalism that fail to interrogate this quest for mastery and meaning are insufficient because they risk reproducing key elements of nationalist thought. This suggests that we need to understand this narrative of modern life as disenchanted in depth in order to appreciate what is at stake in developing a robust critique of nationalism. The next chapter offers another contribution towards that broader aim by turning to another story about the disenchantment of modern life, as presented in this case by Jean-Jacques Rousseau (1712–1778). Of course, Rousseau presents a very different account of politics to Max Weber, but what is interesting is the way in which Rousseau's work is animated by the sense that something, under moder-nity, has been *lost*. The next chapter will argue that a robust critique of nationalism needs to appreciate the way in which this 'sense of loss' (Bennett, 2001: 8) is also central to the nationalist imaginary.

3 Rousseau's legacies

The politics of time, community and loss

We are the creatures of a great thirst. Bent on coming home to a place we have never known.

George Steiner, *Grammars of Creation*

To be modern is to find ourselves in an environment that promises us adventure, power, joy, growth, transformation of ourselves and the world – and, at the same time, that threatens to destroy everything we have, everything we know, everything we are.

Marshall Berman, *All That is Solid Melts Into Air*

Introduction

This chapter addresses some of the writings of the Enlightenment philosopher Jean-Jacques Rousseau (1712–1778). This is not in order to announce that Rousseau was a 'nationalist'; writing before the French Revolution, Rousseau wouldn't recognize the form of 'popular sovereignty' that we now associate with the nation as a constituency that provides legitimacy to the state.[1] Nevertheless, Rousseau forms an important theorist for a study of nationalism because of his portrayal of modern life as constituted in relation to the *loss* of community. This chapter investigates Rousseau's account of the breakdown in community that supposedly engendered the modern era (Nancy, 1991: 9) in order to enquire into the work that it does and the political claims that follow from this foundational narrative. Rousseau offers us another account of modern life as disenchanted, though it is significantly different to that encountered in relation to Max Weber. Rousseau presents an understanding of the modern world as full of discord, noise and 'continual flux' and yearns for a sense of unity and stillness that will keep such discord at bay (Gunnell, 1968; Berman, 1983). The quotation by George Steiner selected to open this chapter echoes Rousseau's craving for a *return* to a simpler and uncomplicated political community, but, as Steiner's quote also suggests, we need to be suspicious of such nostalgia. Whilst accounts of 'loss' have accompanied the Western world from its beginnings, from the 'nostalgia for a more archaic community that has disappeared, to deploring a loss of familiarity, fraternity and conviviality' (Nancy, 1991: 10), this chapter argues that accounts of loss continue to animate attempts at engaging the politics of coexistence.[2] This framing of community therefore forms a key aspect of the nationalist imaginary. Reading Rousseau helps us challenge such nationalist yearnings by asking critical questions about what it *is* that is assumed to have been lost and what is being *forgotten* in the haze of nostalgia for a time when life was ostensibly more straightforward. Finally it also prompts the question of what would it mean to reject the assumption of loss as a starting point for thinking about politics.

The chapter begins by turning to the story Rousseau tells about our 'fall' from an original state of unity and calm to the harsh, discordant state of society, as outlined in *The Discourse on the Origin of Inequality*, first published in 1755, otherwise known as The Second Discourse.[3] The assumption outlined in this text, that 'we' must have been more united, secure and innocent *in the past* forms a powerful backdrop for Rousseau's 'ideal society', that is, a society based upon coherency, commonality and unity, and which is outlined more thoroughly in *Of The Social Contract*, first published in 1762. In reading these two texts, this chapter argues that we need to question Rousseau's 'story of origins' and the series of determinations that he establishes in response to it. These include a modern understanding of freedom and subjectivity as involving self-determination, autonomy and the capacity to perfect ourselves over time.[4] These ideas continue to form key aspects of a nationalist imaginary, yet what is interesting about Rousseau is the way in which he reveals their *contingency*. Rousseau is a thought-provoking figure to contend with because he knows that these are not necessarily starting points that we must accept for political life more generally (Connolly, 1988, 2004). He is a good story-teller, and knows that there are competing understandings of the world and how we might understand our place in it. The chapter therefore closes by introducing other ways of understanding what it might mean to live in common and suggesting that the turmoil, temporality and flux of modern life might instead be embraced as part of what it means to be modern, as the opening quotation to this chapter by Marshall Berman indicates. The chapter therefore reads Rousseau both for the openings and the closures that his work introduces in relation to the task of reimagining political community.

The state of nature

Drawing inspiration from physicists who were hypothesizing about the formation of the world, Rousseau's Second Discourse represents one of the first attempts in Enlightenment thought[5] to offer a temporal account of humanity's development. His desire to understand 'human nature' is not in itself unique, as the idea of a human nature consistent throughout space and time was crucial to Enlightenment thought, as was the idea that it was discoverable through the use of reason. But what is distinctive in Rousseau's case is that he locates the nature of man in a historical epoch (Horowitz, 1987; Hutchings, 2008; Masters, 1976; Wokler, 1987, 2001). For Rousseau, human nature is not static, but assumes a temporal quality which can be described in terms of revolutionary transformations over vast periods of time. Although Rousseau accepts Buffon's theory of the original homogeneity of the species, he makes what would have been considered a radical proposal that mankind (and only mankind) has the capacity to change and adapt to new circumstances and environments. Rather than understand humans, plants and animals as entities that can be empirically observed and transparently represented on a flat table according to their relationships of identity and difference, Rousseau is one of the first to make the argument that men have transformed over time from a 'savage' to a 'civilized' state. This leads him to make what was at the time considered to be a bold and innovative hypothesis: that mankind could have developed from apes (Wokler, 1978).

Whilst Rousseau provides a lucid (and very early) expression of the historicization of things and of consciousness, he is nevertheless also fearful of these developments. On the one hand he offers a powerful analysis of modern life as a condition of 'continual flux' – an analysis that resonates in Karl Marx's work and is picked up later by theorists of modern life including Henri Lefebvre (1995) and Marshall Berman (1983). But, instead of embracing the rhythms of modern life, as Marshall Berman's quotation, used to open this chapter, indicates, Rousseau approaches change with anxiety:

> Everything upon the earth is in continual flux. Nothing in it retains a form that is constant and fixed, and our affections, attached to external things, necessarily pass and change like the things themselves. Always, ahead of or behind us, they recall the past which no longer exists, or they anticipate a future which often will never come to pass: there is nothing there solid enough for the heart to attach itself to.
>
> (Rousseau quoted in Gunnell, 1968: 251;
> also quoted in Bartelson, 2001: 36)

This description of the 'flux' of modern life is important because it forms a persistent shadow over Rousseau's quest for unity, stillness and calm. Rousseau is well known to have disliked the dynamism and discord that accompanied a modernizing and urbanizing society, which led him ultimately to retreat to a life in the countryside practising horticulture.[6] And in consequence, Rousseau yearns to regain a time when forms were fixed and he and the world could be at one with one another. This portrayal of a time of innocence recurs throughout Rousseau's account of the ideal political community, and is what makes it worth investigating further.

As Rousseau sees it, in the state of nature each man (sic) lives in isolation and subsides in plenty. He has all the faculties for self-preservation and his capabilities are never superfluous to his needs. Man's needs, desires and feelings are in accord with those of nature around him and he has not yet had to succumb to the anxieties brought on by society:

> everything takes place in such a *uniform* manner and where the face of the earth is not subject to those sudden and continual changes caused by the passions and inconsistency of peoples living together.
>
> (Rousseau, 1992: 20, my emphasis)

Man in the state of nature is therefore free and autonomous in a way that, crucially, becomes impossible when *people start living together*. Furthermore, this is a state where man is free from servitude and domination, because no man can command another. In all, he leads a fully autonomous life, which includes no relationships of power or chains of dependence. Man is happy, then, because he is *independent*, unlike in society where he becomes *dependent*. He lives a simple life and does not experience the anxiety brought about by the awareness of himself as a temporal (mortal) being. Man only has to live in the immediate present and, interestingly, he has no awareness of the past or the future. He is therefore also free from metaphysical doubt and fear of death:[7]

> His soul, agitated by nothing, is given over to the single feeling of his own present existence, without any idea of the future, however near it may be, and his projects, as limited as his views, hardly extend to the end of the day.
>
> (Rousseau, 1992: 27)

Rousseau's portrait of the state of nature forms an important backdrop to his politics because it will recur to inform his image of what constitutes the ideal political society. The Second Discourse charts this journey from man's original freedom in the state of nature to the state of society, which represents difference, turmoil and discord. As we will see, this is a story about deterioration. Disagreeing with the majority of his Enlightenment counterparts, and in particular with Diderot and d'Alembert, editors of the *Encyclopédie*, Rousseau believes that increased progress will inevitably lead to deterioration and decline. What this means is that nothing can be as perfect as the original state of nature from which we have fallen. The state of nature offers a picture of Rousseau's ideal conditions of autonomy and independence but, significantly, these will forever remain *unattainable*.

From nature to society

Rousseau's picture of the state of nature is often juxtaposed to Thomas Hobbes's well-known depiction of nature as a state in which life is 'nasty, brutish and short' (1996: 86). Unlike Hobbes's war of all against all, Rousseau posits natural man as peaceful and good. As Rousseau describes it: '*Nature, in giving men tears, bears witness that she gives the human race the softest hearts*' (1992: 37). Although Rousseau's natural man is similarly concerned with self-preservation, this doesn't lead him to harm others, because man is independent and doesn't need others to survive. He is compassionate and has pity, which means that he wouldn't hurt others deliberately. Feelings of vanity, pride and self-interest therefore all develop in society, and this is what leads to the possibility of corruption, decadence and decline. Thus, Rousseau appears to offer a contrasting view of the state of nature to that put forward by Thomas Hobbes. However, Rousseau follows Hobbes in a crucial regard. For both Rousseau and Hobbes, self-interest is a problem that demands a sovereign intervention. And significantly, for both, the unstoppable momentum that takes us from nature towards society has the effect of dividing people against themselves and against one another. Rousseau therefore accomplishes an important task: to implant a picture of man's essential nature and a sense of how much that nature has been changed by *time* (Starobinski, 1988: 295). For Rousseau as for Hobbes, it will be impossible to return to the state of nature. Thus, although Rousseau's account appears at first glance to be different from Hobbes's, in that nature represents harmony, unity and an *absence* of conflict, for both thinkers, the state of nature forms a necessary fulcrum for constructing the ideal society.

Rousseau therefore follows Hobbes in an important regard, that is, in claiming that society belongs to a different temporal plane, which destroys and transforms nature forever. For Rousseau, the 'spirit of society' 'change[s] and alter[s] all our natural inclinations' (1992: 70). Thus, although conflict doesn't exist in Rousseau's state of nature, in ensuring the destruction of that state, Rousseau presents us with a Hobbesian problem: how are we to live together when our natural instinct in society is to compete and tear each other apart? Rousseau repeats a Hobbesian dilemma as well as a Hobbesian solution: there is no option other than to unite in a political community under a sovereign authority that can keep our anarchic instincts under control. As with Hobbes's *Leviathan*, Rousseau's state of nature is posited as a rhetorical tool that serves to assert a host of conditions that must follow from it. In juxtaposing the state of nature with the state of society, Rousseau presents a story about the 'destiny of men, caught between the innocence they have renounced and the perdition that is certain to follow' (Starobinski, 1988: 3). Although man can't be free again in his 'natural' state, the possibility of exercising a new form of freedom, based on the laws of reason, in a sovereign political community is open and *must* be taken (Wokler, 1987). This is man's best hope of recreating a dream of independent, autonomous existence. Most importantly then, Rousseau follows Hobbes by using a portrait of the state of nature to *clear the ground* of all other understandings of what it means to be human and to form part of a community, and to *project* a new and modern account of man as a self-determining free agent and of political community united under a sovereign.

This account of the shift from nature to society establishes a new ground for how politics under the conditions of modernity must now be organized. However, with this story, Rousseau also presents us with a paradox, in that it is not clear how we might have moved from the state of nature *to* the state of society. If there was once a time when change was minimal and man lived mainly in the immediate present, how did history gather itself into a force that would bring about man's full faculties? Although Rousseau aims to establish his account of the state of nature on scientific grounds, he is forced to admit that his account of the slow revolutions that formed a civil society also relies on *some measure of conjecture*. In order to account for how this shift from nature to society might have come about, Rousseau introduces the concept of *perfectibilité* (a concept that he also invents). He tells us that men, unlike animals, are 'free beings' and are therefore capable of self-improvement. Each individual's potential for perfectibility eventually leads to an unstoppable struggle which destroys the state of nature forever.

He then speculates that fire would have been invented by 'lightning, volcano, or some fortuitous chance happening' (1992: 45) and that the invention of iron can be explained through 'the extraordinary circumstance of some volcano that, in casting forth molten metal, would have given observers the idea of imitating this operation of nature' (1992: 51). Rousseau knows that it is impossible for him to stand 'outside' history and establish how the world and humanity's place in it might have begun. Yet, despite having to rely on speculation, Rousseau argues that this story nevertheless serves to establish *definite* truths, as this quotation indicates:

> I admit that, since the events I have to describe could have taken place in several ways, *I cannot make a determination among them except on the basis of conjecture*. But over and above the fact that these conjectures become reasons when they are the most probable ones that a person can draw from the nature of things and the sole means that a person can have of discovering the truth, *the consequences I wish to deduce from mine will not thereby be conjectural*, since, on the basis of the principles I have just established, no other system is conceivable that would not furnish me with the same results, and from which I could draw the same conclusions.
>
> (1992: 43, my emphasis)

Although the origins of man and society are impossible to determine with any exactness, Rousseau insists that the conclusions he draws will nevertheless be unquestionable. But what is most interesting about this disclosure is the way in which it *must remain hidden* (Connolly, 2004, 1988). Whilst 'unity' is posited as a pre-social, 'natural' condition, Rousseau is aware that this image of stillness and calm is a fantasy. The key point, then, is that it serves to establish a powerful narrative *about a journey from unity to difference*. This is an important achievement, as not only will the picture of stability and uniformity continue to guide his political thought but, furthermore, and as we will see, from now on, encounters with difference, change and flux will all be haunted by the sense of a 'lost' unity.

The politics of origins

Rousseau attempts to further differentiate himself from Thomas Hobbes by offering a new account of the foundations of political community, and this forms the main aim *Of The Social Contract*. In contrast to Hobbes, who argues that political society is founded on force, Rousseau contends that obedience to political authority should be based upon legitimate grounds. In *Of The Social Contract*, Rousseau boldly states that all other attempts to define the origins of political society have failed to do so properly, either because they assume them to be given by nature (as in the tradition of natural law) or because they have failed to establish a convention that can claim legitimacy (as in the case of Hobbes). Rousseau rejects the idea that obedience should be founded on force because, 'To yield to force is an act of necessity, not of will' (1997: 44). Political right should instead be founded on an act of *will*. This claim leads him to present a challenge: to imagine a form of political community where the people agree to unite together and yet remain as autonomous beings:

> To find a form of association that will defend and protect the person and goods of each associate with the full common force, and by means of which each, uniting with all, nevertheless obey only himself and remain as free as before.
>
> (1997: 49–50)

Rousseau's solution to this challenge is the idea of the social contract, which forms a way for the people agree to unite under a sovereign. The brilliance of the idea, for Rousseau, lies in the fact that 'each giving himself to all, gives himself to no one' (1997: 50). In suggesting that man can be as 'free as before', Rousseau is referring to the freedom man had in the state of nature.

The free will of each member of the community will therefore be advanced as part of a whole: 'Each of us puts his person and his full power in common under the supreme direction of the general will; and in a body we receive each member as an indivisible part of the whole' (1997: 50). This general will, which founds the body politic, and which has 'absolute power over all its members' bears the 'name of sovereignty' (1997: 61). The 'general will' represents the common interests of the community and therefore also reflects the common good. The idea is that the sovereign cannot have any interests contrary to the people, as the sovereign is formed of the people. For example then, obeying the law cannot be contrary to freedom, because it is a law that the people themselves have constituted. Indeed, obeying the law forms another aspect of freedom (1997: 54). The general will is therefore put forward to solve any sense of conflict between the people and the sovereign, or between an individual's will and the community's will, because the people are at both and the same time citizens (participants in sovereign authority) and subjects (subject to the laws of the state). Yet, as we interrogate Rousseau's account further, it becomes clear that maintaining this principle of unity is not as straightforward as he implies.

As William Connolly has argued, what is especially difficult to determine is how and when the act by which the people agreed to form a political community took place (1988, 2004). Rousseau describes that this act was agreed before the formation of laws. He explains that men, having reached the point where they have *left behind* the irretrievable conditions of their natural freedom are now faced with the 'obstacles' of society, where man's self-interest, perfectibility and desire for self-preservation brings him into conflict with other human beings. This primitive state is unsustainable and, according to Rousseau: 'humankind would perish if it did not change its way of being' (1997: 49). There would be a war of all against all. Thus man decides to surrender some of his natural freedoms to gain civil freedom. The problem, however, is that the same conditions that call for the emergence of the social order also threaten its survival. In this sense, we are again presented with a paradox. How can a mass of individuals driven by self-interest, greed, competitiveness and jealousy agree to submit to an authority that will necessarily, sometimes, contradict their own desires? As Connolly maintains, Rousseau is more aware than anyone of this paradox. The question of how a mass of individuals agreed to come together and form a community forms a puzzle of cause and effect:

> For a nascent people to be capable of appreciating sound maxims of politics and of following the fundamental rules of reason of State, *the effect would have to become the cause*, the social spirit which is to be the work of the institution would have to preside over the institution itself, and men would have to be prior to laws what they ought to become by means of them.
>
> (1997: 71, my emphasis)

Yet there is no evidence in the story of the evolution of man and in the development of society (as written by Rousseau) that suggests that this is possible. Indeed, Rousseau admits as much, as this quotation demonstrates:

> The clauses of the contract are so completely determined by the nature of the act that the slightest modification would render them null and void; so that *although they may never have been formally stated*, they are everywhere the same, everywhere tacitly admitted and recognized.
>
> (1997: 50, my emphasis)

The modality of this decision to form a community is crucial. It is projected back into a time before the creation of laws and is now irretrievable. A people find themselves '*already* bound together by some union of origin, interest or convention' (1997: 77, my emphasis). This decision retreats into an abyss that precedes the contract. Of course, Rousseau knows that no such decision will have ever taken place and that there is no community prior to the contract. Yet this fictive account is *necessary* in order to establish the proclaimed *legitimacy* of the social pact.

Indeed, Rousseau briefly admits that this decision 'may never have been formally stated' but what is most significant is his insistence on the *consequences* that follow: the clauses of the contract are 'everywhere tacitly admitted and recognized' (1997: 50). As with the Second Discourse, when Rousseau acknowledges that he cannot know for certain how society began but insists that the implications that follow are indisputable, a similar rhetorical gesture is repeated here. *What Rousseau reveals is that unity will have to be forced*. In erasing the decision through which the people agree to form a political community, Rousseau obfusates the politics at work in securing this 'agreement'. He also dismisses the politics involved in casting aside alternative possibilities. Above all, what Rousseau succeeds in doing is to establish commonality as foundational to political community, and to insist that such commonality cannot be put under question.

Maintaining unity

Rousseau's ideal political community is founded on the principle of unity but, as the first part of this argument outlined, this ideal of unity is haunted by the threat of division, fragmentation and discord. In consequence, Rousseau puts forward a series of measures to maintain unity and to keep disagreement at bay. These include the figure of the lawgiver, who is introduced to remind the people of their original commitment to unity. Despite insisting that the 'general will' is directed towards the common good, Rousseau divulges that some people can make mistakes about what the common good might look like. The problem with a community formed around the 'general will', it seems, is that the general will can err. The lawgiver is introduced to intervene, guide and teach the people to know what they will and secure public enlightenment. Given the limits of deliberative reason, Rousseau needs a higher authority that he can appeal to in order to remind the people of why they came together and submitted to authority in the first place. This higher authority needs to be able to 'rally without violence and to persuade without convincing' (1997: 71). In addition to the lawgiver, then, Rousseau introduces the principle of patriotism. Members of the community must be willing to risk their lives for the state: 'All have to fight for the fatherland if need be, it is true' (1997: 64). Rousseau claims is that this will be preferable to fighting ourselves – which is what we would risk by returning to the primitive state of society. Finally, he insists on the importance of a small polity, which can be subjected to the highest degree of uniformity. This will 'reduce the arrival of new and unforeseen circumstances to a minimum' (Connolly, 2004: 24).[8]

To instill the importance of remaining united, Rousseau banishes all factions and minority group interests. In so doing, he echoes Machiavelli's argument that factions harm republics:

> It is important, then, that in order to have the general will expressed well, there be no partial society in the State, and every Citizen state only his own opinion.
>
> (1997: 60)

Thus the price of maintaining unity lies with the exclusion of particular interests and the silencing of factions, parties, identities, classes and groups (Althusser, 1972: 150). Although Rousseau is occasionally read as a theorist of democracy, given his championing of public assemblies, these assemblies are only designed to reinforce an *already determined* general will. This general will is *more* than an aggregation of voices. It is, he explains, 'constant, unalterable, and pure' (1997: 122). The general will is based on a contract that is now buried in a dark, unreachable origin. And although it can never be unearthed, it is absolute and beyond question. Thus, the general will is not so much the outcome of a procedural politics, as its condition (Barnard, 1988: 74). It's not the task of the people to deliberate what the general will may be because the general will has already spoken. Rather, the people's responsibility is to focus on summoning up this pre-political, constant and pure general will that is a symbol of harmony, unity and virtue. Finally, in order to secure the people's allegiance to sovereign authority, Rousseau introduces the concept of civil religion. The principles of this religion are also closed to debate: 'the dogmas of the civil Religion ought to be simple, few in number, stated with precision, *without explanations or commentary*' (1997: 150). And given that the state cannot sustain conflict between allegiance to a Priest and allegiance to a Master, patriotism must form the primary faith.

Any debate will therefore be bound within the pre-established parameters of the general will. This suggests Rousseau's recurring fear of discord and turmoil. The formulation involves the same underlying tension between the longing for unity and the fear of disunity that we encountered in the Second Discourse. William Connolly argues that the kind of uniformity demanded by Rousseau is so out of step with contemporary conditions that 'the worst kind of nightmare would result if it were to emerge as an active agenda today' (2004: 25). Whilst such a scenario is unlikely, his work is significant because it reveals that: 'To be a sovereign, territorial people, it is necessary to become a highly unified nation' (2004: 25). This implies that strict measures will have to be put in place to maintain this sense of unity. Yet what we find is that, despite Rousseau's attempts to keep difference at bay, this is exactly what keeps on resurfacing. Plurality and contingency – arguably the very stuff of politics – is the stuff of which Rousseau is most afraid. They don't exist in his ideal world of the state of nature, and his ideal political community is built around maxims that reduce the risk of change to a minimum. Yet Rousseau's efforts at maintaining unity also demonstrate that antagonism cannot be expelled completely. Patriotism emerges in an attempt at banishing friction and factions, and this will necessarily involve force.

What, then, are the alternatives to this account of social union laid out by Rousseau? The only option offered in the *Social Contract* is to retreat to the primitive conditions of the state of society. This is the point at which, having permanently left the state of nature, we find ourselves in a brutish state, where people's competitiveness, jealousy, self-interest and dependency all form an unbearable, oppressive melee. Thus, although this is an 'option', Rousseau warns us that it's highly unlikely people would want to 'return' to this abominable state. Whilst the people reserve the right to withdraw their goods and civil freedoms, Rousseau assures us that the contract 'really proves to be preferable to what it had been before' (1997: 63). Thus, man should 'ceaselessly bless the happy moment which wrested him from it forever, and out of a stupid and bounded animal made an intelligent being and a man' (1997: 53). In other words, why on earth would anyone want to give up or contest the social contract? Despite contrasting himself with Hobbes, this is the point at which Rousseau follows most closely in Hobbes's footsteps. He sets up a portrait of the past as consumed by a war of all against all and as the alternative which compels us to accept the security offered by a sovereign political community. The point to remember, however, is that these two options – anarchy or sovereignty – form part of a narrative established by Rousseau. There was no such anarchic, brutish state. This *memory* of chaos and disorder is a fiction that serves to establish why we must accept the authority of the state. In order to contest this conclusion, we must return to address his story of origins about the journey from nature to society, or from unity to difference.

Freedom in time

This narrative about a journey from nature to society, and from unity to difference, enables Rousseau to project a modern understanding of freedom as involving self-determination, autonomy and perfectibility. We have established that Rousseau's state of nature stands *outside* historical time as a point that sets a host of necessary consequences in motion. As such it forms an unreachable, unrecoverable 'void' that makes possible the ensuing tide of history (Starobinski, 1988). This tide allows Rousseau to establish a broad political ontology, about what it means to be a modern subject and to exercise freedom. In the Second Discourse, Rousseau articulates his idea of the kind of subject that emerges with the shift to society: 'Thus we find here all our faculties developed, memory and imagination in play, egocentrism looking out for its interests, reason rendered active, and the mind having nearly reached the limit of the perfection of which it is capable' (1992: 53). For Rousseau, the potential for evolution, development and advancement is now without bounds, though so also is the possibility of decline and degeneration. In an account that would be developed more fully by Immanuel Kant (Cassirer, 1970), Rousseau introduces the idea of man as autonomous, having the capacity to reason, to determine his own future and as capable of experiencing 'real' freedom. Man stands at the centre of the world and is capable of shaping it as he wills. It is this notion of what it means to be a modern subject that later becomes central to modern nationalism: 'The idea that human beings can be understood in themselves as at least potentially self-sufficient, self-contained, and self-moving is vital [to nationalist thought]' (Calhoun, 1994: 315). It therefore forms a central tenet to contest in any attempt at resisting nationalism.

What is especially interesting about this promise of freedom, encapsulated in the idea of the modern subject, is that it won't be available to everyone. Although Europe represents the heights of *perfectibilité* (and of degradation), we learn that other people, including the 'savages of America', 'appear to have remained barbarous' (Rousseau, 1992: 51). Rousseau's idea of the modern subject therefore emerges in relation to a story of development, which enables the possibility of distinguishing between 'those who are thought to belong fully to the present and those who are thought to belong to various positions in the past' (Hindess, 2007: 326). This enables the possibility of distinguishing between modern man and others that aren't capable of arriving at this point of maturity. This doesn't only include people in other parts of the world, beyond European shores. Man also enters the modern stage as already apart and ahead of women, children and animals. For example, we learn that modern subjectivity is divided into 'two sexes', and that the institution of 'conjugal love and paternal love' will now form the most legitimate form of relationship (1992: 48). This gendered and heteronormative account is thus secured by casting out other models of love, sexuality and parenting. It is also secured by discriminating against people and societies that are understood to be at a lower stage of 'development'. The idea that we can identify certain people and societies as *belonging more closely to the past* continues to be extremely prevalent, in conservative as well as in well-intentioned progressive political discourses (Helliwell and Hindess, 2005; Massey, 2005).[9] These ideas of subjectivity and freedom, which remain central to nationalism, are therefore also tied together with the idea that the world can be ordered according to trajectory of progress.

Ideas of 'progress' have been subject to heavy criticism in contemporary political theory and in debates around 'development' especially. Critics of 'development' discourses argue that the classification of the world into First World, Second World and Third World regions relies on assuming that each region corresponds to a different stage of advancement and assumes the superiority of the global north as representing the only model of emancipation to which we should all aspire (Escobar, 1995). It also succeeds in suggesting that vast regions of the world can be understood as sharing something in common, enabling monolithic caricatures such as the 'Third World Woman' (Mohanty, 1991). These critiques are important. But what reading Rousseau allows us to consider further is the way in which narratives of progress also stipulate *particular conditions that will have to be met* in order to be allowed to 'develop' and to join the world of free nations. As Rousseau explains, the Wise Institutor of the political community does not begin his work by drawing up common laws but by establishing *first and foremost* who is 'fit to bear them' (1997: 72). This suggests that some people are 'better suited' to the ideals of freedom, autonomy and self-determination than others. And some people will simply be unable to taste the fruits of freedom given that they belong to a different time: 'Freedom, not being a fruit of every Clime, is not within the reach of every people' (1997: 100). The promise of progress is thus not only problematic for the way in which it projects a very particular account of what freedom must mean. It is also *necessarily* exclusionary because only *some* people will be invited to enter this journey in time.

Rousseau's story of humanity's gradual development is thus universalized as applicable to the entire world, yet it is also limited, in that not all people will be able to achieve full control of their emotions and the capacity to reason, and to become infinitely perfectible. Thus, in order to be able to experience the possibility of freedom, it will be necessary for societies to *unite*. As Rousseau tells us, 'the establishment of a single society rendered indispensable that of all others' (1992: 57) and, in order to join the new, civilized world, '*it was necessary to unite in turn*' (1992: 57, my emphasis). In this passage, Rousseau establishes a condition that continues to be foundational to the modern state system: the possibility of advancement in history is *only* available to those people that are *already* bound within a common – and recognizable – political unit.[10] Unity forms a precondition of becoming political. In the picture that Rousseau paints, it now becomes increasingly difficult to imagine any other way of organizing politically, as 'Societies, multiplying or spreading rapidly, soon covered the entire surface of the earth; and it was no longer possible to find a single corner in the universe where someone could free himself from the yoke and withdraw his head from the often ill-guided sword which everyone saw perpetually hanging over his own head' (Rousseau, 1992: 57). All those communities, movements and peoples who cannot, or refuse to submit to these founding conditions for being political risk being cast as 'barbarian', 'backward' or 'savage'.

The question of being together

The principle of unity is thus all important for Rousseau, and this is founded upon his understanding of subjectivity as, ideally, a life lived in and for oneself. The political theorist Iris Marion Young objects to Rousseau's understanding of subjectivity and of what it means to be together because of the way in which it 'denies, devalues, or represses the ontological difference of subjects, and seeks to dissolve social inexhaustibility into the comfort of a self-enclosed whole' (1990: 230). In contrast to Rousseau's understanding of subjectivity as self-contained, she argues that 'the subject is not a unity, it cannot be present to itself, know itself' (1990: 231): 'Subjects all have multiple desires that do not cohere; they attach layers of meanings to objects without always being aware of each layer or the connection between them' (1990: 232). Rousseau's dream of an individual within a community who, 'uniting with all, nevertheless obeys only himself and remains as free as before' is based upon a mythic understanding of what it means to be human and to be social (Young, 1990: 49). Young's critique is significant, because it helps remind us of the impossibility of unity in the sense that animates Rousseau's political thought. This is important because the dream of unity nevertheless forms a key aspect of the nationalist imaginary, and this is what makes reading Rousseau an important part of unpacking and contesting this way of seeing the world.

Of course, Rousseau was aware that the picture he paints of the ideal state of nature is a fiction and that the idea of a time when communication was straightforward, transparent and life included no 'zones of disorder' is a fantasy (Foucault cited in Young, 1990: 229). Nevertheless, having established this fantasy, the image of life taking place in a 'uniform manner' where man doesn't have to encounter the 'changes caused by the passions and inconsistency of peoples living together' (1992: 20) persistently haunts Rousseau's account of the ideal political community. As Jean Starobinski describes it: 'Henceforth unity is something that must be recovered or rediscovered. Individuals, separated from one another, must achieve reconciliation. The mind, driven from paradise, must embark on a lengthy journey before returning to its original felicitous state' (1988: 10). The point is not only that this condition of original unity is a fiction. It is that it also works to frame political life as involving a choice between identity and difference, order and disorder – a choice that continues to steer many contemporary approaches to politics.

Yet Rousseau is also worth reading because *he is aware* that there are other ways in which we can imagine what it might mean to live together. Put it another way, he is aware that the question of being together is more complicated. This is exemplified in both Bonnie Honig's (2001) and Kimberly Hutchings's (2008) readings of him.

For example, Bonnie Honig argues that Rousseau openly acknowledges that there are other possible worlds available, beyond a world of nations. When Rousseau describes the principle of unity spreading across the earth, as we discussed in the last section, Honig draws our attention to the brief reference Rousseau makes to the '*few great cosmopolitan souls*' that can 'overcome the imaginary barriers that separate peoples and who, following the example of the sovereign being who has created them, embrace the entire human race in their benevolence' (1992: 57, my emphasis). This passage suggests that Rousseau's story of progress is not assumed to be universal after all and that there are alternatives available. This point is further affirmed by Kimberly Hutchings, who argues that Rousseau presents his story of progress, decline and corruption in *both* particular *and* universal terms (2008). That is, Hutchings argues that Rousseau wavers between presenting his story as one that is unique to European society and, alternatively, as representing the fate of the whole world. It is left unclear 'whether all human communities and civilizations eventually evolve in the same direction or whether some develop (decline) further or differently than others' (2008: 38). Hutchings's argument chimes with Honig's because it suggests that Rousseau *recognizes* that there are other ways of imagining community available in the world. Both Hutchings's and Honig's analyses also imply that Rousseau would be aware that the universalization of one account of the political would inevitably be met with resistance.

Thus, if we choose to think both with and against Rousseau, how might we understand the politics of coexistence otherwise? Iris Marion Young posits the *city* as a social imaginary that can counter Rousseau's dream of unity, commonality, and agreement. In the city, she identifies an alternative vision of democratic polity, one that avoids the 'logic of identity' which suggests that 'all participants share a common experience and common values' (1990: 227). For Young, 'city life' offers an alternative to Rousseau's ideal of a highly unified society based around commonality because it forms 'being together of strangers' (1990: 237). Difference is negotiated between clusters of people with mutual affinities, but it doesn't demand that their being together should involve '*a community of shared final ends*, of mutual identification and reciprocity' (1990: 238, my emphasis). Indeed, Rousseau hated the clutter, noise and movement that formed part of an urbanizing society. Yet, despite castigating the city, the political scientist Mira Morgenstern develops an interesting argument when she says that Rousseau *was aware* that the city (in this case, Paris) was instructive in learning what it might mean to live in common. She argues that Rousseau was deeply pessimistic about the changes that life in a modern (and urbanizing) world would bring about, but he was also *intrigued* by urban life. This is why in his other work, *Émile*, written as a treatise on how the ideal citizen might be educated, the fictitious protagonist (Émile) is sent to Paris. Yet, in order to ensure that he maintains an authentic and untainted life, Rousseau insists that '*Émile will be in, not of, the city*: he will participate in the activities of society without being defined by them' (Morgenstern, 2009: 169, my emphasis). Morgenstern argues that Émile was sent to Paris partly in order to develop his personal self-knowledge but also, interestingly, in order for him to *get to know his fellow man*.

Although Émile (like Rousseau) eventually returns to a life in the countryside so as not to be tainted by the 'black mores' of the city (Morgenstern, 2009: 169), Morgenstern argues that the city is crucial in introducing Émile to the question of living in common. It seems appropriate, then, for Iris Marion Young to turn to the city to rework Rousseau's idea of a political community based around commonality and seek to develop instead a form of politics composed of 'diverse social groups' (1990: 240). Yet it isn't enough to celebrate difference as an *alternative* to unity without also challenging the suggestion that we have to choose between one of these two options. As we will recall, Rousseau is responsible for *framing* the politics of imagining community in relation to a *choice* between unity and difference. In opting for one or the other, we fail to interrogate his framing of the options available. What needs to be done is to refuse Rousseau's broader narrative, which begins with his story of modern life as disenchanted, and which succeeds in establishing unity as an ideal that we must recover. Without unpacking this broader narrative, an account of political community that privileges difference will risk being plagued by the accusation that 'we' have 'lost' a sense of identity.

Accepting Morgenstern's remarks that there is something about the city that raises questions for Rousseau about what it means to live together, we can suggest that this social formation continues to offer material for reconsidering what coexistence might look like. We can therefore turn to the city to posit again the question of imagining community. Working with, and against Rousseau, we can ask, what does it mean to live in common? And, furthermore, must '*one live together only with one's like, with someone semblable?*' (Derrida, 2005: 11, my emphasis). Indeed, 'what is a like, a compeer [semblable]' – 'someone similar or semblable as a human being, a neighbor, a fellow citizen, a fellow creature, a fellow man'? (Derrida, 2005: 11). The next two chapters will engage alternatives to the idea that political community must be built upon the principle of unity by turning to attempts at imagining a form of 'urban cosmopolitanism'. Both chapters will examine the extent to which cosmopolitan narratives succeed in going beyond this nationalist dichotomy of unity and difference.

Conclusion

This chapter has engaged with Rousseau's political thought in order to expose how he establishes the question of political community in relation to a narrative of loss. He sets up a fictitious account of the state of nature as a place of calm, uniformity and solidity, which is impossible to realize or to recover. Nevertheless, this picture of a time of innocence forms a recurring guiding ideal for Rousseau, in his idea of a political community based around the highest degree of uniformity, and in his fear of difference, contingency and flux. I have argued that the key point in negotiating the legacies of Rousseau's work is not to argue that we must privilege 'difference' over 'unity', but to reject this binary framing as a starting point for imagining political community. The challenge lies in contesting this founding assumption that community is something that we enjoyed *in the past* and that we need to regain in the future. As the next two chapters will go on to discuss, the idea that we have 'fallen' from a state in which community was simple and more straightforward continues to form an dominant backdrop to debating the politics of coexistence more generally. The next chapter specifically addresses the way in which claims about a form of community that has been lost resurfaced as part of the heightened nationalism of the 'War on Terror'.

This discussion of Rousseau's political thought has also engaged with his ideas about being a modern subject and about freedom as a journey unfolding in time. Again, this idea of subjectivity and freedom as involving autonomy and self-determination is central to nationalist thought and will need to be interrogated as part of any attempt at imagining community beyond nationalism. Chapter 5 in particular will return to this question of subjectivity and how critiques of nationalism remain limited if they cannot also call this idea of a modern subject that is on a journey towards progress and enlightenment into question. The final part of this chapter suggested that Rousseau forms an interesting figure to contend with because of his awareness that there are other ways of understanding coexistence available. These include 'cosmopolitanism' and the possibilities presented by urban life. The next two chapters will address different attempts at reimagining community through urban cosmopolitanism. They will seek to argue against Rousseau's legacies by presenting ways of thinking about living together that refuse to assume that we must share something in common. Nevertheless, the next two chapters will also demonstrate how difficult it is to move beyond the framing of the political offered by Jean-Jacques Rousseau, and his account of time, community and loss which remain persistent.

Part 2
Contesting nationalist imaginaries

4 Urban cosmopolitanism

The return of the nation in times of terror

All community makes somehow, somewhere, sometime – 'common'.

Friedrich Nietzsche, *Beyond Good and Evil*

Introduction

This chapter opens the second section of this book, which engages with different attempts at contesting nationalism. It focuses on political responses to the bombings that took place in London on 7 July 2005 and which killed 52 people and four suicide bombers and injured over 700 people. More specifically, the chapter examines a poster campaign that was displayed across the London transport network in the aftermath of the bombings, announcing: '7 Million Londoners, One London'. This poster campaign offers an example of an urban cosmopolitan account of political community which sought to counteract nationalist rhetoric and mitigate against reprisal attacks on 'Muslim' or 'Arab' minorities in the aftermath of the London bombings.[1] This campaign, run by the then Mayor of London Ken Livingstone has been described as demonstrating a 'commitment to diversity and hospitality' (Massey, 2007: 5), drawing on a tradition of understanding the city as a site of sanctuary. Although the campaign was cautiously welcomed as prefereable to the heightened nationalist rhetoric deployed by the then Prime Minister, Tony Blair (Gilroy, 2006; Tulloch 2006), the chapter argues that this cosmopolitan narrative nevertheless largely operated in tandem with nationalism. Drawing on the discussion developed in the last chapter in particular, about how nationalist ideas of community emerge in the context of ideas about 'loss', this chapter examines the ways in which cosmopolitan ideas often draw upon this nationalist imaginary. This suggests that cosmopolitanism cannot be understood as representing a progressive alternative to nationalism or as something that follows from nationalism in time.[2] Although cosmopolitan ideas are often deployed as an alternative to nationalism, they can nevertheless reproduce a nationalist conceptual vocabulary.[3]

The idea that nationalism and cosmopolitanism can be juxtaposed is widespread and was affirmed in several critical responses to the events of 11 September 2001. Take, for example, Craig Calhoun's claim that 9/11 marked a point when 'the noncosmopolitan side of globalization struck back' (2002: 871) or Martha Nussbaum's comments that, after 9/11, 'we find ourselves feeling sympathy for many people who did not even cross our minds before' (Nussbaum and Cohen, 2002: ix). Although Calhoun and Nussbaum represent different positions, with Calhoun suggesting that the events of 9/11 have worked *against* cosmopolitanism and Nussbaum arguing that they led to its resurgence, both of them understand nationalism and cosmopolitanism as opposing ideas of political community. This chapter places that starting point under question. In contrast, it argues that we need to understand nationalism and cosmopolitanism as ideas that often travel *together* (Fortier, 2008; Grewal, 2005; Robbins, 1998). By way of a discussion of the ideas of space and time underpinning the cosmopolitan narratives that followed the events of the London bombings, the chapter argues that cosmopolitanism provided in this case 'new grammars for national identity' (Fortier, 2008: 4).[4] The key claim is that this forms an example of a cosmopolitanism that celebrates difference, but only so long as 'the general category of the people is still generally understood within a national frame' (Pollock *et al.*, 2000: 582; see also Mignolo, 2000; Seth, 2001).

The chapter also draws inspiration from this poster campaign as well as from broader literatures to suggest that 'urban cosmopolitanism' may nevertheless be conceived differently and could offer openings for disrupting a nationalist imaginary. However, this alternative cosmopolitanism must be able to acknowledge the colonial and imperialist histories that situate global cities such as London as sites in which people find themselves thrown together (Gilroy, 2004; Gunew, 2004; Keith, 2005). It must also be able to recognize difference as more than a 'lifestyle choice' and as instead evocative of 'visceral' and 'affective intensities' (Connolly, 2005). Thus, whilst the main parts of the chapter offer a discussion of the ideas of space and time that were mobilized in the '7 Million Londoners, One London' campaign in order to show how it redeployed a 'nationalist imaginary', the chapter closes by pursuing the idea that the city may nevertheless offer another model of coexistence. The chapter closes by identifying what needs to be done in order to imagine a pluralistic form of political community that can avoid the grip of nationalism.

Summoning unity

In a rhetorical gesture that will seem very familiar, former Prime Minister Tony Blair's immediate response in the wake of the bombings of 7 July 2005 in London was to shore up an image of Britishness and to establish a binary logic between the 'British people' and 'those people [who are trying] to cow us, to frighten us out of doing the things we want to do' (Blair, 2005). People were invited to choose: either they were with the British people, and the British government representing 'our way of life', or they were with the 'terrorists'. This consolidation of British identity was successful insofar as it silenced any seriously threatening criticism of the British government in the aftermath of the bombings. Unlike in Madrid, where the bombings on the transport infrastructure on 11 March 2004 led to sharp political divisions and a change in government following the general election three days later, nothing as subversive happened to the social order in London and the UK: calm was quickly restored, leaders of government and the police remained in their positions and Prime Minister Blair was not compelled to leave office for a further two years. Nevertheless, the Mayor of London distanced himself from this nationalist rhetoric and presented a different account of a cosmopolitan community of Londoners. A large-scale poster campaign publicized across the capital's transport network read, '7 Million Londoners, One London' and, later, 'We are Londoners, We are One'.[5] This campaign sought to celebrate the diversity of the city and it appealed to many who felt critical of the British government's role in the Iraq War in particular (Tulloch, 2006: 196).

In the aftermath of the London bombings, the idea of a solid and identifiable British community was largely consolidated through the image of the Blitz (Manthorpe, 2006: 21–2) which conjured an image of British society in a time of war.[6] As a story of origins, the portrait of the Blitz invokes an idea of the people 'coming together' under the threat of an enemy outside. Paul Gilroy has pointed to the astonishing endurance of the Blitz narrative in providing an image of British culture to which people can aspire. Indeed, it, along with the wartime poster produced by the British Government's Ministry of Information encouraging people to 'Keep Calm and Carry On', seems remarkably persistent as a symbol of British culture. The imagery of the Blitz works to invoke a sense of *loss* for a time when community was more straightforward, less complex and more homogenous. As Gilroy puts it, it summons the idea of 'long-vanished homogeneity', which includes the sense of a lost whiteness (Gilroy, 2004: 95–98). The Blitz imagery and rhetoric therefore proved useful to the British government in narrating the response to the London bombings as a battle between 'good guys' and 'bad guys'. It also served to plant the idea that the bombers must have come from 'outside' the British community. This narrative was later complicated by the discovery that all the bombers lived in the UK, that three of them were second-generation British citizens who grew up on the outskirts of Leeds, in the north of England, and that the fourth was born in Jamaica but grew up in Huddersfield, another northern English city. As the 'Report of the Official Account of the Bombings in London on 7th July 2005' put it, the men were all of generally 'unexceptional background' (2006: 13): they weren't from especially deprived households, and all had varying degrees of further and higher education. Nationalist imagery and rhetoric therefore proved crucial in ensuring that these 'unexceptional' men were portrayed as aberrant and 'foreign'.

Indeed, in the broader context of the political climate of the 'War on Terror', the 'Middle Eastern Muslim male' emerged as 'a new category of visibility' that was deemed to represent danger, risk and threat (Grewal, 2005: 209). Such racialized and gendered categorizations were not altogether 'new' but formed a rearticulation of older colonial legacies (Gregory, 2004; Grewal, 2005: 209). This is one of the reasons why, on 7 July 2005, the UK Islamic Human Rights Commission took the exceptional step of instructing Muslims not to travel or go out unless strictly necessary, for fear of reprisals (*The Independent*, 8 July 2005).

Yet this political climate cannot be understood as straightforwardly 'anti-Muslim'. For example, former Prime Minister Tony Blair would regularly extol the teachings of Islam. Take, for example, his attempt at highlighting the Koran as a 'reforming book', 'far ahead of its time' (2007), a strategy that was later mimicked by President Barack Obama, who, in his first speech in a predominantly Muslim country, lauded the contributions of Islam in developing 'the order of algebra; our magnetic compass and tools of navigation' (2009). This suggests that the representations of Islamic culture in the political climate of the 'War on Terror' worked as part of a *double move*, which both celebrated the contributions of Islam *and* reinforced a fear of difference. Mahmood Mamdani captures this idea of the double image of Islam when he describes it as a practice of distinguishing between 'good Muslims' and 'bad Muslims' (2002, see also Razack, 2008, Volpp, 2002).

This practice is demonstrated in former Prime Minister Blair's statement, released in the immediate aftermath of the bombings:

> I welcome the statement put out by the Muslim Council who know that those people acted in the name of Islam but who also know that the vast and overwhelming majority of Muslims, here and abroad, are decent and law-abiding people who abhor this act of terrorism *every bit as much as we do.*
>
> (Blair, 2005, my emphasis)

What is striking about this statement is the way in which he skillfully distinguishes between Muslims who abhor terrorism and 'we' who also do. In doing so, he establishes 'Muslims' as a distinct and separate community – one that is not 'terrorist' but not fully British either. As a result, 'Muslims' are left hanging between an authentic 'British' culture which they are not fully invited into and the 'terrorists' that are seen as *outside* the time of the international community. The nationalist imaginaries of 'us' and 'them' are therefore ordered according to a scale of progress that, in this case, affirms three distinct communities: British, Muslim and terrorist. In accordance with this temporal scale, the 'British way of life' lies closest to the top, as a community that doesn't have to explain itself. The 'Muslim community', being British and yet not quite British, lies further down the scale, and will from now on be called upon to demonstrate its enlightenment and will constantly encounter the accusation that it may be inclined towards terrorism. The 'terrorists' are, to all effects, off the scale: they do not share the foundational attributes necessary to be able to advance along this journey of progress. They have no sense of reason, or of what civilization might mean. Crucially, this scalar ordering of communities means that the burden of responsibility shifts from any interrogation of the British government's foreign and domestic policies in the aftermath of the bombings and, ironically, away from the bombers too. The burden of responsibility is placed squarely with the so-called 'Muslim community'.

The force of this narrative of progress can be appreciated following our reading of Jean-Jacques Rousseau in the last chapter and, in particular, the way in which he sought to order the people of the world into a *common timeframe*. In

Rousseau's terms, the 'Muslim community' forms an example of a 'primitive' culture that has not quite arrived at the heights of civilization. This point is affirmed in an article published by Tony Blair in *Foreign Affairs* in 2007 in which he describes the 'War on Terror' as representing 'the age-old battle between progress and reaction, between those who embrace the modern world and those who reject its existence – between optimism and hope, on the one hand, and pessimism and fear, on the other'. This article eloquently and perniciously reworks Samuel Huntington's infamous essay on the 'Clash of Civilizations'[7] (also published in *Foreign* Affairs, in 1993) to suggest that the 'War on Terror' should not be understood as a clash *between* civilizations but as a clash *about* civilization. Although Blair seems in the first instance to reformulate Huntington's thesis in more inclusive terms, for example, when he says that:

> 'we' are not the West. 'We' are as much Muslim as Christian, Jew, or Hindu. 'We' are all those who believe in religious tolerance, in openness to others, in democracy, in liberty, and in human rights administered by secular courts
> (2007)

his narrative follows the same logic in that it orders the world into a trajectory of progress and skilfully distinguishes between those who are civilized and *within* the international community and those who are barbaric and *outside* the time of human-ity. This all suggests that it wasn't so much the case that celebrations of difference disappeared off the political agenda in the context of the 'War on Terror'. Indeed, in the aftermath of the London bombings, political leaders seemed overtly keen to talk about 'difference'. What needs to be examined is the way in which cultural difference is understood as something both to be feared *and* celebrated.

Urban nationalism

The image of the Blitz that circulated in the aftermath of the July 2005 bombings in London offers an example of the way in which a nationalist idea of community is imagined in relation to narratives of loss. Yet this was accompanied by another idea of community as cosmopolitan, symbolized by the motif of the Olympic Games. By chance, the International Olympic Committee had announced on 6 July, the day before the bombings, that London had won the bid to host the Games in 2012. London's bid had been built on a platform selling the idea of London as a 'cosmopolitan city'. In the event of the bombings, the successful bid to host the Olympics served as useful in projecting an image of London (and, through it, Britain) as a tolerant community, at ease with its multicultural, post-national self. This is demonstrated in *The Guardian*'s leading commentary on the day follow-ing the bombings: 'London has won the Olympics because it is an open and tolerant city. The way Londoners responded to the vicious attacks on them has vindicated the Olympians' confidence' (Editorial, 8 July 2005). Whilst the Blitz conjured the image of a distinctly white Britishness, this image of the Olympics affirms an idea of London as an open and multi-ethnic community.[8] The Mayor of London's poster campaign chimed with this cosmopolitan understanding of London and seemed to offer a more progressive, less nationalistic response to the bombings than that offered by Prime Minister Blair. But what is striking is the way in which the spirit of cosmopolitanism, encapsulated by the Olympic Games is invoked as something that Londoners have *lost*. This celebration of difference is projected along a trajectory of progress, as multicultural solidarity is cast as something we once had and which we must now recover again. In this sense, cosmopolitan narrative abides by the logic of a nationalist imaginary.

In seeking to project an alternative account of political community, the Mayor's statement in response to the bombings announced that: 'This was not a terrorist attack against the mighty and the powerful.... It was aimed at ordinary, working-class Londoners, black and white, Muslim and Christian, Hindu and Jew, young and old' (2005). In many respects, his words invoked a different image of community to that espoused by Blair, as Livingstone sought to promote an idea of London's unique role in acting as host to Arabs of various origins as well as Jewish communities (Jabri, 2009: 51–52). Yet this celebration of difference nevertheless cautions against *division*, in a way that echoes a nationalist imaginary:

> As I said to the International Olympic Committee, the city of London is the greatest in the world, because everybody lives side by side in harmony. *Londoners will not be divided* by this cowardly attack. They will stand together in solidarity alongside those who have been injured and those who have been bereaved.
>
> (7 July 2005, my emphasis)

In this statement, 'difference' emerges as something that is to be celebrated *and* feared. Like Blair, Livingstone succeeds in casting out the terror caused by the four bombers from anything to do with the community of Londoners. Of course, Livingstone's *tone* is very different, and this is not an insignificant point. This explains why leaders of civil liberties organizations and Muslim associations were more willing to work with Livingstone to try and contain reprisal attacks in the aftermath of the bombings. This was demonstrated in another poster, released on behalf of the Mayor of London as well as on behalf of the civil liberties pressure group Liberty, the Secretary General of the Muslim Council of Britain, the Muslim Association of Britain and representatives from a range of community organizations and faith groups. This poster, which was again publicized across the transport network, declared, 'Only united communities will defeat terrorism and protect civil liberties'.[9] This message sought to provide a collective show of solidarity across different communities and faiths and to insist on the need to protect civil liberties. Yet, in order to deliver the statement, this protest again insists upon *unity* as a foundational principle. The question to ask here is, why should a *united* identity form a condition for organizing to defend civil liberties? This poster campaign offers another example of the way in which nationalist discourse sets the terms through which progressive political movements can make their voice heard.

The '7 Million Londoners, One London' posters were accompanied by another campaign launched in the aftermath of the bombings by Transport for London. These additional posters were often to be seen displayed next to the '7 Million Londoners' message and declared simply: 'It's Up to All of Us'. The press release that accompanied the launch of this set of posters tried to explain what exactly was 'up to us' in more detail:

> One of the best security measures we have is the eyes of our customers. We are asking everybody to remain vigilant. Do look after your own luggage and belongings when travelling...
> *Don't be afraid to speak up...*
> If you spot something suspicious, don't be afraid to tell a member of staff or a police officer. It's up to all of us to keep London secure.
> (28 November 2005)[10]

Through the circulation of this poster, and by way of a broader discourse that affirmed its message, Londoners were invited to police their fellow passengers. The problem with this invitation, however, is that Londoners were not told what it was that they should be on the lookout *for*. This poster succeeded in cultivating suspicion toward an ultimately mysterious object. Londoners, especially tube and bus travellers, had their reasons to be anxious in returning to their everyday journeys in the aftermath of the bombings, as several hundred survivors were caught in the blasts on that day and were injured to varying degrees. In capitalizing on what may be understandable fears, these posters did not encourage Londoners to extend a 'presumptive generosity' (Connolly, 2005: 126). Rather, passengers were invited to 'to speak up' against their fellow passengers and to act as 'petty sovereigns' (Butler, 2006: 65). In being placed alongside the '7 Million Londoners' message, these posters seemed to firmly undo any good intentions suggested by the cosmopolitan agenda.

The one and the many

This example of the '7 Million Londoners, One London' campaign suggests that nationalist narratives of unity can be put to work in cosmopolitan and in urban settings. This means that the task of resisting nationalist narratives of unity will need to involve more than shifting from the national to the cosmopolitan, or from the national to the urban, and will need to offer another account of difference. Flat, ahistorical celebrations of difference offer a one-dimensional and ultimately apolitical picture of difference-within-unity, in a gesture that defends against accusations of *in*tolerance on behalf of the state, but nevertheless continues to establish determinations between insiders and outsiders (Fortier, 2008: 18; see also Weber, 2010: 81). Whilst the '7 Million Londoners' campaign emphasizes the plurality of this global city, it also reveals the forceful practices at work in establishing who 'we' are. The critical question to ask is whether this campaign forms a critical attempt to initiate a 'crisis' in the construction of a collective national identity, or whether it reaffirms a liberal understanding of tolerance as 'patriotic citizenship' (Weber, 2010: 81). This is a question that Cynthia Weber asks in a study of the adverts released by the American Advertisement Council in the wake of the events of 9/11. These adverts introduced a range of people from different ethnic backgrounds, representing a diversity of age groups and occupations, all staring to camera and declaring one after another 'I am an American'. The effect was to produce an image of 'multicultural' America that 'welcomes' immigrant communities but which is notable for the way in which only *some* minoritized subjects acquire legitimacy and the right to speak as citizens' (Weber, 2010: 80). This statist celebration of cosmopolitanism echoes with the '7 Million Londoners' campaign and again suggests how cosmopolitanism and nationalism often travel together. The adverts all feature happy patriotic citizens and there is very little sense of the force required to ensure that citizens keep their faith in the nation. Critically, the adverts all close with words drawn from the US national motto, 'Out of Many, One', or *E Pluribus Unum*. As with the London poster campaign, this example of cosmopolitanism provides 'new grammars for national identity' (Fortier, 2008: 4). The challenge, then, is to interrogate the persistence of this notion of community based upon unity. As the post-colonial critic Homi Bhabha argues, a critical interrogation must question 'the progressive metaphor of modern social cohesion – *the many as one*' (2004: 204). He argues that this task involves fracturing the 'we' in a way that reveals the ambivalence of the nation, thereby re-presenting cultural difference in a way that shifts from the question of 'the other outside' to the question of the immanent presence that disturbs and informs the nation every day. For Bhabha, the critical task is to 'question the otherness of the people-as-one' (Bhabha, 2004: 215).

Cynthia Weber has developed a film project in response to the 'I am an American' Ad Council adverts, which can be understood as a response to the challenge of questioning the 'otherness of the people-as-one'. The project enquires into the stories behind the declaration, 'I am an American', as Weber invites differently placed American citizens (as well as non-citizens, and those with uncertain status) to tell their stories to camera. In a series of four-minute films, titled *I am an American: Portraits of Post 9/11 US Citizens*, a multifarious picture and a range of experiences of 'belonging' to the US nation emerges. The project forms an example of 'narrating the nation' (Bhabha, 1990) that traces the limits of an American national community in a way that highlights a complex array of coexisting subject positions. And, in direct contrast to the Ad Council films, which finish with the US motto, *E Pluribus Unum*, Weber's short films end by subverting the closing motto, to proclaim, 'out of one, many'. This technique of reversing the motto and interrogating the stories behind the declaration of belonging exposes what Homi Bhabha has described as the 'ambivalence' of the nation (2004). When compared with Livingstone's poster campaign, Weber's film project helps highlight some of the limitations of his account of London as a community of differences. For example, whilst Livingstone's poster campaign relies on an ahistorical narrative that fails to allow for an appreciation of how *certain bodies* come to be read as more inclined to commit violence than others

(Grewal, 2005: 201), Weber's project seeks to recover an account of the force required to uphold narratives of 'happy multiculturalism' (Ahmed, 2010: 122).

Although the benevolence shown by celebrations of cultural pluralism may be well intentioned, the point is that they often 'fail to acknowledge the critique of modernity that minoritarian cosmopolitans embody in their historic witness to the twentieth century' (Pollock *et al.*, 2000: 6). Pollock and his co-authors argue that it is refugees, peoples of the diaspora, migrants and exiles that represent the spirit of the cosmopolitical community. And in the context of the London bombings and their aftermath, it may be possible to understand Jean Charles de Menezes as one such 'minoritarian cosmopolitan'. Menezes was a Brazilian citizen living in London at the time of the bombings and working as an electrician. This young man was shot eight times at close range by British anti-terrorist officers on 22 July 2005 and was killed in the police search for what was said to be a second failed attempt to bomb the capital on 21 July 2005. Although the Metropolitan Police Commissioner Sir Ian Blair initially announced that the decision to shoot was directly linked to the search for the bombers, it quickly emerged that Menezes had no connection to the events at all (Vaughan-Williams, 2009a). Menezes was killed in a case of 'mistaken identity'. Menezes' death illuminates the terror that forms the condition of defending the authority of the state and the unity of the political community. It also reminds us that London cannot be understood simply in a normative vein as a site that suggests another imagining of coexistence. It must also be understood as a key node in the violent geographies of the 'War on Terror', in its participation in the use of torture and rendition, and in its support for the wars in Afghanistan in 2001 and Iraq in 2003.

This all suggests that a cosmopolitan account of community doesn't necessarily do enough to contest the violent stakes of nationalism. In contrast to the '7 Million Londoners' campaign, Cindy Weber's 'I am an American' project follows Homi Bhabha's recommendation that we unpack the turbulent stories that uphold the nation. In this sense, Cindy Weber's project can be read as a critical attempt to introduce a tremor into the idea of a united community and in the 'construction of a collective US national identity in which body is nation, diversity is identity, and tolerance is patriotic citizenship' (Weber, 2010: 81). As such, it aims to recover the force involved in producing accounts of 'unity' and the contestations that underpin accounts of community as 'one'. It offers a contrast to liberal multicultural interventions because in revealing the many differences that constitute the US nation, the point is not to arrive at a 'better' representation. Rather, the aim is to tease out the 'critical difference' between the 'lived reality of US citizenship for unsafe US citizens during the War on Terror measured against the ideal of the tolerance of difference as the foundation and lived reality of the US nation-state' (Weber, 2010: 83).[11]

These films therefore enact an important critical gesture. However, we may also ask whether this shift in emphasis – from the one to the many – ultimately does enough to disrupt a nationalist imaginary. Does this attempt to subvert the terms of the debate offer a robust enough strategy or does it risk reproducing key elements of a nationalist imaginary? In asking her participants to 'narrate their story [and] reflect upon their experiences of citizenship and patriotism after 9/11' (Weber, 2010: 82), we find that many of the participants are keen to reaffirm the idea of 'America the Beautiful' and the ideals of democracy, freedom and justice, *despite* their experiences of injustice and exclusion (Ling, 2010: 100). Thus, whilst the films begin with an inquiry into the declaration, 'I am an American', they often lead to an intensified patriotic declaration: 'I am an American!' (Luke, 2010). The point here is not to blame people for being patriotic. Rather, it is to query the effectiveness of attempts at revealing the differences *within* the nation when such critical gestures also risk reaffirming a nationalist imaginary. It is because of the limits of continuing to work within the terms of nationalism that I return to the city as a site that potentially offers another way of imagining coexistence.

Urban cosmopolitanism as everyday encounters

How might London as a global city, with all its contradictions, present a different understanding of coexistence to one that abides by a nationalist imaginary and reinforces the sovereignty of the state? In touching upon a tradition of thought that understands the city as a place where people 'come to be free, they come to live the life they choose, they come to be able to be themselves' (2005), Livingstone articulates the very opposite of Rousseau's position, which understands the city as corrupting man's essential autonomy. Of course Livingstone's description is overly romantic. People occasionally come to the city because they are fleeing for their lives. Or as the urban theorist Fran Tonkiss argues, people don't necessarily come to the city to *celebrate* their 'differences'; they also come to get *away* from being 'different' (2005: 22–24). With her intervention, Tonkiss draws upon sociologist Georg Simmel's account of 'metropolitan individuality' (1971: 325) to rework the idea of being in the city. Writing at the turn of the twentieth century, Simmel describes the way in which the metropolitan character must navigate 'the swift and continuous shift of external and internal stimuli' (1971: 325).[12] Tonkiss develops this work to argue that, whilst the idea of walking in a crowd, of being surrounded by a thousand faces and not knowing any of them represents what some might understand as a *lack* of community, for others, this offers *another example* of community. Tonkiss reflects on the art of city living, which involves pushing past people in the busy street or metro carriage while carefully refraining from getting too close to develop an argument about a form of community based around an 'ethics of indifference' (2005: 22–24). This image of community reflects some elements of Iris Marion Young's work (1990) discussed briefly at the end of Chapter 3, in that it is radically opposed to Rousseau's idea of community as involving face-to-face encounters (Sennett, 1971). Drawing on Simmel, Tonkiss reworks ideas of sociality so that what may appear as 'dissociation' is instead understood as a 'basic form of urban sociation' (2005: 11). Difference is therefore approached according to another set of terms, 'as a profoundly spatial reality, lived over and over in the glancing encounters of the street' (2005: 18).

Although her work is informed by the experience of minorities navigating cities, she nevertheless seeks to get away from the language of 'group identity' which she rightly argues continues to 'hang around' urban literatures (2005: 9). Tonkiss seeks to rework an understanding of social life which assumes certain identity categories in advance. She also refuses the idea of a *bounded* political community as suggested by the '7 Million Londoners' campaign. Thus, it is not a question of *staging* encounters between different identity groups, but of acknowledging everyday encounters between urban strangers (see here also Amin, 2012). In drawing upon the experiences of women walking the city as well as men 'whose bodies are marked in terms of racial, sexual or cultural difference' (2005: 23), she evokes the freedom of being able to walk and travel 'unhindered, unremarked and unbothered' (Tonkiss, 2005: 10). These 'relations of indifference' may be 'fragile, grudging, uneven' but they are nevertheless *ethical*, she argues (2005: 10). Crucially, these encounters are not laden with a sense of *meaning* (an aspect of the nationalist imaginary that we explored in Chapter 2) but, rather, they are 'transitory, instrumental or incidental' (2005: 13). This chimes with the work of political geographer Joe Painter, who reworks community through an account of neighbourly urban encounters, which he describes as 'hostile as well as friendly, indifferent as well as interested, passive as well as active' (2012: 524). Both Tonkiss' and Painter's interventions counteract the celebration of difference as a 'good thing' by emphasizing the *ambivalence* of social relations. They also posit the heterogeneity of the global city as what is *already there*, and so it doesn't necessarily have to be conjured or honoured. This emphasis on urban encounters disrupts accounts of community underpinned by the principle of unity because it works with a very different set of terms, that crucially refuses the language of the 'one and the many' which we have explored as derivative of a nationalist imaginary. It also cuts through the distinction between 'unity' and 'difference'. Evoking urban encounters does not necessarily mean dismissing all celebrations of difference, which of course remain preferable to 'the praise of purity' (Nancy, 2003: 280). The point is to try and understand 'difference' according to another set of terms. We will return to this idea of rethinking community through urban encounters in Chapter 6. Before that, we will turn to another example of urban cosmopolitanism as involving a post-colonial journey in time.

Conclusion

This chapter began by arguing that cosmopolitanism should not be understood in opposition to nationalism, thereby inviting the question of which might form the most suitable model of political community, or how we might *extend* community to accommodate differences. As this chapter has demonstrated, cosmopolitan ideas of community often travel alongside nationalism and reproduce elements of a 'nationalist imaginary'. Rather than assume that celebrations of 'difference' must provide an alternative to nationalism, this chapter has argued that critical interventions must engage with the spatio-temporal logics that make different ideas of community possible. This point enables a critique of Martha Nussbaum's position, for example, when she argues in her response to the events of 9/11 that 'we form intense attachments to the local first, and only gradually learn to have compassion for people who are outside our own immediate circle' (Nussbaum and Cohen, 2002: xii). The problem with this approach is that it presumes a tension between 'home' (the nation) and 'away' (beyond the nation) and reproduces a static and bounded understanding of space, place and identity.[13] It fails to consider how many American citizens and residents have attachments to several places at once, reflecting a much more complex and cross-cutting account of difference. It also maps the question of empathy for others in relation to a trajectory of progress, whereby we might *gradually extend* compassion to others beyond the nation. Rather than accept the suggestion of a tension between cosmopolitan and nationalist forces, this chapter has argued that it is necessary to adopt another way into the debate, which will involve acknowledging an 'actually existing cosmopolitanism' and the reality of 'multiple attachments' (Robbins, 1998: 3).

This chapter also discussed the ordering of different communities according to a scale of progress as part of the political climate of the 'War on Terror', where 'Muslim communities' were cast as yet to arrive at the heights of civilization. This suggested that the problem does not only lie with identifying certain communities as 'other' but with the *double strategy* of celebrating and recognizing 'differences' whilst simultaneously banishing and excluding them from the national community. As the discussion of the '7 Million Londoners, One London' poster campaign outlined, the challenge does not lie in opting for 'unity' or 'difference' but in establishing how unity and difference emerge together as two options that comply with a nationalist imaginary. This suggests that a nationalist imaginary can also inform *critical* responses to nationalism. For example, although political interventions such as Cynthia Weber's 'I am an American' film project work well to reveal the contestations that underpin images of national unity, they nevertheless continue to work within the terms of the 'one' and the 'many' and thereby risk the reaffirmation of nationalist categories. The final part of this chapter has begun to sketch a form of urban cosmopolitanism that gets away from the language of group identity and from the *celebration* of difference. It was suggested that everyday encounters between urban strangers might be understood as another way of imagining community. This point will be developed more fully in Chapter 6. Before getting to that material, however, Chapter 5 will pursue further the spatial and temporal logics that underpin critiques of nationalism in order to press further the question of what an effective critique of nationalism must involve.

5 Nationalism and its limits

The politics of imagination

'In those days', continued Ishvar, 'it seemed to me that that was all one could expect in life. A harsh road strewn with sharp stones and, if you were lucky, a little grain – '

'And later?'

'Later I discovered there were different types of roads. And a different way of walking on each.'

Rohinton Mistry, A Fine Balance

Introduction

This chapter addresses critical responses to the events of 11 September 2001 that sought to write *against* a heightened US nationalism. Primarily, it engages with a novel by the author Mohsin Hamid called *The Reluctant Fundamentalist* (2007) that became a bestseller on account of saying '*dangerous things in dangerous times*' (Halaby, 2007). This novel offers a critique of the nationalist imaginaries of 'us' and 'them' from the perspective of a minoritarian subject navigating his life in New York City in the aftermath of the events of 9/11. It engages with the politics of 'mistaken identities' and is especially interesting because it narrates a disjuncture between 'national' and 'urban' understandings of coexistence. As such, the novel demonstrates the political implications of a heightened rhetoric of 'us' and 'them' whilst intimating that the political landscape of the global city offers a different model of community that can defy national containment (Jabri, 2009: 56). This chapter therefore pursues many of the themes discussed in relation to the '7 Million Londoners' poster campaign in the last chapter by addressing another example of urban cosmopolitanism, which in this case also involves a post-colonial journey in time. It thus continues with the theme of how nationalism and cosmopolitanism often travel together, in this case, by demonstrating the persistence of a linear, progressive understanding of time.

I argue that this novel is interesting for the way in which it stages a critique of nationalism, whilst simultaneously reproducing elements of a nationalist imaginary. The novel is therefore read in the light of the work done in Chapters 2 and 3 to explore the key tenets of a nationalist imaginary by way of the works of Max Weber and Jean-Jacques Rousseau. In particular, the chapter pays attention to the temporal narratives that underpin this specific novel. As will become clear, *The Reluctant Fundamentalist* replicates a narrative of disenchantment, which involves a quest for meaning, mastery and enlightenment. It thus brings together ideas about loss and about freedom as involving a progressive journey in time. The key argument that this chapter develops is that, despite the novel's well-intentioned aim of contesting nationalism, in reproducing a narrative about freedom and progress in time, it also operates in tandem with nationalist ways of seeing the world. This can be gleaned in the way in which the novel relies upon the literary format of the *Bildingsroman*.

Having developed this argument, the chapter then seeks to draw out the novel's ambivalent relationship to nationalism and, in particular, the gestures it makes towards another understanding of coexistence. This is exemplified in the different understandings of 'loss' that the novel invokes and how 'loss' might lead to an understanding of subjectivity as 'incomplete' rather than as something that must be recovered and restored in a 'self-enclosed whole' (Young, 1990: 230). In order to develop these possibilities for thinking the relationship between subjectivity and loss differently, and in an emphatically anti-nationalist vein, the chapter then turns to an essay by the feminist political theorist Judith Butler, called 'Violence, Mourning, Politics' from the book, *Precarious Life*, (2006), which she published in response to the events of 9/11. This essay offers an alternative response to grief, mourning and loss to that presented by nationalism. It also extends the possibilities for an alternative understanding of political community presented in *The Reluctant Fundamentalist*. The final part of the chapter debates the openings and closures presented by both Hamid's and Butler's interventions for undoing a nationalist imaginary.

Cosmopolitanism and its limits

The main protagonist of *The Reluctant Fundamentalist*, Changez, is a young man from Lahore, Pakistan, educated at Princeton and living in New York City before, during and after the events of 11 September 2001. In the course of the novel, Changez shifts from being seen as an 'exotic other' to being coded as a 'suspected terrorist'. The novel exposes the deleterious effects of being 'on the lookout' for 'suspicious people' in the political climate of the 'War on Terror', a subject that was also discussed in the last chapter. However, this book largely became known as a result of one passage in the book deemed to represent a controversial response to the events of 11 September 2001 (Hussein, 2007; Olsson, 2007). This is the moment when the main character, Changez, watches the twin towers fall from a hotel room in Manila and, in the immediacy of that moment, responds with a smile:

> I stared as one – and then the other – of the twin towers of New York's World Trade Center collapsed. And then *I smiled*. Yes, despicable as it may sound, my initial reaction was to be remarkably pleased.
>
> (Hamid, 2007: 72, my emphasis)

This passage contributed to the novel's remarkable success in the international literary market place: the book made the New York Times bestseller list and was shortlisted for the Man Booker Prize, as well as for the Index on Censorship's annual T.R. Fyvel Book Award.[1] It became a novel that was worth discussing because it was considered to reveal the view of America *from other parts of the world*. In this sense, it also formed a response to one of the questions that circulated in the United States in the aftermath of the events of 11 September 2001, that is: '*Why do they hate us?*'

Changez tells us that, although he was 'never an American[,] I was *immediately* a New Yorker' (2007: 33).[2] In this way, the novel invokes an experience of urban belonging that complicates and surpasses the national. This involves being able to travel unseen and unhindered through the city's landscapes, blending in at 'the middle of the colour spectrum' (2007: 33) and feeling 'at home' in 'the fact that Urdu was spoken by taxi-cab drivers; the presence, only two blocks from my East Village apartment, of a samosa- and channa-serving establishment called the Pak-Punjab Deli' (ibid.). New York City is presented as a site that hosts multiplicity in a way that offers a reprieve from the nationalist geographies of 'us' and 'them'. Yet, in the aftermath of the events of 11 September 2001, a heightened nationalism takes precedence over the alternative possibilities expressed by being a 'New Yorker'. As the responses to the events of 11 September 2001 unfold, we find that Changez is less able to move undisturbed through the city. He's 'mistakenly' described as a 'Fucking Arab'. And Changez is repeatedly asked to explain his relationship and commitment to the United States:

> 'What is the purpose of your trip to the United States?' she asked me.
> 'I live here,' I replied. 'That is *not* what I asked you, sir' she said. 'What is the *purpose* of your trip to the United States?'
>
> (2007: 75)

The novel offers cutting critiques of the politics of statist security measures. It also raises questions about how quickly the achievements of liberal multiculturalism were undone in 'times of terror' (Amin, 2010: 3). For example, the reader is made aware of the ways in which 'differences' are only embraced when they agree to conform. Take, for example, the main character's experience of joining a prestigious valuation firm, which supports 'diversity' in the workplace:

> Two of my five colleagues were women; Wainwright and I were non-white. We were marvelously diverse ... and yet we were not: all of us, Sherman included, hailed from the same elite universities – Harvard, Princeton, Stanford, Yale; we all exuded a sense of confident self-satisfaction; and not one of us was either short or overweight.
>
> (2007: 38)

The reader is aware that it is not *in*significant that it is a heterosexual, privileged, articulate, slim and well-dressed minority that is invited to enjoy the privileges of a good salary. Given that the reader knows that the events of 11 September 2001 are about to take place, we are also aware that Changez's ability to access the exclusive cultured spaces of Manhattan will gradually turn out to be unreliable. The novel therefore exposes the *limits* of liberalism's embrace of multiculturalism.

Yet what is especially interesting about this critique of multiculturalism, is the way in which the novel's format relies on affirming what the reader *already knows*. This is a key narrative technique of the *Bildungsroman* and the novel is largely written in this format. It thus follows the story of an individual on a journey 'from youth to meaningful life, first through civil society and then through the state' (Cheah, 2003: 243). As such, it resonates with the trajectory of modern nationalism in its portrayal of an autonomous and self-determining subject on a journey towards freedom and enlightenment in time. Whilst much has been written on the coeval relationship between the novel and the nation, and how the image on a knowable community in the literary realm developed alongside the possibility of understanding ourselves as belonging to an 'imagined community' (Anderson, 1991; Bhabha, 2004; Williams, 1985), what is distinctive about the *Bildungsroman* is the way in which the main protagonist is socialized in the process of learning for oneself what everyone else already knows (Slaughter, 2007: 3). In this case, the reader knows in advance that Changez's journey towards progress, citizenship and becoming American will not be straightforward and that these promises will turn out to disappoint.

This can be gleaned through Changez's relationship with his almost-girlfriend, Erica (a play on Am-Erica). Throughout the novel we sense that Changez forms no more than a passing interest for Erica, a stage in the process of coming to age. Erica is initially drawn to Changez because of his strong sense of home, and she finds in him a sense of *stability* and *roots*. The reader is aware of the racist undercurrent that informs her view of him. Erica's cosmopolitan, metropolitan circle of friends spend their time *consuming* culture, whilst seeing Changez as *tied* to his culture (Mamdani, 2002). It is presumed, then, that the reader is sympathetic to the view that America is unable to be self-reflexive. As Erica's father welcomes Changez into the family home, he tells him: 'You guys have got some serious problems with fundamentalism' (2007: 54). The reader is invited to laugh along at the irony of this jibe and at Erica's father's inability to see America's own fundamentalisms. But what is notable about these critical moments is the way in which they nevertheless keep the idea of a world divided into 'us' and 'them' in place. Thus, although these moments nicely reveal how celebrations of 'difference' often keep the structures of power in place, they don't necessarily suggest how nationalist imaginaries might also be undone.

Stories we like to hear

In its engagement with the limits of nationalism, the novel appeals to a well-meaning, liberal audience that wants to show the United States how its actions might be seen in other parts of the world. But what is troubling about it is the way in which it seems to reproduce a nationalist imaginary in the course of critiquing it. For example, it gradually becomes impossible for Changez to stay in New York

City and to find alternative forms of being together in that city; he returns to Pakistan. In this sense, the plot of the novel affirms a Hegelian plot of alienation and return as Changez moves away from, but ultimately returns to, his nation of origin (Slaughter, 2007: 97). This conclusion serves to suggest that national identities will defeat other possibilities of living together presented by the city. It reproduces a notion of belonging that can be traced back to a point of origin (understood as language, race, ethnicity, or place) in contrast to a more 'diasporic imaginary' (Axel, 2002). Thus, whilst the novel may become successful because it satisfies a desire to reveal *what people in other parts of the world think*, what is disconcerting is the way in which it also reaffirms a geography of 'us' and 'them'. In offering a choice between becoming American or retreating to origins, the plot of the novel collaborates with a nationalist imaginary. Despite the possibilities offered by the hospitality of the global city, the suggestion is that national identities will ultimately triumph.

This implies that the critique of cosmopolitanism offered by this novel travels alongside a reaffirmation of nationalism. For example, when Changez can't in the end secure Erica's love, he blames it on the fact that he doesn't really know *where he belongs*: in America or in Pakistan. He slides into a state of disenchantment with the world, which leads him to become a university lecturer(!) At this point, the novel again follows in the format of the *Bildungsroman*, as the chief protagonist goes on a search for meaning and moral purpose that can offer an antidote to modernity's upheavals (Cheah, 2003: 243). In this way, the novel narrates a quintessentially modern understanding of freedom as involving a progressive journey towards autonomy, self-determination and self-awareness, which as Chapters 2 and 3 discussed, resonates with a nationalist imaginary. This seems to confirm Joseph Slaughter's provocative argument that post-colonial novels become well known and are marketed to literary audiences in the global north, not because they disturb or challenge familiar representations, but because they reproduce *views of the world that we already hold* (2007). Thus, although the novel suggests a certain 'anti-Americanism' and was marketed to an international literary public hungry for stories *from the other side of the world*, what we find is that the story narrated by this particular novel is largely familiar. This novel doesn't so much offer another way of *seeing* the world as reaffirm a recognizable understanding of freedom as involving a straightforward path towards meaning and enlightenment. Regardless of whether the journey leads towards inclusion or exclusion, progress or disappointment, it is animated by the idea of a solid organism travelling along a journey in time. As such, it is steeped in a nationalist vocabulary.

The plot and techniques of critique

The heightened nationalisms that formed part of the political climate of the 'War on Terror' were enabled by a 'conception of freedom that is understood to emerge through time, and which is temporally progressive in its structure' (Butler, 2008: 3). This is what facilitates a view of the world in which some people are understood to be 'advanced' and others 'backward', a theme that we discussed in

Chapters 3 and 4. This understanding of freedom as secular progress is also expressed in the genre of the *Bildungsroman* (Cheah, 2003). It celebrates the idea of an autonomous individual, in charge of his (*sic*) own destiny, capable of overcoming the burdens of the past in order to become enlightened. Significantly, this time of progress is understood as potentially restorative of something that has been lost and needs to be regained in the future. In the case of the *Bildungsroman*, that which is understood to be lost is the connection between the main protagonist and the world, which sends him (originally, predominantly, but not exclusively a 'him') on a search for meaning. This forms another version of the story of modern life as disenchanted. Yet this novel is somewhat more complicated because, even in its affirmation of a narrative of disenchantment, it seeks to caution *against* concluding that disenchantment leads to a 'necessary nationalism'. Thus, although its plot and format may follow a narrative of progress that is anchored in a nationalist imaginary, the story nevertheless actively engages with challenging nationalist (and essentialist) categorizations. For example, in comparing the United States and Pakistan, and the complex geopolitical relationship between the two countries, Changez says: 'It seems an obvious thing to say, but you should not imagine that we Pakistanis are all potential terrorists, just as we should not imagine that you Americans are all undercover assassins' (2007: 183). The novel aims to challenge nationalist stereotypes but, even as it does so, the problem lies with how its framing of political life continues to distinguish between the citizens and nations within and the enemies and others outside (Walker, 1993).

The novel appears to play out an oppositional critique, which wants to hold up a mirror to the nation. The problem with oppositional critiques however, is that they don't necessarily lead to the undoing of nationalist categories. In this sense, the form of critique enunciated by this novel echoes with a short film directed by Mira Nair, released as part of the collective project, 11'09"01 (2002). Nair's film tells the true story of a mother's search for her missing son, Muhammad Salman Hamdani, in the wake of the fall of the twin towers. Much like *The Reluctant Fundamentalist*, Nair explores the politics of 'mistaken identities' that characterized this political climate and how young 'Muslim' or 'Arab' men (or rather, men who *looked* 'Muslim' or 'Arab') were targeted for representing potential risks to the nation. Salman Hamdani was suspected by the FBI for being a terrorist, but months later it was discovered that he was killed running into the twin towers to try and help. After months of being named a terrorist, Muhammad Salman Hamdani is at the end of the film renamed as a national hero. Nair's film chimes with Hamid's novel because both expose the problem of 'mistaken identities' and both reveal the conditional welcome of liberal multiculturalism – insofar as that this is a welcome that can easily be withdrawn. Indeed, The 'War on Terror' was in many ways epitomized by the demand to *prove* one's allegiance to the nation. This is demonstrated in this film when Salman's mother pleads with the FBI that 'he likes reading science fiction books and playing video games; *Salman's a regular American boy*'. In this political context, pastimes, travel movements and purchasing habits were all liable to be read as suspicious (Amoore, 2006, 2007) and therefore could also be held up as 'evidence' of good citizenship. But, as

Jasbir Puar argues, to understand these instances as examples of 'mistaken identities' is to miss the politics of what is at stake (2007: 167). In discussing assaults
on Sikh, turbaned men mistaken for Muslims in the US following 9/11, Puar
argues that explaining these as 'mistakes' suggests that the viewer 'is open to and
willing to discern the visual difference between Sikh turbans and Muslim turbans'
(2007: 167). This point – that there might be more at stake than a straightforward
'mistake' – has resonance for the case of the shooting of Jean Charles de Menezes
in London, which was discussed briefly in the last chapter. This is because the
idea of a 'mistake' effaces the force of sovereign power just as it also brushes
aside the complexities of racism. This critique of the idea of a 'mistaken identity' therefore also reveals the limits of both Hamid's and Nair's interventions.
Although both the novel and the film demonstrate the dangers of the sovereign
demand to prove that one 'belongs', and the way in which this demand operates
by way of a racialized imaginary, they suggest that the critical task lies with
'correcting' mistaken impressions. In so doing, the interventions risk working
within the terms that they aims to critique.

This point is captured in a key moment in *The Reluctant Fundamentalist* when
Changez contemplates the way in which he was co-opted by America. In reflecting on the way in which his faith in the nation has only led to disappointment,
Changez compares his situation to the Janissary, the Christian boys who were
captured by the Ottoman army and re-educated as Muslims to become their most
loyal fighters. We arrive at something of a Messianic moment in the novel, as the
light shines for Changez, and he describes taking off a veil that had hitherto
obscured his vision:

> my blinders were coming off, and I was dazzled and rendered immobile by
> the sudden broadening of my arc of vision.
>
> (2007: 145)

This extract encapsulates perfectly the predominant form of critique offered by
this novel: that is, that critical work should be engaged in *extending* and *improv-
ing* our ways of seeing – either to show how others see the world differently or to
see the world for what it really is. In this sense, critique is enunciated as a process
of unveiling and this implies that our pictures of the world might be improved
with better *vision*.[3] Whilst this understanding of critical work as involving an
extension in what we are able to see is well intentioned, and forms an aim that is
not easily dismissed, it is underpinned by a narrative of progress and enlightenment that suggests we *will* arrive at a greater degree of understanding. This
account of what critique involves operates in tandem with a nationalist imaginary
because it affirms the sense of a common journey in time. This critique of nationalism is therefore limited by the way in which it borrows and reproduces the
language of nationalism. As such, it represents a vulnerable critical strategy. In
suggesting that what needs to be done is to *extend* our compassion to others, this
critical gesture fails to place the values *that we already hold* under question. It
keeps the very idea of who 'we' are intact.

The time of imagination

This suggests that the problem doesn't so much lie with the (mis)identification of the 'civilized' and the 'uncivilized', the 'citizen' and the 'terrorist', but with the persistence of this *framework of options* as a way of making sense of global politics (Butler, 2008). Critical work needs to be able to overturn these terms as the grounds and conditions for political debate. This would indicate that the critical strategy of insisting that other people in the world are 'just as civilized' is insufficient. This is the technique used in *The Reluctant Fundamentalist* when the narrator says, 'Four thousand years ago, we the people of the Indus river basin, had cities that were laid out on grids and boasted underground sewers, while the ancestors of those who would invade and colonize America were illiterate barbarians' (2007: 34). This extract aims to challenge dominant images of 'progress' and 'civilization', but it once again operates by way of an oppositional critique which may subvert ideas about what 'progress' represents but nevertheless keeps the terms of the debate intact. It also continues to affirm a homogenous, empty understanding of time, which both frames and limits the kind of debate that can be had. This is exactly the point that Judith Butler makes when she says that the challenge lies with thinking beyond 'that teleology that violently installs itself as *both origin and end of the culturally thinkable*' (2008: 19, my emphasis). That is, the problem with ideas of 'progress' does not lie with the question of *who* is deemed to be 'advanced' or 'backward', but with this homogenous, empty understanding of time and the way in which this marks out both the *origins* and *limits* of what we are able to *imagine*.[4]

This indicates that the problem does not only lie with the ways in which *some* people *see* the world, and that what is required is to tweak, adjust, improve or correct that which we are *able to see*. Such critical gestures immediately lead us back to a subject that portrays the other (wrongly or rightly) as 'other'. There is more at stake in the challenge of imagining another form of politics than is captured by the idea of (mis)representations. This point applies to Derek Gregory's critical engagement with the political climate of the 'War on Terror' (2004) when he outlines the kinds of questions that should guide a study of the 'imaginative geographies' of 'us' and 'them':

> First, who claims the power to fabricate those meanings? Who assumes the power to represent the other *as* other, and on what basis? . . . This attempt to muffle the other – so that, at the limit, metropolitan cultures protect their powers and privileges by insisting that 'the subaltern cannot speak' – raises the second question. What is the power of those meanings? What do those meanings *do*?
>
> (2004: 8)

The first of these questions assumes a distinction between the *imagined* and the *real*. It is a distinction that also hovers at the edges of Edward Said's *Orientalism*, from which Gregory borrows the concept of 'imaginative geographies'.[5] As

Robert Young argues in his reading of Said's *Orientalism*, the binary between the real and the imagined leaves us caught in a puzzle that revolves around the relationship between representation and its object (2004: 168–171). On the one hand, the suggestion is that there is *no* relationship between representations and their objects (representations are fabrications). On the other hand, it is assumed that representations work to control and dominate their objects (the framings absorb everything). As Young points out, whilst there is no ready answer to the question of how representations connect (or not) to the real, what we're presented with is a closed system, in which we're shuttling back and forth between 'reality' and 'fiction'.

This problem of closure is 'fundamental' to Said's *Orientalism*, argues Young, and it is a problem that also haunts Gregory's study. Take, for example, his analysis of how racism works through representations that control and dominate their objects: 'This culture (which is to say 'their' culture) is [understood as] closed and stultifying, monolithic and unchanging – a fixity that is at the very heart of modern racisms' (Gregory, 2004: 22). The trouble with Gregory's formulation of the problem is that techniques of discrimination are more sophisticated than this emphasis on acts of seeing is able to capture, and this is a point that became especially prevalent in the context of the 'War on Terror', as works that have engaged with data-profiling practices intimate (Amoore, 2006, 2007). It is for this reason that Ash Amin asks whether an anti-racist politics based around appeals to 'human particularity, recognition and reconciliation' can offer enough to 'discursively and practically unsettle the elaborate machinery of fear, suspicion and discipline... being put in place by the new biopolitics of emergency' (2010: 15–16). Similarly, Jasbir Puar argues for a shift away from a study of racism that focuses on regimes of visuality towards a study of the circulation of emotions and, in that context, draws on the work of Sara Ahmed in order to understand how images of fear 'stick' to some bodies more than others (2007: 186–189). This approach enables a better understanding she argues, of how fear can be 'materialized in any body within a particular profile range' and that the figure of the terrorist retains a potent 'significatory ambiguity' – enabling fear to 'stick' to bodies that 'could be' terrorists (2007: 186).

Gregory's first question about 'who' has the power to 'represent the other as other' makes it difficult to ask questions about the shifting discursive marker of 'the terrorist'. It suggests a straightforward relationship between agency and representation, which implies that 'mistaken identities' can be corrected. Gregory goes on to say that part of the problem with the political climate of the 'War on Terror' lay with attempts to 'muffle the other' (2004: 8). Yet, as this reading of *The Reluctant Fundamentalist* attests, the problem does not necessarily lie with *silencing* 'the other' so much as with the forms and techniques through which 'others' *are invited to speak*. Racist practices don't operate simply through the denial of difference, but also through techniques of accommodating and containing differences (Butler and Spivak, 2007: 5). This is why the second question that Gregory provides is much more useful – what is the power of those meanings and what do they *do*? This question detaches the problem from one of enunciation and enquiries into the ways in which different representations circulate. This is an important shift because it opens up the question of how closed representations can also resonate in *critical* interventions.

Gregory is of course fully aware of the problem of 'closure' and how critique can either lead to the further entrenchment of a political system or contribute towards its undoing. As he puts it, 'every repertory performance of the colonial present carries within it the twin possibilities of either reaffirming and even radicalizing the hold of the colonial past on the present or undoing its enclosures and approaching the horizon of the postcolonial' (2004: 19). The key problem, then, is how we might distinguish between 'effective' critical gestures that contribute towards nationalism's undoing and those that threaten to reaffirm nationalism's dominance as a way of framing what it means to be political. This reading of *The Reluctant Fundamentalist* has indicated that a critique of nationalism must in the first instance question the homogenous empty understanding of time that underpins this modern account of freedom and subjectivity. The challenge of 'approaching the horizon of the postcolonial' may therefore lie in understanding the present as shot through with multiple temporalities (Hutchings, 2008: 154–177).

As the post-colonial critic Dipesh Chakrabarty argues, there is a connection between understanding time as plural and the question of political imagination. Although the European category of 'imagination' has a long and complex history (2008: 174), it is nevertheless often understood as something pertaining to the mental capacities of a subject[6] and assumes that the present can be neatly demarcated from the past and future. It is this idea of imagination that largely animates *The Reluctant Fundamentalist*. For example, readers are invited to recognize the view of the present as *what they already know*. A 'critical' audience can therefore congratulate itself on identifying essentializing and mistaken views of 'others' at work. But, ultimately, the novel asks nothing of a left-leaning and liberal literary public in the global north that *already* understands itself to have an 'open' understanding of 'others'. It therefore fails to ask readers to consider ways of seeing and understanding the world that lie *beyond* interpretations of their own present (Hutchings, 2008: 165). In suggesting that 'imagination' might signal a different orientation towards the present and future, Chakrabarty argues that the concept indicates 'heterogeneous practices of seeing' (2008: 149). This chapter will now turn to explore this point further by addressing how this novel also points to other understandings of living with difference. This will involve a discussion of how the politics of loss might be approached outside of a linear account of time. This will be supplemented by a discussion of Judith Butler's writings in response to the events of 9/11.

An anti-nationalist sense of loss

Literary texts offer a key site through which a sense of nationhood is evoked, but the process of articulation is an ambivalent one that reveals the 'wide dissemination through which we construct the field of meanings and symbols associated with national life' (Bhabha, 1990: 3; see also Bulson, 2007). *The Reluctant Fundamentalist* follows in the format of the *Bildungsroman*, but it also offers a critique of the spatio-temporal coordinates of nationalism. This is achieved primarily in the urban portraits of New York and Lahore which are posited as sites that complicate and surpass a nationalist framing of the world. For example, we learn that Lahore is 'layered like a sedimentary plain with the accreted history of invaders from the Aryans to the Mongols to the British' (2007: 7), suggesting that differences are not building blocks that make us 'more interesting' but are formed through complex relations and fractious histories, including colonial histories. This city is thus less a container of multiple 'identities' than a node that hosts a plurality of urban dwellers, including bats and other urban animals. In these moments, the novel suggests cosmopolitanism, but not in the sense of a point that lies at the end of a journey in time or as something that needs to be managed, encouraged or praised. In contrast to cosmopolitanism as an ideal, these urban images suggest that 'we already are and have always been cosmopolitan, though we may not always have known it' (Pollock *et al.*, 2000: 588). The main protagonist occasionally assumes the role of a post-colonial *flâneur*, who finds his mental life mirrored in the constantly changing montage of the metropolis around him. The novel thus also draws on a tradition of writing the urban experience as a disorderly and disorientating experience – as in James Joyce's *Ulysses*, Virginia Woolf's *Mrs Dalloway* or Alfred Döblin's *Berlin Alexanderplatz*. Furthermore, the novel draws on a tradition of post-colonial novels that reveal the absurdity, as well as the violence, of aligning territory with identity – as in Chimamanda Ngozi Adichie's *Half of a Yellow Sun*, Rohinton Mistry's *A Fine Balance* or Bapsi Sidhwa's *Ice Candy Man*.[7]

The portraits of Lahore therefore offer openings for thinking what it means to be in the world differently. Following the loss of what Changez hoped to find in America (and with Erica), he decides to give up on his yearning for security and certainty and instead learns to live with fragmentation and incompleteness. We are presented with a different understanding of subjectivity, as something that works against the principles of nationalism and which refuses the search for completion. He reflects that he cannot 'be made whole again': 'try as we might, we cannot reconstitute ourselves as the autonomous beings we previously imagined ourselves to be. Something of us is now outside, and something of the outside is now within us' (2007: 172–3). In this case, the city serves as another kind of port in the storm of modern life, which seeks to accommodate brokenness rather than enable redemption. In Lahore, Changez can allow himself to become a 'divided subject' (Shapiro, 2010). In this part of the novel, Hamid draws on another understanding of mourning and melancholia, which is anti-nationalist insofar as it doesn't aim to *overcome* trauma but, rather, to encircle it (Edkins, 2003). Whilst an affective community may be produced by 'sharing an object of loss', this form of melancholia involves a failure to 'get over loss' (Ahmed, 2010: 141) and a refusal 'to participate in the national game' (Ahmed, 2010: 142). This, alternative understanding of loss resonates with Judith Butlers response to the events of 9/11 and in her reflections on how we might *refuse* to respond to traumatic events by opting for a heightened nationalism (2006). For example, Butler suggests that moments of high insecurity that produce strong individual and collective grief potentially offer moments for contesting nationalist narratives and recrafting understandings of what it means to live together.

By remaining critical of the 'reaffirmation of solidarity and nationhood' (Edkins, 2003: 19) that followed the events of 11 September 2001, Butler attempts to think loss in a way that offers a 'reorientation for politics' (2006: 28). Butler is especially concerned to draw out the complex character of loss – that we do not necessarily know when mourning is successful or complete, or that we cannot necessarily exactly pinpoint what it is that we have lost. This echoes some of what Mohsin Hamid hints at in the latter parts of *The Reluctant Fundamentalist*. For Butler, however, the points draw on her earlier work on the way in which grieving the loss of a gay or lesbian partner means facing a loss that is often 'ungrievable' within established familial structures and traditional practices of mourning (Butler, 2004; Bell, 1999; Lloyd, 2008). She extends that work to suggest that *certain* lives that are lost in conditions of war are never recognized or acknowledged in any official sense as having been lost. She asks: 'Who counts as human? Whose lives count as lives? And … What *makes for a grievable life?*' (2006: 20). We have all lost, she says. But instead of establishing this as a point of originary commonality, Butler suggests that mourning might make a 'tenuous "we" of us all' (2006: 20). She refuses to think of loss as a foundational moment from which we might move on 'together'. Instead, she draws out the continuing and complex experience of loss to argue that this is not something that can be easily located or atoned for through nationalism and retaliation. This is in marked opposition to President George Bush's announcement on 21 September 2001 that the time for mourning was over and that now was the time for action (Butler, 2006: 29).

Butler suggests that loss exposes the inescapability of our vulnerability. Whilst security practices might suggest that this is something we have to defend against or overcome, Butler suggests that vulnerability is ultimately unavoidable and that coming to terms with that may lead to another understanding of being. For example, she argues that grief, loss and vulnerability challenge the myth of an autonomous and self-determining subject: 'Something is larger than one's own deliberate plan, one's own project, one's own knowing and choosing' (2006: 21). Thus, rather than understand community as something that is built around autonomous citizens agreeing to a common contract, she suggests that the idea of individuals as autonomous agents needs to be challenged. In this sense, grief poses a 'challenge [to] the very notion of ourselves as autonomous and in control' (2006: 23). This leads Butler to argue for an understanding of political community as formed around an unavoidable relationality.[8] This is somewhat reminiscent of the work of philosopher Jean-Luc Nancy (1991, 2000), who argues that we are always already with others and that being can only be understood as such.[9] As Butler puts it, we don't encounter, lose, or fall in love with other autonomous beings; rather, we are transformed, turned upside down and unsettled by those encounters: 'It is not as if an "I" exists independently over here and then simply loses a "you" over there, especially if the attachment to "you" is part of what composes who "I" am' (2006: 22). This is not a relation that links a solid me with a separate you, but rather concentrates on the *tie* through which we find ourselves already negotiating our place in the world. Butler's account of relationality therefore draws partly on some of Nancy's work, but it also derives from her interest in *bodies* – in how 'the skin and the flesh expose us to the gaze of others but also to touch and to violence' (2006: 21). She is explicitly interested in resisting an account of subjectivity as mastery. In this respect, her work offers a counter-narrative to the political thought of Max Weber and Jean-Jacques Rousseau, discussed in Chapters 2 and 3. It also signals an alternative orientation to time, which refuses the determinism of an account of the present and future as already known.

Critique, co-optation and ambivalent nationalisms

One of Butler's key aims in this essay is to suggest that the question of imagining community needs to be approached again. But she is specifically concerned about how difficult it was to express any sort of critical position in the aftermath of the events of 11 September 2001, without risking the accusation of being 'unpatriotic' (see also Brown, 2005). Thus, although her essay seeks to challenge a nationalist account of community, it is caught in a bind where any suggestions she makes risk appearing as a form of 'anti-Americanism'. This might explain why Butler seems to go far in showing that she identifies with an American national community. Take for example the following quotation:

> *Our collective responsibility* not merely *as a nation*, but as part of an international community based on a commitment to equality and non-violent cooperation, requires that we ask how these conditions came about, and endeavor to re-create social and political conditions on more sustaining grounds. This means, in part, hearing beyond what we are able to hear. And it means as well being open to narration that decenters us from our supremacy, in both its right- and left-wing forms.
>
> (2006: 17–18, my emphasis)

Given that Butler's reading community assumes a more complex and international form than an exclusively American reading public, it is fairly surprising that she chooses to position herself as an American addressing her fellow citizens. She may have felt this was an imperative position to take given the highly sensitive political context and what she herself describes as 'a rise of anti-intellectualism and a growing acceptance of censorship within the media' (2006: 3). This may have formed an attempt to *make her voice heard* under conditions that made it difficult to offer *any* critique of the United States administration and its foreign policy. Yet we may also ask whether, in assuming this rhetorical stance, Butler contradicts her efforts to problematize and contest a nationalist imaginary. Whilst we may understand the move as a 'tactical strategy', this fleeting appeal to a national community might also suggest the persistence of nationalism in offering the dominant terms through which it becomes possible to narrate critique, dissent and resistance, especially in 'times of terror'.

This 'tactical strategy' is shared by Wendy Brown in an essay called 'Political idealization and its discontents' (2005). In that essay, Brown seeks to respond to the 'You're either with us or against us' cry of the 'War on Terror' by rethinking the relationship between citizenship, love of country and critique. To do so, she turns to Plato's *Crito* and *The Apology* to recover an argument that critique of the regime can also form an expression of *love* and *loyalty* to the regime. In this sense, she argues that critique can form a way of practising virtue and justice, and so goes hand in hand with civic loyalty:

> If one loves another Athens, another America than the one whose actions or laws we decry in the present, what is the place of loyalty in mediating between this love and the polity as it presents itself now, here? Or, if one loves what one is harboured by but is also ruthlessly critical of and devoted to trying to improve, is this loyalty?
>
> (2005: 21)

Brown's argument is compelling even if it does amount to what she herself qualifies as a 'nonrevolutionary' form of dissent (2005: 18). But, what is striking about it is that it nevertheless keeps us tied to a political imaginary that privileges the space of the nation. The question to ask in this context is, why must critique reterritorialize around a national community? And what are the risks in reproducing this entrenched understanding of what politics is and where it must take place?

This is effectively a question about the relationship between critique and co-optation, or what forms a critical reworking of the nation and what risks reproducing another figure of nationalism. This is a problem that Butler is very familiar with (McRobbie, 2006: 77) and it is what makes drawing on her work so fruitful. She asks: 'Is it that easy in practice to be able to determine what forms a critical re-working of the nation and what risks becoming a "new nationalism"'? (Butler in Butler and Spivak, 2007: 61). This is an important question, and what this chapter has sought to do is to point to how some critical gestures seem so deeply rooted in a nationalist imaginary that they are unable to offer an effective critique of nationalism. In this respect, Butler's position is different from Hamid's, in that she strategically appeals to the idea of the nation but simultaneously works to undo the presumption of autonomy, self-control and self-determination. Nevertheless, this is what also makes Butler's fleeting appeal to an American national community surprising. We find that 'there is … an inescapable irony in Butler's position. She chooses to speak within the frame that she critiques' (Zehfuss, 2009: 423). She will be aware of the risks involved in reproducing the exclusionary categories that she sets out to struggle against. As Butler tells us in earlier writings, often subjects have no choice but to take such a stance and, when 'utterly subjected', to 'reiterate the law of their genesis' (1999: 135). But did the conditions of thinking and writing in the United States in the aftermath of the events of 11 September 2001 represent a time when critical theorists ostensibly had no choice but to frame their critiques in national terms? The problem with endorsing this tactical strategy is that Butler also warns us about the need to be 'suspicious of any and all forms of national homogeneity, however internally qualified they may be' (Butler and Spivak, 2007: 32). The other problem with it is that it suggests that the events of 11 September 2001 were primarily *attacks on America*, although they killed citizens from many different parts of the world and ultimately had to be *talked* and *written* into a national frame (see Smith quoted in Elden, 2009: xvi). Butler would of course appreciate these points; nevertheless, it seems that this momentary appeal to the US nation offers an example of nationalism's relentless ability to determine the terms of debate.

To borrow Butler's earlier question: who is able to hear this call to decentre 'us' from 'our' supremacy? Who is she addressing and who might feel excluded by this call? She argues that experiences of loss have the potential to lead to a reorientation for politics and towards another understanding of political community. Yet it is interesting that she articulates this point *as a citizen of the United States*. In doing so, she seems to suggest that what is required in the task of rethinking political community is to turn *inwards*, to a conversation that takes place *within* the United States before the US can emerge *back into the world* to establish different kinds of ties, as this quote suggests:

I consider our recent trauma to be an opportunity for a reconsideration of United States hubris and the importance of establishing more radically egalitarian international ties...the notion of the world itself as a sovereign entitlement of the United States must be given up, lost, and mourned, as narcissistic and grandiose fantasies must be lost and mourned. From the subsequent experience of loss and fragility, however, the possibility of making different kinds of ties emerges.

(2006: 40)

This framing of the problem seems to rub against Butler's invocation of a form of politics that begins with the ties between us rather than with autonomous units that 'reach out' into the world. My point here is that even Butler's critical undoing of a nationalist imaginary seems to come close to reaffirming nationalism in this case. Whilst she encourages us to consider ways of seeing and understanding the world that lie beyond what is already familiar (Hutchings, 2008), she also revivifies a well-established political imagination. It seems, then, that more is required to open up 'heterogeneous practices of seeing' (Chakrabarty, 2008: 149) and to imagine a form of politics beyond what we already know. This return to the nation may be countered by revisiting the different understanding of coexistence elaborated through the site of the global city, which in its 'complex terrain of transnational movement and affiliation' potentially offers a different understanding of what it means to live together to the 'conceptual fixities associated with the state or nation' (Jabri, 2009: 45). The next chapter will return to the site of the city as an opening for rethinking what it means to live together in more detail.

Conclusion

This chapter has addressed a novel that engages with the political climate that followed the events of 11 September 2001 and which became a bestseller on account of saying 'dangerous things in dangerous times' (Halaby, 2007). The novel seeks to expose and contest heightened nationalisms at work and, in particular, the problem of 'mistaken identities' that emerged in this context. But this chapter has argued that the form of critique narrated by this particular novel is indebted to a nationalist imaginary. This is especially the case in terms of the homogenous, empty understanding of time it reproduces and the idea of subjectivity as involving a search for mastery and meaning. It is also the case in relation to the way in which it enunciates critique as the task of extending that which we are able to see. The chapter argued that the form of critique offered in *The Reluctant Fundamentalist* ultimately owes too much to a liberal imaginary to be able to offer a robust critique of the politics of the 'War on Terror'. As an intervention, it largely works by affirming to a liberal audience that which it already thinks it knows rather than encouraging other ways of thinking about what it means to be in the world. The key point here is that it risks asking nothing of a left-leaning literary audience that assumes it *already* holds an enlightened view of 'others'.

The chapter has nevertheless also identified several potential openings for thinking coexistence differently – through reworking ideas of subjectivity, community and loss, and also through portraits of the global city. Both these avenues have offered fruitful material for undoing nationalism, in particular because they offer possibilities for complicating the spatio-temporal coordinates of nationalism. The layers of history forming the city of Lahore suggest a form of living together that doesn't rely on a common understanding of the present. And the idea of reworking community through a focus on encounters that move, transform and unsettle us, and reveal the way in which we are all constituted incompletely in relation to one another, is promising. The next chapter takes up these possibilities by enquiring further into an urban account of coexistence and also by seeking to recover ideas of loss from the grip of nationalist thought. It does so by departing momentarily from the political context of the 'War on Terror' to study sites of memory in the city of Berlin.

6 Sites of memory and the city as a melee

> Berlin is... a place whose identity is based not on stability but on change. Berlin can appear solid and secure at one moment, but its history has shown the dangers of taking the image for granted. It is a volatile place, and many have found to their cost that the veneer of normality can vanish as quickly as...sand slips through the fingers.
>
> Alexandra Richie, *Faust's Metropolis*

Introduction

This chapter aims to take the glimpses of a non-nationalistic understanding of coexistence encountered through the city in Chapters 4 and 5 further. It does so by way of a discussion of sites of memory in the city of Berlin. The chapter therefore departs from debates surrounding the political aftermath of the events of 11 September 2001. Yet, as Judith Butler's reflections in the aftermath of 9/11 suggest, debates around memory, loss and trauma are significant because they engage directly with the politics of nationalism (2006). Whilst the nation will 'co-opt the dead into its own narratives' (Edkins, 2003: 95), there will be attempts at contesting that co-optation, to try and remember the dead differently, and outside the categories imposed by the state. This chapter engages with the ways in which we can read critiques of nationalism into the designs of Holocaust memorials in the city of Berlin.[1] It discusses three examples of sites of memory, including the Jewish Museum designed by Daniel Libeskind – opened as a building in 1999 and as a museum in 2001, the Memorial to the Murdered Jews of Europe designed by Peter Eisenman, which opened in 2005, and the 'Missing House' (1990) designed by Christian Boltanski. It also discusses two art installations by the artist Gustav Metzger, who arrived in Britain from Germany in 1939 with the help of the Refugee Children's Movement.

The chapter argues that these sites of memory can be read as contesting a nationalist imaginary. This is because their architects have drawn on an experience of time as non-linear, non-unifying and which breaks out in several directions at once. In experimenting with this alternative idea of time, the architects draw on an experience of modernity that counteracts nationalist narratives of meaning, rationality, continuity and homogeneity – the kind of experience of modernity that we traced through the first part of this book as forming a backdrop for the possibility of nationalism. These architects have brought this other experience of modernity – as irrational, discontinuous and meaningless – to the forefront of their designs, and this is what makes them interesting in providing another entry point to the study of nationalism. These architectural designs evoke a different way of understanding modern life – an experience that has been fleshed out by figures including Walter Benjamin, Georg Simmel and Friedrich Kracauer (Frisby, 1985) – writers who, incidentally, all wrote at different points about the experience of living in Berlin. They all make this 'discontinuous experience of time' and an understanding of space as 'transitory, fleeting and fortuitous' a central concern (Frisby, 1985: 4). Given how this book has argued that an experience of modernity as rational and linear in many ways makes nationalism possible, this chapter will address what possibilities emerge for understanding coexistence when we approach modernity and time differently.

The chapter begins by turning to Walter Benjamin's attempts to draw connections between a non-linear, non-unifying understanding of time and the experience of urban life. It then goes on to consider how this offers a different entry point to the task of contesting nationalism by way of a discussion of sites of memory. In contrast to critiques of nationalism that nevertheless reproduce a narrative of progress in time, as encountered in the last chapter, this chapter develops a different approach. Specifically, it addresses the question of how these particular sites of memory offer responses to loss that refuse to congeal around the sense of a united community. In doing so, the chapter also draws on the work of the philosopher Jean-Luc Nancy and his description of the city as a 'melee' (2003). Nancy's idea of the city as a 'melee' is interesting because it refuses to understand identities and differences according to a binary choice, in the way that we have established is typical of a nationalist imaginary. According to Nancy, the notion of a 'melee' works on another register, which undoes the assumption of a constitutive unity. The overall aim of this chapter is to present an alternative approach to the challenge of 'imagining community' through the notion of 'urban encounters'.

The time of the city

Benjamin's life-long friend, collaborator and critic, Gershom Scholem, recounts that Benjamin would often ask him whether time, which must have a sequence, must also have a particular direction (Scholem 2001: 41). Indeed, Walter Benjamin (1892–1940) offers a persistent critique of 'homogenous empty time' and several attempts at thinking the experience of time outside the time of progress (Smith 1989: xxvi; Buck-Morss 1991; Scholem 2001; Crang 2001). His writings on *cities* in particular offer an important resource for thinking time differently (Amin and Thrift, 2002; Shapiro, 2010)[2] and are directly connected to his attempt at rethinking the experience of modernity. Benjamin began writing against the backdrop of the First World War in 1914 and the Bolsheviks' October Revolution in 1917; he witnessed the rise of Nazism in Germany and died seeking to escape that terror, committing suicide on the border between France and Spain. He understood the conditions of modern life as presenting both spectacular achievements and great violence – and therefore as necessarily ambivalent. Yet Benjamin *responds* to the conditions of modern life in a very different way to the insistence on the necessity of a modern nation-state and the figure of an autonomous, self-determining individual that we encountered in the work of Max Weber in Chapter 2. Instead of opting for the state as a solution to the *meaning-lessness* of existence, and placing his faith in processes of rationalism and rationalization, Benjamin seeks in the fabric of the city (of Berlin and Paris mainly, but also other cities including Naples, Moscow and Marseilles) material for capturing the contradictory forces of modern life. In so doing, his writings offer openings for resisting a politics that insists on the centrality of the nation-state. They also suggest a counter-narrative to an account of modern life as based upon rationality.

Suggestive of movement, flow, energy and contradiction, cities have of course long formed something of a metaphor for writers, painters, musicians and artists interested in an understanding of modernity as a fragmented, disjointed experi-ence: 'The cultural chaos bred by the populous, ever-growing city, a contingent and polyglot Tower of Babel, is enacted in similar chaos, contingency and plural-ity in the texts of modern writing, the design and form of Modernist painting' (Bradbury, 1976: 98). This understanding of modernity is indebted to Charles Baudelaire, the quintessential poet of modern life, who wrote about the changing understandings of space and time that he saw reflected in the streets of nine-teenth-century Paris (Frisby, 1985, 2001). Walter Benjamin (along with Georg Simmel and Friedrich Kracauer) can be understood as working within this tradi-tion established by Baudelaire – to 'set up his house in the heart of the multitude, amid the ebb and flow of motion, in the midst of the fugitive and the infinite' (Berman, 1983: 145; Frisby, 1985). Although Benjamin writes almost exclusively about the cities of the global north, the point about the connection between an experience of modernity, urbanity and a disjointed temporality is just as relevant in the global south (Mbembe and Nuttall, 2004: 361). The point is not that this experience of time as non-linear and unpredictable corresponds directly to the experience of life in cities, or in particular cities. Rather, it is that writings on cities often reveal the Janus-face of modern life (Magnusson, 2000) and that, for example, the 'division between urban planning geared towards urban growth and development, and that which focuses on attempts at place annihilation or attack, is not always clear' (Graham, 2004: 33; see also Berman, 1983; Davis, 1990, 2000, 2002; Graham, 2010; Harvey, 1989, 2003; Sandercock, 1998).

As the social theorist Georg Simmel (whose lectures Benjamin attended) describes in 'The Metropolis and Mental Life' (published originally in 1903), cities present a plurality of experiences of time.[3] Specifically, Simmel describes two expe-riences of time at work in modern cities, which he saw reflected on the streets of Berlin at the turn of the twentieth century. One experience of time echoes the 'calculating exactness of practical life', which transforms 'the world into an arith-metical problem' (1971: 327). This experience means that, 'if all the watches in

Berlin suddenly went wrong in different ways even only as much as an hour, its entire economic and commercial life would be derailed' (1971: 328). Yet, all importantly, this experience of time only emerges in relation to its opposite:

> Punctuality, calculability, and exactness, which are required by the complications and extensiveness of metropolitan life...are conducive to the exclusion of those irrational, instinctive, sovereign human traits and impulses which originally seek to determine the form of life from within instead of receiving it from the outside.
>
> (1971: 328–329)

Thus, although, as financial centres, cities require strict clocks and calendars and an idea of time as something that can be measured and quantified, cities also form sites for spending time, to wander in the city's crowds and to walk without direction. Crucially, the point here is not to romanticize cities as sites of 'openness, chance and getting lost' (Massey, 2005: 161). Rather, it is to recover an experience of modernity that is often cast aside by political theorists who prefer to emphasize an ethos of order, rationality and continuity (Magnusson, 2000, 2012). It is this experience of discontinuity, openness and flux that Michael Shapiro, drawing on the work of Walter Benjamin, describes as 'the time of the city' (2010). In terms of developing another political imaginary, the idea of 'the time of the city' is interesting because it suggests that the future need not be understood as bound within a nation-statist model of politics but as instead open to 'alternative actualizations' (Shapiro, 2010: 29).

What Benjamin offers is a wide-ranging critique of the time of progress, which extends from the way in which this underpins a particular approach to writing history to the way in which it enables the forward march of capitalism.[4] For example, Benjamin argues that the idea of progress weighs on the writing of history by treating the past as already over and ordering events into a continuous sequence, 'like the beads of a rosary' (1968: 263). He tells us that progressivist accounts of history thereby serve as the tools of the ruling classes by obfuscating stories of struggle, disagreement and resistance. He also argues that the concept of progress has succeeded in keeping the working classes in their place, by selling the idea that it was moving with the current: the promise of self-improvement and 'liberated grandchildren' come to replace memories of 'enslaved ancestors', concealing class antagonisms and structural inequalities (1968: 260). Yet, according to Benjamin, it is not enough to attack this idea of progress. Rather, any critique of progress must begin by interrogating the experience of 'homogenous empty time' that makes the concept possible. As he puts it:

> The concept of the historical progress of mankind cannot be sundered from the concept of its progression through a homogenous, empty time. A critique of the concept of such a progression must be the basis of any criticism of the concept of progress itself.
>
> (1968: 261)

It is this concept of 'homogenous empty time' that forms the central hurdle in closing off alternative ways of understanding history and politics and, as such, according to Benjamin, must form the focal point of critical work.

From his early work on 'A Berlin Chronicle', to his essays on 'Naples', 'Moscow' and 'Marseilles' (Benjamin, 1978), and his reflections on Paris in *The Arcades Project* (1999), Benjamin's urban writings can be read as offering critiques of the idea of 'homogenous empty time'. This is evident partly in the style of writing that he deploys. For example, in *One-Way Street* (1978), Benjamin experiments with an anti-academic writing style that is composed of aphorisms, anecdotes and observations, all collated under particular themes that serve as 'thought-images'[5] for reflecting on social-political concerns. This technique is extended further in *The Arcades Project*, which forms a social and cultural history of nineteenth-century Paris and at the same time serves as a history of the origins of the present moment (Buck-Morss 1991). The *Arcades* is written in a way that deliberately works against the idea of a continuous, linear and contained text. It is disjointed, uneven and incomplete (partly because of the impossibility of offering a 'complete' representation of Paris, but also because the work was interrupted by Benjamin's untimely death). *The Arcades Project* offers a 'literary montage' of thought-images, reflections, historical anecdotes, quotations and commentaries, spanning politics, philosophy, literary studies, art and history. Its style is intended to reflect and reinforce the transient and splintered experience of urban, modern life. Benjamin doesn't aim to represent the city as a whole, since his basic understanding of the city as fragmented makes such a task impossible. Similarly, he doesn't set out to present a theory that captures modernity fully, since if modernity is a disjointed experience, then it also cannot be explained as a totality (Frisby, 1985). In contrast, Benjamin's snapshot style works both as a mirror and as an expression of this discontinuous, ephemeral experience of life in the city and of the conditions of modernity.[6] As we will see, this particular experience of time has been emulated by architects in their designs of sites of memory in Berlin.

Sites of memory and another grammar of identity/difference

Sites of memory are well known loci through which nationalist discourses and imagery are mobilized (Edkins, 2003; Anderson, 1991). The practice of national commemoration acts as a form of national communion where remembering the dead becomes a way of affirming the endurance of the nation. This practice of commemoration and of establishing a narrative of loss and continuity is not an innocent process. Rather, the state must manage a multiplicity of historical narratives and 'impose coherence on what is actually a series of fragmentary and arbitrary conditions of historical assemblage' (Shapiro, 2000: 80). Unifying accounts of time and history are thus central to nationalist modes of remembering, and this process relies upon a politics of force and of forgetting. Yet several sites of memory in the city of Berlin deliberately work against such 'nationalist' models of remembering. They do so by invoking another experience of time as fragmented and disjointed, thereby challenging accounts of modern life as based around order, rationality and measurable progress. For example, these selected memorials to the victims of the Nazi terror suggest that the Holocaust cannot be understood as an aberration in what is otherwise a collective journey from barbarity in the state of nature to the heights of reason, progress and order. Rather, following Zygmunt Bauman, they suggest that the Holocaust forms an example of 'the hidden possibilities of modern society' (2008: 12) and it must therefore be understood as *part* of modernity's drive towards progress, order, reason and uniformity (Bauman, 2008: 93).

These sites of memory in the city of Berlin are therefore explicitly political, and two of them commemorate the lives of murdered Jewish citizens specifically. However, I want to argue that their *designs* undermine the idea of remembering according to 'identitarian' categories. In the context of Berlin, and the building of the Memorial to the Murdered Jews of Europe specifically, there were heated debates around the decision to commemorate the *Jewish* victims of the Holocaust specifically rather than *all* victims of the Nazi programme of killing, including the Roma and Sinti, homosexuals and trade union members (Schlör, 2005).[7] There are, of course, good reasons to remember different 'communities' in their specificity and the fact that 6 million of the 20 million killed were Jews. For example, it is important to make clear that people were killed on account of being *of* a particular community, one that was considered to be a deviation from a 'pure' model of German identity. But I want to argue that the *designs* of both the Jewish Museum in Berlin and the Memorial to the Murdered Jews of Europe narrate a form of remembering that evokes people as having plural identities and complex affiliations. As such, the designs affirm 'the pluralism of the human world' (Bauman, 2008: 93).

In order to develop this point, I draw on the philosopher Jean-Luc Nancy's explicit attempts to reorient ideas of being together in ways that defy the idea of self-contained 'identity groups'. Specifically, I turn to an essay of Nancy's called 'In Praise of the Melee' (2003) in which he reworks the idea of political community in a way that undoes the constitutive principle of unity. This is relevant for this book insofar as Nancy develops this alternative account of community by drawing on reflections about *cities*, specifically, and the way in which cities challenge the very possibility of a homogenous identity. But it is also relevant in the sense that this work is written in response to another example of ethno-nationalism, that of the Balkan conflicts in the 1990s. Whilst not wishing to erase the very different historical contexts of Sarajevo's and Berlin's encounters with ethnic nationalism, the point is that this subject is important to all studies of nationalism.[8] Written for the city of Sarajevo in March 1993, Nancy begins the essay by stating that Sarajevo had in the 1990s become 'the name for a complete system of reduction to identity' – where a City maps onto a Nation, onto a State (Nancy, 2003: 277–278). Against this understanding, Nancy suggests that we might understand Sarajevo as less the name of one identity and instead as 'the locus of a melee' which is never the name of one person, one identity, one community, but the marking of 'crossing and halt, of entanglement and commerce, competition, release, circulation, scattering of lights' (Nancy, 2003: 278). This portrait of the city as a *melee* concurs with Walter Benjamin's analysis of cities as multiple, fragmented and splintered and, thus, suggests a way of thinking identity that rejects an idea of completeness. It also suggests that the desire for 'unity' and 'purity' that underpinned the Holocaust cannot be understood as 'exceptional', but rather as more broadly indicative of a modernist desire for order. This concurs with Bauman's position that 'the conditions that once gave birth to the Holocaust have not been radically transformed' (2008: 86).

In contrast to celebrations of cosmopolitanism that nevertheless reproduce a form of nationalism, as explored in Chapters 4 and 5, Nancy is critical of what he describes as 'the praise of mixture' (2003: 278). His point is a conceptual one, in that he argues that the practice of *praising* mixture suggests that 'identities' form in the first instance, 'pure substances' that can *then* be mixed together (2003: 278). This presumption makes no sense for Nancy because, as we briefly discussed in the last chapter, Nancy refuses to understand identity in isolation. He argues that identities are established through the constitution of a *relation* (Coward, 2009a: 95; see also Nancy, 2000). Any understanding of identity as a 'pure substance' relies upon obscuring relations with others that are essential to the possibility of all identities. Using the example of a painter working with colours, Nancy points out that it wouldn't occur to a painter to 'praise the blending of colors' (2003: 278). This is because the painter is not interested in 'pure colors' but in the 'infinite derivation and melee of their nuances' (2003: 279). To be clear, it is not the case that Nancy's critique of ideas of 'mixture' leads us back to 'purity', as Nancy is even more critical of the 'praise of purity' (2003: 280). As he puts it, it was dreams of purity that sought to reduce 'Sarajevo' from its constitutive heterogeneity to 'some substance or some presence that measures up to the "nation" or the "state"' (2003: 278). What Nancy seeks to do rather is 'shift accent and genre' (2003: 279) in the way we think about difference, away from the notion of mixture and purity and towards the idea of the melee.

This analysis is useful for the critique of 'celebrations of difference' encountered in Chapters 4 and 5. This is because the idea of the melee refuses an account of difference that relies on a quantitative discourse. The melee does not presume the existence of coherent substances that can then be accumulated or brought together. Whilst identities may appear self-contained and distinct from one another, they exist in relation to a 'constitutive alterity whose very existence counters their existence' (Coward, 2009a: 95). This suggests that 'there has never been anything "pure" that one could or should "mix" with some other "purity"' (Nancy, 2003: 280). It is necessary at the outset, then, to refuse the suggestion that we are dealing with 'maintaining some happy medium between these opposed theses' (2003: 280), that is, 'purity' and 'mixture'. This corresponds with the argument developed in Chapters 3 and 4 of this book about rejecting 'unity' and 'difference' as two poles that we are then invited to choose between.[9] As Nancy puts it, this only leaves us with the 'endless catechism of unity within diversity, of complementarity, and of well-tempered differences' (2003: 280). It also leads to a failure to address 'the very things that are at stake' (Nancy, 2003: 280). Thus, whilst liberal democratic governments honour diversity for contributing towards 'mutual enrichment', Nancy argues that the idea of the melee 'escape[s] diversity' (2003: 282). It works according to a different grammar. In this sense, the melee cannot be reduced to some presence that can be identified wholly or captured. Perhaps there is 'never any such thing as a melee "pure and simple"' (2003: 281). In contrast to an idea of community as something that has 'substance', Nancy argues that, with regard to the melee, 'we would be better off speaking... of an action' (2003: 281).

There is therefore a connection between Walter Benjamin's attempt to capture the city as a transitory site that is constantly evolving and Jean-Luc Nancy's attempt to understand the city as a melee. This is because the melee 'is' nothing, but, rather, 'It happens, it emerges' (2003: 282). In this sense, Nancy is drawing on a tradition of writing the urban experience as a practice rather than as static (see also Thrift, 2000; Amin and Thrift, 2002). In contrast to an approach to knowledge that is driven by a search for essence, this method refuses from the outset the suggestion that there is an essence to be uncovered. It involves a different ontology, which draws attention to the moments, collisions and encounters which produce different subject positions. It therefore allows for the possibility of thinking coexistence differently. In this sense 'communities' are not assumed in advance but rather are formed through encounters in time. We can suggest, then, that cities form interesting sites for rethinking what it means to live together, not because they evoke *mixture as opposed to purity*, but because of the way in which they *exceed* both the idea of 'purity' and of 'mixture'. The notion of the melee draws our attention away from identity categories that are deemed to come into contact with one another and shifts the focus to the crossings, weavings and encounters that produce and transform subject positions. It suggests something close to Amin and Thrift's notion of a set of 'coming urban communities' which are transitory, mobile and cannot be entirely fixed in space (2002: 31). It forms another way of understanding coexistence and, as such, overturns the foundational starting points of nationalism.

The Jewish Museum (Daniel Libeskind)

The Jewish Museum, designed by Daniel Libeskind,[10] and situated on Lindenstrasse in the Kreuzberg district, portrays two understandings of time: one that is continuous and linear, and one that is discontinuous and disrupted. This is reflected in Libeskind's pet name for the project, 'Between the Lines', where 'one is a straight line, but broken into many fragments; the other is tortuous and complex, but continuing indefinitely' (1992: 86). This building recalls Georg Simmel's point that it is impossible to disentangle an experience of time as involving 'punctuality, calculability and exactness' (1971: 328) from an experience of time as open, fluid and multidirectional. This point is echoed by Libeskind who claims that, in designing this project, he sought to work with both 'the paradigm of the irrational' and the rational (1992: 82). However, reflecting on the history of the Holocaust, he claims that the 'best works of the

Figure 6.1 The zinc-clad exterior of the Jewish Museum, Berlin, with its jagged window
        panes. Designed by Daniel Libeskind.
        Source: Picture taken by Angharad Closs Stephens, April 2009.

contemporary spirit come from the irrational, while what prevails in the world,
what dominates and often kills, does so always in the name of Reason' (1992: 82).
This point echoes Zygmunt Bauman's approach to the Holocaust, which, he
argues, arrived 'in a factory-produced vehicle, wielding weapons only the most
advanced societies could supply, and following an itinerary designed by scientifically managed organization' (2008: 13). Indeed, this building is designed to
acknowledge the Janus-face of modern life, of rational and irrational forces.

The visitor enters the Jewish Museum through the Colliegenhaus Baroque
building that formed part of the old city museum, where visitors are obliged to

walk past at least one security guard and enter through airport-style metal detectors. The Libeskind-designed building (winner of an open competition) and the old building are connected by an underground passage that takes the visitor towards an exhibition that follows the journey of 'Two Millennia of German-Jewish History'. This part of the museum conforms to a homogenous, linear understanding of time which tells the story of 'two communities' and 'the cultural border between Jewish and non-Jewish citizens', and the way in which the border has 'opened and closed, disappeared and reappeared over time' (Jewish Museum Berlin, 2001: 18). But this is countered by a fragmented experience of time that is etched onto the building in the form of the jagged window panes that mark the zinc-clad exterior (Figure 6.1). These zigzag window panes capture the idea of the 'time of the city' by suggesting that time doesn't only follow a straightforward course but can also be understood as involving multiple flows and offshoots. In this sense, they juxtapose narratives of completion, and instead emphasize disruption or interruption. According to Libeskind, they form the 'writing of the addresses [of the lost citizens] by the walls of the Museum itself' (2007: 27). This suggests a form of remembering that works against bounded identity categories and also contests the idea of a community that can rebuild according to a linear

Figure 6.2 The E. T. A. Hoffmann Garden (or Garden of Exile) at the Jewish Museum, Berlin.
Source: Picture taken by Angharad Closs Stephens, April 2004.

journey in time. These window panes evoke marks and scars that cannot be completely healed or atoned for through nation-building.

In designing this museum, Libeskind drew on works that embraced the idea of thinking modernity as involving disruption rather than stability. In contrast to political theorists who tend to be more concerned with systems of order, as discussed in the first part of this book, Libeskind draws inspiration from an experience of 'aesthetic modernity' that disturbs systems of rational or objective thought.[11] He began the project by plotting a hexagonal figure, somewhat resembling the Star of David, and went about plotting the names and addresses of some of the city's most well known German Jewish citizens who were lost: 'Kleist, Heine, Rahel Varnhagen, E. T. A. Hoffmann, Mies van der Rohe, Schönberg, Paul Celan, Walter Benjamin' (1992: 83). He then worked his way through two large books listing the names of murdered Jewish citizens, with their dates of birth, dates of deportation and the presumed places where they were killed. He also drew from Schönberg's unfinished opera, *Moses and Aaron*, written in Berlin, and on Walter Benjamin's autobiographical writings in *One-Way Street*. He used these raw materials to develop a physical matrix that would form the basis of the site (Libeskind, 2007: 27). Although these resources could be understood as building on a sense of an identifiable 'Jewish-German community', the way in which Libeskind gathers his material, following a rather eclectic method, and the *kinds* of artistic works that he draws upon – most notably Benjamin's disjointed writings – suggest a dispersed, plural and scattered understanding of citizens lives. It also suggests an approach to loss that refuses to transfigure the dead into the substance of one community, 'be these homeland, native soil or blood, nation' (Nancy, 1991: 15). Instead, the approach embraces an idea of community that can never be fully complete.

At the heart of this museum is the 'Holocaust chamber', which forms a dark empty room that visitors are invited to stand in as a heavy concrete door closes behind them. All that can be seen from the room is a shaft of light in the ceiling and all that can be heard is the very distant sounds of the city. This room suggests the 'impossibility' of representing the Holocaust, in that the visitor is simply invited to encounter 'absence'. Indeed, this chamber queries the very capacity of different systems of representation, and explores notions of 'silence' and 'voids' in ways that seem to be much more mainstream in architecture than in the political sciences.[12] It also rejects the idea of a linear journey in time as, in this chamber, time is at a standstill. In this sense, the chamber forms a direct contrast to the E. T. A. Hoffman Garden (or the Garden of Exile and Emigration) that sits behind the museum. This garden contains a grid of 49 large, white, concrete pillars, all filled with earth, with plants growing from the top of each pillar (Figure 6.2).[13] The pillars are designed to signify the birth of the State of Israel in 1948 and are filled with earth from Berlin; the additional one (the 49th) signifies the city of Berlin and is filled with earth from Jerusalem. This garden presents a very different reflection on the Holocaust to that of the dark chamber. It also suggests an alternative understanding of time to that evoked by the zigzag windows of the building. Put simply, this garden suggests a nationalistic response to loss by drawing an association between community, soil and continuity: in this case, the brutality of death is tempered by the attainment of a meaningful life in a community. Furthermore, in this garden, identities are territorialized into distinct units and Berlin appears as a nation that 'is purified of its heterogeneity' in order to serve as a basis for the nation-state (Butler in Butler and Spivak, 2007: 32).

The pillars of the garden and the connections they draw between Berlin, Germany and the state of Israel are thus more suggestive of a politics of cultural 'diversity' than a politics of cultural 'melee'. As Jean-Luc Nancy argues,

> Cultures – or what are called cultures – don't add up. They encounter one another, mix with one another, alter one another, reconfigure one another. All cultures cultivate one another: they clear one another's ground, irrigate, or drain one another, plough one another, or graft themselves onto one another.
> (Nancy, 2003: 282)

Nancy's sense of cultures irrigating, draining and ploughing one another offers a very different understanding of the relationship between community, soil and continuity to that offered by nationalism and by this garden. Nancy gestures towards the impossibility of keeping total order in a garden, of forbidding cross-pollination, and keeping plants from growing into and through one another. This part of the building thus seems more suggestive of the paradigm of the rational than the irrational, and reproduces nationalist ways of seeing. Perhaps this is one among many reasons why the philosopher Jacques Derrida in his response to Daniel Libeskind's design for the Jewish Museum wondered what Walter Benjamin would have made of the design, 'remembering that he died during the War, on a border, committing suicide in a very strange situation on a border' (1992: 94).

The Memorial to the Murdered Jews of Europe (Peter Eisenman)[14]

Remarking on its location, just a stone's throw away from the *Bundestag* (the German parliament), a review in an architecture journal provocatively describes the Memorial to the Murdered Jews of Europe as representing the equivalent of the United States building a memorial to American slavery in front of the Washington Monument with views directed towards the White House and the Capitol (Page, 2005). This memorial represents the result of another competition, in this case to design a site to remember the murdered Jews of Europe, and it opened on 10 May 2005.[15] The visitor doesn't enter this memorial in the same way that one enters the Jewish Museum. Rather, it forms an open site, in the former 'Ministry Gardens' of the Third Reich's foreign minister,[16] 170 metres from the Brandenburg Gate and adjacent to the new fortress that is the US embassy.[17] The case for a memorial was made by the 'Society for the Promotion of the Memorial for the Murdered Jews of Europe', who argued that the site must be built in an 'authentic' place of suffering. Although this site responds to that demand, it also reveals the impossibility of

Figure 6.3 The Memorial to the Murdered Jews of Europe, Berlin. Designed by Peter
Eisenman: 'In this monument there is no goal, no end, no working one's way
in or out' (2005, p. 52).
Source: Picture taken by Angharad Closs Stephens, April 2009.

ascertaining an 'authentic' site of suffering. Like most parts of Berlin, it reveals
many layers of history, as although it formed a key location for the Third Reich, it
was also heavily bombed in the air raids of 1944–1945, and later became part of
the death-strip between East and West Berlin (Schlusche, 2005: 18). The site is
strikingly vast (19,073m$_2$), and contains 2,700 grey, concrete pillars, all of the
same width (0.95m) and length (2.38m), but ranging in height from 0m to 4.7m,
and tilting from 0.5° to 2° (Figure 6.3). Some of the concrete pillars are taller than

the visitor, others are shorter, and people are invited to walk among the columns according to a path of their choosing, which is only wide enough for one individual at a time. Peter Eisenman insists that the field of columns that forms this memorial is not the structure of a labyrinth or a maze, because such structures work with an assumption of an underlying order. In contrast, 'In this monument there is no goal, no end, no working one's way in or out' (Eisenman, 2005: 52). This structure is therefore designed in a way that works against the idea of a homogenous, linear experience of time. It also refuses to think of time as involving a single start and end point. It is therefore more indicative of an experience of 'city time' than the progressive understanding of time we have explored as underpinning a nationalist imaginary.

Similarly to Libeskind, Eisenman experiments with a design that reflects the confluence of rational and irrational paradigms. For Eisenman 'all closed systems of a closed order are bound to fail' (2005: 52). This monument therefore seeks to recover the experience of modern life as discontinuous, open and unpredictable, in the way that Georg Simmel and Walter Benjamin both sought to do. For example, the difference between the ground plane and the top plane is deliberately random and arbitrary. Inspired by the fabric of the city, Eisenman explains that each plane is determined 'by the intersections of the voids of the pillar grid and the gridlines of the larger site context in Berlin' (2005: 52). His design works in tandem with the plurality of gridlines traversing the city in order to prompt the effect of a 'slippage in the grid structure', 'causing indeterminate spaces to develop within the seemingly rigid order of the monument' (2005: 52). In this way, the design invokes a fragmented and unstable experience of space/time, which results in a disorientating experience for the visitor as the light and sounds of the city shift and accentuate according to one's position in the grid. Eisenman's design evokes the messiness of city-space which counteracts a nationalist imaginary of identities that fit into territorial units. In this sense, the memorial implies a form of being-together that refuses the assumption of a common journey that we can all organize around. Crucially, it works in a similar vein to Jean-Luc Nancy's notion of the melee because it addresses identities and differences according to another 'accent and genre' (Nancy, 2003: 279). Eisenman's Memorial to the Murdered Jews of Europe evokes crossings, exchanges and encounters, without suggesting that such experiences must be underpinned by a common order. Eisenman's design thus works against identitarian categories.[18] It suggests a political ontology that begins with encounters rather than with bounded units. The design points towards 'countervalence and encounter', 'resemblance and distancing', 'contact and contraction', 'concentration and dissemination', 'identification and alteration' (Nancy, 2003: 282). In the same way that Nancy insists there is nothing unitary in a melee (2003: 282), there is nothing unitary about this site of memory. Indeed, Eisenman is explicitly interested in spatial forms that defy an ontology of units.[19]

Finally, this site is interesting because it isn't organized around a central 'message'. Unlike the Jewish Museum, its aim is not necessarily to educate us about the 'lessons of war' (Lisle, 2006b: 853) – whatever they may be – but, arguably, to create a space in which people can gather together. The memorial doesn't tell the story of the Holocaust as something that 'belongs to the past' but as a 'memory that is active in the present' (Eisenman, 2005: 52). In contrast to homogenizing experiences of time, this memorial encourages a different understanding of the relationship between past and present. Drawing on Walter Benjamin, we can suggest that the monument doesn't seek to show the past 'the way it really was' (1968: 255) but to conjoin the past and present in a way that forces a new understanding that 'blasts open the continuum of history' (1968: 262). This means approaching 'what has been' 'not historiographically... but politically, in political categories' (Benjamin, 1999: 392). Eisenman's design doesn't draw a line under the past (Schlör, 2005: 38) suggesting perhaps that enthic nationalism is not a problem that has gone away. This also means that it isn't altogether clear how one should encounter this site of memory or what 'lessons' we should take away with us. In this sense, it stands in marked contrast to those war exhibitions where, as Debbie Lisle argues, we often *know in advance* what we are going to find. As Lisle says, 'visitor responses to war exhibitions cannot be legislated, no matter how 'serious' the subject matter is' (2006b: 845). It is therefore especially interesting that the German federal government insisted towards the end of the building of this monument that it *had* to be accompanied by an exhibition space – *contrary* to Eisenman's original design. An open understanding of time and history was ultimately deemed to be too risky, and this is why the exhibition space at this memorial is tucked underground – it was the only place left to build it.

'Flailing Trees' and 'Historical Photographs' (Gustav Metzger)

Gustav Metzger's installation, 'Flailing Trees', is a work that engages with the legacy of the Holocaust but in a way that is less explicit, and again offers a different reflection on the relationship between past and present. This site-specific installation was first displayed at the Manchester International Festival, from 3– 19 July 2009, by the Peace Garden, near to the Manchester Art Gallery (Figure 6.4). The installation was free to encounter for the duration of the festival and formed an interruption to people's everyday journeys across the city. This is a different kind of work in that it forms an art installation rather than an architectural design/building; it is also radically smaller in scale and cost.[20] It features 21 inverted willow trees, with their deep brown, dying roots facing towards the sky, in a canopy effect. Each tree is moulded into a concrete slab that forms the structure. The design is interesting for the way in which it combines trees and concrete, but in a way that disrupts the image of the sprouting trees encountered at the Jewish Museum Garden of Exile. These trees are dead and they are buried into (rather than growing out of) concrete. They will also decompose further in time. Following Metzger's long-standing interest in the relationship between creation and destruction,[21] this installation doesn't present a straightforward idea of death and renewal, as we find under nationalism. Rather, it presents a meditation on the time of decay: the installation will continue to move and take shape, unlike a

Figure 6.4 'Flailing Trees' by Gustav Metzger, displayed at the Manchester International
Festival from 3–19 July 2009: 'What is more brutal, than taking willow trees,
favourites of so many poets, in so many languages, cutting off their canopies,
as we plan to do, sticking them into a concrete platform with their roots
exposed to the sky?' (Metzger, 2009).
Source: Picture taken by Rhodri Davies, 3 July 2009, and reproduced with
his permission.

design that is finished and complete. As such, it forms a staging of protest: 'protest to me is the central intention of this work' (Metzger, 2009b).

The project forms part of Metzger's long-standing interest in critical responses to the Holocaust, from which he escaped as a young boy, arriving in London in 1939 with the help of the Refugee Children's Movement, having lost his parents and family. It also expresses his concern with ecological politics. The significance of the sculpture lies with the way in which it echoes the use of trees at the Garden of Exile in the Jewish Museum, but in a way that works against identitarian categories of remembering. Although the willows are deliberately selected, Metzger seeks to push against a romantic and nationalist tradition as much as possible. So, although each tree belongs to the same genus, they are uprooted. This sculpture is designed to *show* brutality, then, rather than offer a response to it. As the artist makes clear in an introduction to the project:

> This project is essentially about brutality. The brutality with which we human beings treat and mistreat nature. What is more brutal, than taking willow trees, favourites of so many poets, in so many languages, cutting off their canopies, as we plan to do, sticking them into a concrete platform with their roots exposed to the sky?
>
> (Metzger, 2009a)

In this way, Metzger's installation attempts to offer a jolt in people's experiences of the present and to 'blast open the continuum of history' (Benjamin, 1968: 262). It forms an open provation to consider the connections between ideas of continuous time and forms of destruction.

In this sense, the project concurs with another of Metzger's works, the *Historical Photographs* series. This work presents a series of familiar photographs of the Holocaust and of the Nazi command, but they are deliberately concealed behind galvanized zinc and wooden shuttering boards (Wilson, 2005; Metzger, 2007). The first two photographs in the series, *Historic Photographs: No 1: Hitler Addressing the Reichstag after the Fall of France, July 1940* (1995) and *Historic Photographs: No 1: Liquidation of the Warsaw Ghetto, April 19 – 28 days, 1943* (1995) are selected precisely because they have become so *familiar* as pictures of the Nazi command. But, in making them more difficult to view, Metzger encourages us to encounter them *anew*. In this way, the series potentially initiates a political debate about the way in which these photographs have come to act as signs that require no further explanation, or as representing a 'sequence of events like the beads of a rosary' (Benjamin, 1968: 263). In staging a different relationship between past and present, Metzger hopes to invite what Walter Benjamin describes as the flash of a new awareness or recognition. This work therefore offers an experience of the present as disjointed and, in so doing prompts a reconsideration of those views of the world that we already hold. Metzger encourages a disruption to homogenizing accounts of time and history to challenge the suggestion that *we already know* what happened during the Holocaust and what this must mean for the present and future.

The Missing House (Christian Boltanski)

Zygmunt Bauman argues that in understanding the Holocaust as a *Jewish* tragedy specifically or even as an event in *Jewish history* (2008: x), the Holocaust is too easily 'shunted off into the familiar stream of history' (2008: 2). In this sense, it appears as a subject of interest for historians, but not for those interested in rethinking the politics of the present. It also suggests that the Holocaust can be explained as 'a cancerous growth on the otherwise healthy body of the civilized society' (2008: 7) or as a 'deviation from an otherwise straight path of progress' (2008: 7). In order to reflect critically on the legacies of the Holocaust then, and the logic of nationalism expressed in this extreme example of ethno-nationalism, it is necessary to trouble linear ideas of time. This is reflected in another site of memory, designed to a much smaller scale, which, in this case, refuses to remember victims according to their 'identities' and, instead, much like Metzger's 'Flailing Trees' installation, invokes an account of the present as out of joint.

The Missing House (1990) is a site-specific installation designed by Christian Boltanski that stands at 15/16 Grosse Hamburgerstrasse, in the former East Berlin (see Figure 6.5). The site was originally blasted away by the allied bombings of 3 February 1945, destroying a building containing several apartments, killing or maiming the people who lived in those apartments, but sparing the buildings as well as those who lived on either side of number 15/16 (Solomon-Godeau, 1998). As the two remaining parts of the building were reconstructed, a vacant space was left between the two supporting walls. Boltanski's installation consists of 'a series of 12 black and white plaques, 120 x 60cm, mounted on the facing walls, storey by storey, indicating the family name, profession, and period of residency of each tenant who had lived in the bombed out apartments' (1998: 3). What is interesting about this work is that it doesn't seek to name particular 'communities'; rather, it remembers the everyday encounters of ordinary (and perhaps anonymous) citizens who lived in apartments in the city (see also Painter, 2012). It therefore forms a site of memory that works against identitarian categories of representation and instead suggests 'partial connections' (Bell, 2007: 32). It refuses to write the dead into a narrative of nationhood or homeland and, rather, represents the dead in terms of a 'gap' in the everyday encounters of the city.

In this sense, the Missing House operates in a different mode from that of museums and exhibitions that seek to *tell the story* of the Holocaust. Signalling perhaps the sheer impossibility of fully conveying the crimes of the Holocaust, this installation doesn't aim to portray any kind of 'message', nor does it seek to neutralize 'difficult stories of trauma, violence and loss ... through comforting narratives of commemoration and education' (Lisle, 2006b: 843). This installation engages the memory of the Holocaust by revealing simply a distressing image of the 'everyday'. This is not to say that there aren't important historical lessons to be learnt. The point here is that the legacies of the Holocaust are still being negotiated, debated and contested. This is especially the case if we accept that aspects of modern life that made the Holocaust possible are still around us –

Figure 6.5 The Missing House, Berlin, designed by Christian Boltanski (1990).
Source: Picture taken by Joe Painter, April 2009, and reproduced with his
permission.

namely the desire for a fully ordered, unified world. However, there is no need to make a special journey in search of 'memory' or to pay a fee to learn the 'lessons of war' through this site. Rather, it forms a simple but powerful interruption in people's journeys across the city.

In contrast to nationalist approaches to history that formulate the relationship between past and present according to a journey of national time, this installation suggests a different formulation. It engages with questions of memory, loss and trauma in a way that refuses to subsume those experiences into a narrative about the recovery of a community. It works with a different temporality from that of 'homogenous empty time' by emphasizing disruption rather than continuity. It thus reflects the experience of modern life emphasized by Benjamin as involving a transient and splintered experience of time. As a critical gesture, it operates in an anti-nationalist vein, which is affirmed further in the understated presence of the installation. It offers an alternative to imposing, statist memorials or conventional war exhibitions that place their emphasis on patriotism and education (Lisle, 2006b) by revealing the 'illuminating power' of the seemingly marginal and ephemeral, in a way that Benjamin always sought to do (Richter, 2007: 47). This site invokes a sense of the present time as disjointed, in contrast to nationalist understandings of time that emphasize how 'we' are sharing in a common temporal journey. It refuses to prescribe where such an interruption in the present might lead. The site is thus open and suggests no formula about what the lessons of the past may be. This openness stands in marked opposition to the way in which museums and war exhibitions often keep a tight rein on understandings of the present, past and future (Lisle, 2006b). The Missing House thus suggests an approach to politics that affirms an experience of time as discontinuous and fractured and, as such, potentially invokes the 'flash' ('aufblitzen') of a new understanding of the past and present (Benjamin, 1968).

Reimagining community

The sites of memory discussed in this chapter are interesting for the ways in which they suggest an understanding of the present as disrupted and as shot through with multiple temporalities. They work against the understanding that 'we' are all sharing in the same present and that, furthermore, the present can be clearly demarcated from the past and future (Hutchings, 2008). As such, they echo the work of Walter Benjamin, and resist the nationalist inclination to declare the past as over and that we know what the implications of that past are for the present and future. In contrast to a statist account of politics that declares that we already know the best way of organizing political community, these sites of memory indicate an openness towards the future. They therefore address the challenge of 'imagining community', but not in the way outlined in the first chapter of this book, where the concept of imagination was bound to the further continuation of the nation. Rather, these sites of memory address the question of 'imagining community' differently, by indicating a future that is not yet known. This understanding implies that imagination is an active political concept, unlike those studies that assume that the work of 'imagining' a political community has already been done. This is indicated in the different meanings of the term 'imagination', which points both to 'the process of forming a conscious idea or mental image of something' and also to an 'idealized or poetic creation' (Webster's Dictionary, 1971: 1128). This sense of 'imagining' as involving a *productive* imagination and as associated with forming something unknown has become lost in the much reproduced concept of 'imagined communities', suggesting that we almost know in advance what the process of 'imagining' might involve and where it must lead. The critical task lies with recovering a tremor in the idea of imagination, which may be inspired by architectural and artistic designs, as suggested in this chapter, or in works of fiction, as indicated in the last chapter. In sum, they suggest the possibility of a future beyond what is ready and available.

Thus, these sites of memory are interesting because they can be read as invoking a different relationship to time, beyond the nationalist assumption of homogeneity, linearity and progress. As a result, they provoke questions about critical imagination. But, finally, these sites also evoke a different approach to the politics of coexistence. This is the case in relation to the Memorial to the Murdered Jews of Europe in particular, which suggests 'the poetics of multiple durées coming together' (Bachelard quoted by Crang, 2001: 190). This site indicates another understanding of 'community' in that it refuses the presumption of a bounded unit or a unified temporality. It suggests an understanding of being together that cannot be contained within a unifying narrative. Much like the city itself, this sense of community 'leaks and flees' (Mbembe and Nuttall, 2004: 353). This site therefore sonates with Jean-Luc Nancy's notion of the melee, because it suggests that 'what we have in common is always also what distinguishes us and differentiates us' (2003: 286). There is no 'pure identity' that we must strive to resurrect. But there is no 'mixture' either, as mixture presupposes that there are already identifiable and distinct identity categories to begin with. These assumptions all betray an understanding of temporality as something that may be distilled and separated into distinct flows. In contrast, the design of the Memorial to the Murdered Jews of Europe proposes that *all* there is 'is the always-incessant mix-up of one with the other' (Nancy, 2003: 287). It suggests heterogeneity as 'an existential condition' (Coward, 2009a: 90) and, as such, it doesn't need to be praised, conjured or mourned. Heterogeneity is already there, and nationalism – in contrast – represents the attempt to impose order on the melee of urban life.

These sites of memory all in different ways suggest a reframing of community as involving everyday encounters. Given that such encounters are temporal and unpredictable, they will involve 'surprise and conflict' (Ahmed, 2000: 6). This element of conflict is intimated in the concept of a melee, which suggests 'both the promise and the possibility of catastrophe' (Shapiro, 2010: 162). Thus, there is no way of knowing in advance the nature of a given encounter, which will always be uncertain. In this sense, this understanding of encounters corresponds to an account of the present as disjointed. It ties in with the art installations of Gustav Metzger, who warns us about the dangers of assuming that we already *know* the best way of organising political life. Drawing on his artwork as well as these other memorials, we might say that encounters have the potential to 'shift the boundaries of the familiar, or what we assume that we know' (Ahmed, 2000: 7). The critical challenge lies with recovering those moments of openness, which gesture towards another possible way of understanding political community. This chapter has presented an account of coexistence as formed through crossings, exchanges and encounters which produce, transform, and unsettle subject positions. These are the encounters of the everyday and, as such, they may be transitory and indifferent, and undermine an idea of community that is built around a heavy sense of *meaning*. But the key point is that community does not appear as something that has been lost and must be regained, but as what is already present in the melee of urban life.

Conclusion

This chapter has read sites of memory in the city of Berlin in order to develop a different entry point towards a critique of nationalism. Whereas the last chapter touched upon attempts at thinking of loss outside of a nationalist framework, this chapter has taken that work further by drawing attention to sites of memory that refuse to work with identitarian categories and which also refuse a search for meaning and reconciliation through the nation. The chapter has also sought to contest the 'homogenous empty' understanding of time that underpins national-ist modes of remembering by attending to the notion of a 'time of the city'. This time of the city is distinctive for the way in which it refuses the principle of total-ity and instead affirms disruption and chance. In drawing on a particular tradition of writing the city, the aim was not to privilege a particular spatial form as somehow anti-nationalist so much as to use writings about cities and urban designs to open up the question of what it means to be-in-the-world (Mbembe and Nuttall, 2004: 347).

Jean-Luc Nancy's notion of the melee is especially useful in recasting how we might understand coexistence. The idea of the melee suggests a different grammar for thinking questions of identity and difference by refusing to begin from the assumption of settled identities that come into contact with one another, and instead evoking a political ontology that begins from the collisions, encounters and moments through which identities are enacted. This chapter has developed a differ-ent understanding of time and space to that which we associated with a nationalist imaginary in the first part of this book. It is also different to the accounts of 'urban cosmopolitanism' addressed in Chapters 4 and 5, which, it was argued, were still indebted to a nationalist imaginary. This is not an idea of space that can be stretched to accommodate differences, because the melee works against an idea of space as bounded and therefore that identities are distinct and separable. This marks a differ-ent political ontology, one that doesn't depart from or return to an originary unity, but one that points towards another conceptual imaginary. Finally, this alternative political imaginary doesn't necessarily comprise of something that 'we already know'. Rather, it signals that the critical task lies with considering the politics of coexistence beyond what is already familiar to us.

Conclusion

The aftermath of nationalist imaginaries

> But the real question is how to make a move, how to get through the wall, so you don't keep banging your head against it.
>
> Giles Deleuze, *Negotiations*

National–global–communal

This book began with the concept of 'imagined communities' and with the suggestion that this has become 'a tag phrase – almost a mantra – in academic and para-academic discussions of nationalism' (Redfield, 1999: 60). As a 'tag phrase', the concept suggests that nations are not natural but have to be imagined, narrated and performed into existence. Whilst this point is important, it doesn't necessarily enable an engagement with the *politics* of nationalism. For example, it doesn't always allow us to ask how we might *resist* the repetition of the nation-form and the persistence of nationalism in the contemporary world. Indeed, the work of thinking about alternatives to nationalism is often obscured or at least made more difficult by debates around the 'constructedness' of the nation and by the series of binary options that dominate debates in the field. These include the question of whether the nation is real or imagined, old or new, as well as the question of whether the nation is here to stay or about to wither away.[1] Thus, despite Benedict Anderson's argument, made some time ago, that what matters is not the falsity/genuineness of a community but the style in which the nation is imagined (1991: 6), the idea that *it is possible* to distinguish between false and genuine communities remains powerful and haunts many critical studies of nationalism. This becomes evident in the residual assumption that there is something *more powerful* about national identities than other identity categories. It is also manifest in debates around the possibility of a post-national future, which often appears as something to fear or even as a symbol of the end of politics as such. The problem here lies with the way in which the very possibility of alternatives to nationalism are often considered *through* a nationalist imaginary, where political community can only be debated through narratives about the 'loss' and/or 'recovery' of a people that hold something in common. This matters because it demonstrates the persistence of nationalism in framing our capacity to talk about global politics. This can be gleaned in two well-recognized attempts to think 'beyond the nation' – by way of the cosmopolitan and the global, respectively.

The sociologist and critical theorist of nationalism Craig Calhoun has written widely on the relationship between nationalism and cosmopolitanism and offers what might be described as a 'communitarian' critique of cosmopolitanism (2002, 2007a, 2007b, 2008). His argument is that an abstract form of 'liberal cosmopolitanism' fails to appreciate the ties people feel towards place, culture and language. According to Calhoun, it is insufficient to present individuals as able to rise above, or opt in and out of, their attachments. As he puts it, people are not abstract individuals who can decide whether or not to enter group formations. Rather, they find themselves *already* part of different 'social contexts in which people are moved by commitments to each other' (2002: 875). Calhoun makes some important points about how people don't *precede* their cultures but are formed *through* culture. He also supplements this critique with an attack on the elitism of particular accounts of cosmopolitanism that posit a world made up of 'frequent travellers' (2002). What is interesting, however, is the way in which Calhoun moves from his critique of an abstract form of cosmopolitanism to conclude that national attachments *continue to matter*.[2] As he puts it:

> Imagining a world without nations, a world in which ethnicity is simply a consumer taste, a world in which each individual simply and directly inhabits the whole, is like imagining the melting pot in which all ethnicities vanish into the formation of a new kind of individual. In each case this produces an ideology especially attractive to some. It neglects the reasons why many others need and reproduce ethnic or national distinctions.
>
> (2008: 437)

What is problematic about Calhoun's argument is his assumption that, because cosmopolitanism fails to appreciate the persistence of local attachments, the only option available is to reassert the national as the best (if not the only) way of articulating social ties. Whilst Calhoun's decision to defend the nation may not be surprising, the problem lies with the way in which he presents the reader with a choice between a national *or* a cosmopolitan world – a choice that is enabled by a nationalist imaginary, where the possibilities available are ordered according to a homogenous, linear account of time. We can either choose to move forward to a world in which 'ethnicities vanish' or defend the status quo. This approach steers and limits the debates we can have about a cosmopolitical future, as it can only appear in relation to the *loss* of the nation and therefore 'lacking [of] a strong account of solidarity' (Calhoun, 2002: 873). Thus, it also reveals a decidedly conservative position in that we can only choose to continue with the world as it is or opt for a world that threatens to destroy everything we have. The framing of the question allows for very little space to consider how else world politics could be imagined – or indeed – might already be organized. What hovers over Calhoun's analysis is the assumption of an originary commonality that must ground political life – a commonality that is secured for him by the nation. Whilst

Calhoun makes several important points about the limits of particular understandings of cosmopolitanism and their ability to take cultural attachments seriously, what is at stake is the way in which Calhoun refuses to understand cultural attachments in anything other than nationalist terms. The question to ask, then, is whether cultural attachments can *only* be accommodated by nationalism. How might we open up the question of 'imagining community' beyond that which is already familiar?

Globalization literatures represent a very different position on nationalism, as these literatures generally aim to consider a form of political space beyond the nation-state. Manfred B. Steger's work on the rise of the 'global imaginary' (2008) represents such an attempt, in his claim that national identities have in the contemporary world become destabilized. Steger argues that several transformations in the twentieth century have led to a situation in which a global political imaginary has displaced the nation as the primary vehicle through which we conceive of, and practise politics. Arguing that nationalism formed the dominant 'social imaginary' in the northern hemisphere from the time of the American and French revolutions to the Second World War, he claims that we have since witnessed a shift toward a global imaginary which serves as the new framework of the political. Steger accounts for the arrival of this new world order by referring to new ideas generated by social elites, which gradually 'seep' into the public consciousness (2008: 130) as well as an increasing sense of *mixture* between cultures and peoples. However, the trouble with this way of imagining the relationship between a national political system and a global political system is that it again reveals the assumption of a homogenous empty experience of time. The image of the future is tied into an account of 'mixture', where more mixture signals more globality. This suggests that, once upon a time, we had a simpler understanding of identity. Yet, as this book has argued, this narrative about a time in the past when identities were less complex relies upon a nationalist imaginary. The idea of a unitary identity is never simply indicative of a time gone by, but is rather reflective of a nationalist ideal and a condition that has to be *forced*. Indeed, this framing ignores the fact that nationalism was in early twentieth-century Europe *formed* from the mass movement and mixture of people (Hobsbawm, 1990). We can suggest that the very idea of a pure identity only makes sense in relation to an opposing image of mixture, which can either appear threatening, as it does for Calhoun, or liberating, as it does for Steger. In both of these narratives, however, what is secured is the nationalist (and modernist) ambition to separate the pure from the mixed, and to understand the political possibilities available according to a binary framework.

In narrating this shift from the national to the global, Steger makes it difficult to raise questions about other ideas of political community that jostled against the national or were forgotten in the trail of its domination. The national imaginary has of course been heavily resisted, fought and countered at repeated historical points and in various geographical contexts: Ernest Gellner hinted at such resistance in noting that 'a territorial political unit can only become ethnically homogenous ... if it either kills, or expels, or assimilates all non-nationals'

(1983: 2). Yet, rather than pursue such moments, Steger stages a shift from one time of history to the other. Steger appeals to an increasing sense of global connectedness brought about through new technologies, cosmopolitan café culture, jet travel and globe-trotting careers to establish a progressive rhythm that explains the shift from one social order to the next. But the question to ask here is, how did we succeed in moving from one stage in history to the next? Steger is ultimately responsible for authorizing this shift. Thus, once we have arrived at this new global imaginary, the only choices available are to catch up, join in or get left behind. The problem with Steger's rhetorical gesture is that the critical energies that go into the work of 'imagining' seem to retreat once this global political imaginary is set up. This global spatio-temporal framework is universalized as *the* dominant system that we now have available and the possibility of resistance is limited to those modes of objection that make sense *within* the global political imaginary. So, although we can choose between the forces of the 'New Left' or the 'New Right', there is little possibility of objecting as such to this new 'communal frame of the political' (2008: 9). The work of imagination is confined to the moments of 'rupture' that have already constituted the new global imaginary (2008: 12). The question to ask in this context is, what, then, is left to imagine?

Craig Calhoun and Manfred Steger's positions are significantly different: the former is suspicious of 'cosmopolitan dreams' and insists that the nation continues to form the best model of political community available; the latter is instinctively suspicious of nationalism and suggests that we now live in a world in which the very idea of identities based upon national membership has become 'destabilized' (2008: 11). What is striking, however, is that both analyses rely upon an experience of time as progressive and linear. Consequently, both narratives also deploy a nationalist conceptual toolkit in trying to make sense of the possibilities of political life beyond nationalism. This indicates the persistence of nationalism in framing the ways in which we are able to debate politics. It also suggests the difficulties of prising open the question of imagining a future beyond nationalism. This book has argued that the task of thinking 'beyond' the nation will require questioning the broader imaginary that makes nationalism possible, and in particular the ideas of space/time, subjectivity and freedom that underpin it. This suggests that the challenge lies with introducing a *tremor* back into the concept of imagination so that the work of imagining is not tied to an account of a present and future that we already know. The possibility of developing a robust critique of nationalism relies upon being able to acknowledge a plurality of temporal trajectories.

Troubling the common time of the political

The quotation by Raymond Williams used to open Chapter 1 suggests that imagination has a structure, 'at once grammatical and historical, in the tenses of past, present and future' (2009). The question of imagination is therefore directly related to the question of how we imagine the present, pasts and futures of political life. This is a point affirmed by the post-colonial theorist Dipesh Chakrabarty, who aims to 'breathe heterogeneity' into the concept of imagination by shattering an understanding of politics guided by the sense of sharing in a *common time* (2008: 149). But what would it mean to imagine a form of politics that doesn't rely upon commonality? Chakrabarty argues that this involves becoming open to the idea of time as multiple and to appreciate 'that the field of the political is constitutively not singular' (2008: 149). This suggests that it might be possible to understand the future as unfolding in several different ways and as not shackled to the further continuation of the nation. It also implies that politics might not be understood as that which takes place *within* a common unitary framework but rather, as struggles over different ways of practising political community. This does not mean a battle between 'our' community and 'their' community, but rather, struggles over the very ways in which political community is conceptualized, negotiated and actualized. As the International Relations theorist Kimberly Hutchings argues, reading world politics as 'heterotemporal' suggests being open to futures that are *unfamiliar* and represent something beyond that which we already know and recognize (2008). In this sense, she argues that post-colonial theorists as well as feminist theorists offer useful suggestions for thinking time – and world politics – differently.

Indeed, in the context of the 'War on Terror', feminist theorists offered sharp analyses of the depoliticizing effects of reading the world through a common timeframe. Take, for example, the way in which the war with Afghanistan (2003) was framed as an attempt to liberate Afghan women from the 'past' and from their 'uncivilized' countrymen (Eisenstein, 2002; Shohat, 2002). This framing of the war resuscitated the narratives of enlightenment that we explored as part of the discussion of Jean-Jacques Rousseau's work in Chapter 3. In situating Afghan women on a journey of development towards education, sexual freedom and neoliberal enlightenment, such ideals were cast as unproblematic 'good things' and as conditions that 'Western women' already enjoy and can therefore extend to others. This narrative of progress universalizes a particular account of what development and freedom must mean and erases all questions of historical and cultural context (Frankenberg and Mani, 1993; Mohanty, 1991; Pedwell, 2010). In this way, feminist theorists have long been engaging with the problems that follow from framing the political in relation to a universalizing and progressive temporal trajectory. After all, the idea of animating narratives of progress through stories about women's freedom and women's bodies is not new, but played a key role in the history of colonial missions (Ware, 2006: 528) and in a particular form of 'Western feminism' (McClintock, 1995; Spelman, 1990).[3]

Such debates have been revitalized in contemporary attempts at contesting the claim that 'we' now live in a 'post-feminist' society in which we are 'all agreed' on the importance of women's rights. This issue is addressed by Angela McRobbie (2009), who questions how to respond politically to a context where gender equality appears on the one hand as 'common sense' and when, on the other hand, sexual violence and discrimination persist. McRobbie addresses directly the temporal experience implied by the claim of 'post-feminism' and the challenges presented by the way in which feminism appears 'outmoded' to many young women and as something that belongs *to the past*. She challenges this narrative by first of all contesting the idea that there was once a fixed and singular thing called 'feminism' and a clear object that activists could organize around. She also examines the force of this narrative of progress about 'women's rights'. This is not to say that there have not been significant achievements in the field of gender equality and also in attitudes towards sexual orientation. Rather, the point is to query the way in which a *particular* form of feminism – one 'which permits offices of government to claim that women's interests are indeed being looked after' (2009: 154) – has been instrumentalized and a 'respectable' form of feminism has been mainstreamed. McRobbie argues that feminist politics operates in the context of a 'double entanglement', where previously marginalized or excluded groups are invited to enjoy the benefits of full citizenship, whilst new forms of banishment and exclusion take place. One example she offers is the extension of entitlements to gay and lesbian couples by way of civil partnership and adoption rights in European and North American countries. These welcome measures have been accompanied by further punitive measures against those who choose to live outside the two-parent economic unit.[4] This 'double entanglement' presents a challenge for thinking about how to intervene politically, in a context where particular freedoms are understood as 'having been won', and where questions of discrimination on the grounds of gender and sexual orientation are cast as belonging to the *past*, suggesting agreement on how we think the present.

This notion of a 'double entanglement' is useful also for the study of nationalism and this is for two reasons. Firstly, it suggests that power operates both by way of expulsion, banishment or outlawing, *and* through the extension of rights and privileges and 'the mode of a certain containment' (Butler and Spivak, 2007: 5). This addresses directly the ways in which the nation extends its promise of full citizenship to some previously marginalized groups, whilst simultaneously strengthening its borders and security practices to keep others out. The second point that makes the concept of the 'double entanglement' useful for the study of nationalism is that it acknowledges that ideas about self-determination, autonomy and independence cannot be easily rejected or put to one side. These are ideas that we 'cannot not want' (Spivak, 1996: 9), which means that political interventions have to be thought through in much more careful terms than to position a movement 'for' or 'against' particular achievements. Whilst the promise of a nation of one's own or complete autonomy cannot be straightforwardly understood as 'good things', they cannot be dismissed as ambitions from 'another time' either (Bell, 2007) or that we've already 'been there, done that' (Hindess, 2008). Perhaps the critical challenge lies with articulating such struggles in terms that simultaneously unravel the discourses of nationalism.

How, then, might we intervene critically in so-called 'post-feminist' times? For McRobbie, it means insisting on the multiplicity of the present and of the political, and she offers an example by way of the feminist classroom. She suggests that this forms a 'contact zone' that offers an encounter with the possibility of a life that is not wholly determined by marriage and motherhood (2009: 164–167), as young women of different ages, sex, class and nationalities begin to negotiate the 'tension, anxiety, and sheer uncertainty of a life to come' (2009: 165). McRobbie posits the classroom as a potential space of encounter in a global city in which different subject positions and identity categories are challenged. As such, this contact zone forms a portal for renegotiating forms of being in the world where unfamiliar encounters lead to surprising and potentially affirmative social formations. This is not an attempt to sketch out a new political space in which subjects can come together, agree a common project and forge a new community. Rather, it forms an attempt at imagining what it might mean to develop political solidarities in unusual or unexpected moments of contact. In this sense, it suggests a form of politics that is informed more by *disagreement* than *agreement*. But such disagreement is not necessarily a negative thing, which is what it means when we are set on searching for commonality. This sense of disagreement does not reflect a problem that needs to be overcome, but rather, it forms a constitutive condition. Furthermore, this is not disagreement in a context in which certain rules and norms have already been agreed, as in political debates between 'left' and 'right' that must first of all agree on the primacy of the nation-state as the space in which politics must take place. Rather, it is intended to signal the very impossibility of bringing all differences into a common framework. As Jacques Rancière puts it, this sense of disagreement does not refer to a speech situation in which one interlocutor says white and the other says black. Rather, it reflects the 'conflict between one who says white and another who also says white but does not understand the same thing by it or does not understand that the other is saying the same thing in the name of whiteness' (1999: x). This form of disagreement affirms the plurality of the political.

It is this sense of disagreement as constitutive of the political that animates Sara Ahmed's study of the way in which the promise of happiness works to shape particular worlds and to establish a consensual political community (2010: 1–2). Ahmed develops a critique of the ways in which feminist, queer and migrant subjects are frequently posited as 'difficult' or 'killjoys' for refusing or being unable to 'go along' with normative images of happiness offered by marriage, motherhood or a heterosexual identity. She argues that these figures appear as threatening to the coherence of particular worlds and the stable distribution of identities. In reclaiming the stories of those who may be described as struggling *against* happiness through feminist, queer and anti-racist archives, Ahmed challenges consensual accounts of the present as a place where we can all be 'happy' as offered both by sexual norms and also by the promise of multicultural nationalism. In giving 'the killjoy back her voice' (2010: 20), Ahmed insists on heterogeneity and disagreement as a constitutive aspect of the political. Furthermore, and in a way that echoes the work of Chakrabarty (2008) and Hutchings (2008), Ahmed argues that the category of the future must be understood in ways that disrupt the promise of a stable journey in time. For example, in calling for 'the freedom to be unhappy' (2010: 195), she draws inspiration from the ways in which queer theorists have made an affirmative politics of a *refusal* to embrace the future (2010: 161; for more see Edelman, 2004), when the idea of the future is heavily tied together with normative ideas about children, and continuity through the nation. This book explored a similar point in relation to Max Weber's insistence that politics involves the 'struggle to preserve and raise the quality of our national species' (1994a: 16). The challenge lies in recovering the idea of the future as open to many different actualities.

In this vein, Sara Ahmed encourages us to recover the 'hap' of happiness – the element of chance that dictates that no future is fully knowable and to embrace the way in which futures often turn out differently to what we might have imagined for ourselves. This form of happiness would be 'alive to chance, to chance arrivals, to the perhaps of a happening' (2010: 198).[5] This understanding echoes Walter Benjamin's formulation of a future that is heavy with anticipation but that holds no solutions. It also suggests an understanding of politics as involving more than an invitation to sign up to a model of political community that has already been laid out. In this sense, feminist and queer writings allow for an appreciation of the problems of reproducing political categories that are already familiar and which have proved to be oppressive. This is why it isn't enough to call for *extending* the limits of the nation, or to reassure ourselves of the merits of 'good' versions of nationalism or patriotism. As the feminist theorist Elizabeth Grosz argues, feminist, anti-colonial movements and anti-racist movements have all at times seemed 'terrified by the idea of a transformation somehow beyond the control of the very revolutionaries who seek it' (1999: 17). But, whilst it may be unsettling to give up on normative, dominant or long-cherished ideas about liberation, preserving these categories might also be harmful and injurious. The refusal to consider the possibility of a future politics outside the continuation of what we already know represents not only a conservative and deterministic position, but an exclusionary one, as it relies on shutting down and casting out other forms of organizing political community that make themselves momentarily available.

The technique of shackling the future into a particular model of politics therefore assumes that we can know in advance what liberation must look like, suggesting that there is a timeless ideal that we can arrive at if only we continue to focus on the journey ahead and ignore the forceful practices required to keep that sense of a common journey intact. But, as Elizabeth Grosz asks: 'If the future revolution can carry no guarantee that it will improve the current situation or provide something preferable to what exists now, what makes it a sought-for ideal? What prevents it from blurring into fascism or conservatism?' (1999b: 17). To be open to the chance of the future necessarily involves taking a gamble, but the key point here is not to understand the options available as a choice between a future that we already know and a future that is unknowable and therefore too risky. There are risks also involved in reproducing the status quo. The challenge, then, is to encourage a more open and pluralistic understanding of the present in order to be able to be responsive to new ideas, possibilities and solidarities. What this requires is being able to 'acknowledge the capacity of any future eruption, any event, any reading, to rewrite, resignify, reframe the present, to accept the role that the accidental, chance, or the undetermined plays in the unfolding of time' (Grosz, 1999b: 18).

One of the primary concerns of this book has been to draw attention to the persistence of the normative framing of the political as a struggle between 'us' and 'them' and the challenges of thinking and writing against this nationalist account of politics. Whilst the book has addressed different attempts at *extending* political community towards the 'global' or the 'cosmopolitan', it has argued that such well-intentioned aims nevertheless assume an originary commonality that can anchor political life. This suggests that the challenge lies in identifying those modes of thinking and acting politically that do the most to undo or displace a unifying framework. In this sense, feminist theorists offer significant routes forward in their attempts at thinking time as open and plural. Yet feminist theorists encounter a similar set of limits, as they come up against the 'double entanglement' of tarrying with ambitions that form both the problem and that which they 'cannot not want' (Spivak, 1996: 9). For example, in 'speaking back' from the perspective of those banished, expelled or forced out and 'how it feels to inhabit that place' (2010: 20), as Sara Ahmed does, we find ourselves still caught within a framing of politics as set up between the forces of 'us' and 'them'. Ahmed seeks to avoid this trap by focusing on the circulation of 'feelings' (2010: 14) rather than 'marginalized subjects', but the fact that this framing recurs and persists shows how difficult it is to get away from an account of politics as anchored around the realization of a subject in time. It may therefore be necessary to draw on a broader conceptual toolkit for thinking community *without* commonality, and it is in that context that this book seeks to bring together the feminist and post-colonial work on thinking time as plural, with a focus on the city as a site of encounters.

Urban encounters

This book has gestured towards the city as a site for unpacking another way of imagining what it means to live together. Cities are routinely presented as sites for thinking about the politics of difference on account of their mixture. This is not, then, a new gesture. But, as the second part of this book has argued, 'mixture' cannot straightforwardly be understood as a 'good thing' or as an anti-nationalist thing. This is where Jean-Luc Nancy's work, which argues for an understanding of the city as a *melee*, becomes useful (2003). A 'melee' translates from French to English as mixture, as 'a confused mingling together of often incongruous elements', and also as a 'fight', 'contest' or 'brawl' (Webster's English Dictionary, 1971). Thus, a melee doesn't suggest 'happy cosmopolitans'; nor does it suggest an absence of violence. What it offers is another grammar for imagining community which avoids the false opposition between identity, stability and stillness on the one hand and mixture, turmoil and difference on the other hand. In thinking the city as 'the locus of a melee', Nancy suggests that the city never represents the name of one person, one identity, one community, but the marking of crossings, entanglement and circulation (2003: 278). Cities are interesting because of the way in which they potentially exceed both 'purity' and 'mixture' and defy the sense of a common substance. This is not a form of community that is already familiar to us – as evoked by Calhoun and Steger. Rather, the idea of the melee points towards the possibility of another way of imagining community and, indeed, to imagine community *as* encounters.

The encounters of a melee evoke a mode of thinking about politics that is drawn less towards a substance or essence and is instead attentive to moments of contact and contraction, identification and alteration (Nancy, 2003: 282). These are not encounters that can be identified in advance. And this way of thinking about encounters rejects the assumption of predefined subjects or groups as coming into contact with one another. Recalling McRobbie's idea of the 'contact zone', it suggests moments of renegotiating forms of being in the world. As such, encounters may involve 'surprise and conflict' (Ahmed, 2000: 6). They may be 'fragile, grudging, uneven' (Tonkiss, 2005: 10) as well as 'transitory, instrumental or incidental' (Tonkiss, 2005: 13). These are not encounters that are laden with a sense of meaning or a clear outcome: they may be 'hostile as well as friendly, indifferent as well as interested, passive as well as active' (Painter, 2012: 524). This sense of urban encounters is therefore different to approaches that ask how we might generate the kind of social encounters that would lead to a 'respect for difference' (Valentine, 2008: 325). Such understandings assumes an account of politics that is agreed in advance, and we are left with the task of determining what constitutes a critical or a regressive encounter. An approach to urban encounters informed by the works of Fran Tonkiss, Sara Ahmed, Angela McRobbie and Jean-Luc Nancy is quite different in this respect, in that it resists the suggestion that encounters may be encouraged (or limited) in order to extend or deepen 'liberal values' (Valentine, 2008: 330). It also refuses to assume that encounters form instances that may be scaled up to 'produce social change' (Valentine, 2008: 330), because this position suggests a geography of scale where the state is still assumed as the proper site of politics (Isin, 2007). Finally, in contrast to the idea that encounters take place between 'minority and majority groups' (Valentine, 2008: 330), this book has proposed a notion of urban encounters that defies a group based ontology and instead advocates that encounters are *productive* of political identities, which are both contingent and multiple.

In contrast to an approach that suggests that urban encounters form potentially progressive moments that politics needs to tap into, then, the approach outlined in this book invokes the encounters of the melee as the *actual institution of politics itself*. This understanding doesn't point to struggles between distinct, ahistorical and identifiable subjects or constituencies. Rather, it has been argued that multiple struggles constitute different subject positions and communities, which change and shift in time as part of a 'difference machine' (Isin, 2002). This is how the notion of urban encounters gestures towards a way of thinking politics beyond nationalism, because it forms a way of thinking coexistence that defies the forces of unification. The chapters in this book have all argued that the task of thinking beyond nationalism will require undoing a *unifying* way of conceptualizing space, time and subjectivity. In situating nationalism as part of this broader imaginary, one that relies on the assumption of state sovereignty and that draws upon powerful narratives about what it means to be modern, the book has unpacked what is at stake in thinking against this deeply entrenched way of understanding the political. It has also addressed different forms of critique that seek to go beyond nationalism, whilst suggesting that many of them nevertheless reveal the ways in which nationalism often informs the ways in which we aim to escape it. The central claim of the book is that nationalist imaginaries are persistent despite the many well-intentioned attempts to undo their force.

In gesturing towards urban life, the aim is not to put forward a new normative ideal, nor to suggest a new unifying concept where we are all expected to become urbanites. Rather, urban life names 'the plane upon which people – circling, touching, avoiding, attaching – come together, sometimes kicking and screaming, as an infrastructure' (Simone, 2011: 356). It thus names the *stuff* of political life – contestation, disagreement, melee. Politics under nationalism involves being in agreement and unifying around a common cause. It involves taking up a position after the rules have been drawn and the subject positions have been demarcated. In contrast, an approach to political life that attends to encounters displaces the search for community. It is precisely such encounters that Ernest Gellner, Max Weber and Jean-Jacques Rousseau sought to avoid, in that they carry the possibility of a redrawing of the rules on how politics is organized. It is these kinds of encounters that post-colonial, feminist and urban literatures more often evoke – in their sense that politics may be understood in another mode, in another tense and through another account of coexistence in disjointed times.

Notes

Acknowledgements

1 '"Seven Milion Londoners, one London": National and Urban ideas of Community in the Aftermath of the 7 July Bombings in London', in *Alternatives: Global, Local, Political*, 32 (2007), 155–176, by SAGE publications Ltd, http://online.sagepub.com.
2 'Beyond imaginative geographies? Critique, co-optation, and imagination in the aftermath of the War on Terror', in *Environment and Planning D: Society and Space*, 29(2011), 254–267 by Pion Ltd, London, www.pion.co.uk, www.envplan.com.
3 'Citizenship without Community: Time, design and the city', in *Citizenship Studies*; 14(1) (2010), 31–46, http://www.tanfonline.com.

Introduction: the persistence of nationalist imaginaries

1 In forming these questions, I have drawn on Ash Amin's work on the persistence of 'race' and racism, when he asks 'why the steady achievements of multiculturalism and the politics of diversity in general in the last decades of the 20th century... melted away so fast' (2010: 3) and how it is that 'racism persists and quickly resurfaces even when thought to be thoroughly dismantled' (Amin, 2010: 2).
2 The 'Global War on Terror' has provoked an enormous response in terms of critique, which has included international demonstrations, theatre performances, artistic installations, novels and films, as well as debates and active interventions by lawyers, journalists and academics. For a selection of critical academic approaches to the politics of the 'War on Terror', see Anderson and Adey (2011); Amoore (2006, 2007, 2009); Amoore and De Goede (eds) (2008); Boothe and Dunne (eds) (2002); Butler (2006, 2008); Closs Stephens and Vaughan-Williams (eds) (2009); Devji (2005); Elden (2009); Gregory (2004); Gregory and Pred (eds) (2007); Gokay and Walker (2003); Hill (2009); Jackson *et al.* (eds) (2011); Jarvis (2009); Masters and Dauphinee (2007); Mayer (2009); Neal (2008, 2010); Pain and Smith (2008); Puar (2007); Razack (2008); Reid (2009); Volpp (2002), Zehfuss (2002b).
3 George W. Bush said: 'Our war on terror begins with al-Qaeda, but it does not end there. It will not end until every terrorist group of global reach has been found, stopped and defeated'. See http://georgewbush-whitehouse.archives.gov/news/releases/2001/09/20010920-8.html. The obscure meanings and geographies of a 'War on Terror' was precisely what was most useful – and controversial – about this particular concept.
4 'War on Terror – A Term that No Longer Applies', *The Guardian* news blog, 15 January 2009, www.guardian.co.uk/news/blog/2009/jan/14/war-on-terror-david-miliband-mumbai; 'Declining Use of 'War on Terror'', BBC News, 17 April 2007, http://news.bbc.co.uk/1/hi/uk_politics/6562709.stm.
5 'Obama Moves to Make the War on Terror Permanent', *The Guardian*, 24 October 2012, www.guardian.co.uk/commentisfree/2012/oct/24/obama-terrorism-kill-list.

6 In the UK, these have included measures passed as part of the Terrorism Act 2000, the Anti-Terrorism Crime and Security Act 2001, the Prevention of Terrorism Act 2005, the Terrorism Act 2006, and the Counter Terrorism Act 2008.

7 I am not saying here that this represents either Billig's (1995) or Anderson's (1991) positions, but their works are often cited as 'signposts' for a case about the social construction of the nation. For a critique of the social constructivist approach to nationalism, see Campbell, 1998a.

8 For more on how this nationalist understanding of community came to dominate our understanding of political community more generally, see Bartelson, (2009).

9 In deploying the concept of 'imagination', they are all indebted to the works of Edward Said and Michel Foucault, among many other figures. They are specifically interested in questions of representation and in how different ways of approaching the world carry with them particular ontological assumptions.

10 This argument is expanded in Chapter 1. In contrast, Hage develops a critique of the tendency to differentiate between Eastern and Western forms of nationalism by arguing that practices of nation building, regardless of their differences, are steered by a national imaginary (1996). Chatterjee (1993) argues against the tendency to distinguish between Eastern and Western forms of nationalism and says that this distinction is informed by a unitary, modern and bourgeois-liberal understanding of knowledge. For a robust critique of the distinction drawn between civic and ethnic nationalisms, see Xenos (1996).

11 There are exceptions to this trend, and studies that are explicitly interested in the affective atmospheres of nationalism; see, for example, Berlant (1991, 1997, 2008).

12 Such attempts can be gleaned in the distinction between 'nationalism' and 'patriotism' (which, it is worth noting, doesn't exist in all languages) that is sometimes deployed as a way of distinguishing between 'good' and 'bad' forms of nationalism (Viroli, 1995).

13 Balibar argues further that, historically, this effect of unity has been secured through an idea of language or race (1991: 96). This point has been put another way by the geographers Prem Kumar Rajaram and Carl Grundy-Warr, who state: 'the community of the nation-state emphasizes, at its bottom line, a commonality that cannot be put under direct questioning' (2007: xvii)'.

14 In his book, *Being Political: Genealogies of Citizenship*, Engin Isin demonstrates how ideas about 'being political' are historically and geographically contingent (2002: x). Echoing Walter Benjamin, he argues further that dominant images of 'being political' are bequeathed by the victors and are produced through struggle, violence and conflict.

15 See, for example, Campbell (1998a, 1998b); Der Derian and Shapiro (eds) (1989); Dillon (1996); Edkins (1999, 2000, 2003); Huysmans (2006); Inayatullah and Blaney (2004, 2010); Lisle (2006a); Shapiro (2004, 2010); Shaw (2008); Sylvester (1994); Vaughan-Williams (2009b); Walker (1993, 2009); Weber (1995); Zehfuss (2002a).

16 Judith Butler's work remains my primary inspiration for asking how we might think about practices of being political outside of a model of statehood. Although questions about the modes of being political have long underpinned Butler's work in relation to her analysis of the feminist subject, her more recent work addresses the question of nationalism more explicitly through her engagement with the contemporary politics of Israel/Palestine. In terms of challenging established ways of thinking and acting politically more generally, I draw on the following feminist texts: Ahmed (2000, 2010); Bell (1999, 2007); Braidotti (1994, 2002); Brown (1995, 2001, 2005); Butler (1992, 1999, 2004); Butler and Scott (eds) (1992); Grewal (1996, 2005); Grosz (1994, 1995, 2005); Haraway (1991); Hemmings (2011); Hooks (1982, 1984, 1989); McRobbie (2009); Mohanty (1991); Riley (1988); Sedgwick (1990); Ware (1992).

17 Bhabha (1990, 2004); Chakrabarty (2008); Chatterjee (1987, 1993, 2004); Fanon (1971); Harootunian (2000); Mignolo (2000); Nandy (1987, 1988, 1994); Seth (2007); Spivak (1988, 1999).

18 This phrasing borrows from Audre Lorde's point about patriarchy, when she says, 'What does it mean when the tools of a racist patriarchy are used to examine the fruits of that same patriarchy? It means that only the most narrow perimeters of change are possible and allowable' (2007 (1984): 110–111).

19 The dilemma has been addressed by several post-colonial theorists, feminist and queer theorists, who argue that the tools we rely upon in articulating a political struggle don't lie outside power and therefore can't be understood to lead straightforwardly to 'freedom'. For selected examples of the argument, see Butler, 1999; Butler and Spivak, 2007; Chatterjee, 1993; Grosz 1999a, 1999b; Nandy, 1987, 1988, 1994; Puar, 2007. Of course, the inspirations for these works vary and they are addressing different historical problems – from the case of anti-colonial political movements in India (Chatterjee, 1993) to the politics of feminist movements (Butler, 1999).This is also an issue that was addressed by Michel Foucault, who forms an inspiration for some of these writers. In *The History of Sexuality*, he argues that we cannot understand 'sex' as a causal principle, as this makes it more difficult to discuss how it is implicated in a 'multiple and mobile field of power relations', which includes the production and dissemination of knowledge or the regulation of sex at multiple points of authority outside juridical power, including in the family, in schools, medicine, prison and so on (1979: 102).

20 I return to questions about the temporality of this critical positioning in the Conclusion, through a discussion of Angela McRobbie's (2009) and Sara Ahmed's (2010) works.

21 Key texts on the experience of cities and urban life that have influenced the argument of this book include, Amin and Thrift (2002); Benjamin (1999); Berman (1983); Coward (2009a); Davis (1990, 2000, 2002); Donald (1999); Frisby (2001); Graham (2004, 2010); Graham and Marvin (2001); Harvey (1989, 2003); Magnusson (2000, 2012); Massey (2007); Mbembe and Nuttall (2004); Mumford (1973); Park *et al.* (1967); Pile and Thrift (eds) (2000); Sennett (1971); Simmel (1971); Simone, (2004); Soja (1996); Tonkiss (2005); Young (1990).

22 There have been several attempts in the field of Human Geography to conceptualize a form of politics based around the idea of 'urban encounters'. These include Amin (2002); Amin and Thrift (2002); Painter (2012); Swanton (2010); Valentine (2008); and Wilson (2011).

1 Beyond 'imagined communities': nationalism and the politics of knowledge

1 As Marc Redfield argues, the concept of 'imagined communities' has become

> a tag phrase – almost a mantra – in academic and para-academic discussions of nationalism…a powerful set of expectations seems to hold sway: no matter what the critic's agenda or methodology, she or he can usually be counted on to affirm – usually more or less in passing, with a bare nod at Anderson's actual arguments – that nations are 'imagined communities'.
>
> (1999: 60)

For interesting attempts at engaging with this question of the relationship between nationalism and imagination, see Chakrabarty (2000); Redfield (1999); and Axel (2002). For a more detailed discussion of how social constructivism has formed a dominant approach in the social sciences more generally, see Hacking (2000).

2 The idea that solid identity categories must be understood as fluid, changing and contingent, and that these are constructs that only make sense in relation to their opposites: man/woman, white/black, us/them has become the widely accepted mantra in disciplines including Geography, Sociology, Media, Cultural Studies and Feminist Studies.

3 In talking about 'Anglo-American studies of nationalism', I refer to some of the key texts that represent 'canonical texts' in this minor discipline and which regularly form

key readings for academic programmes on Nations and Nationalism in the UK and North America. These include Anderson (1991); Gellner (1983); Hobsbawm (1990); Kedourie (1993); Kohn (1967); Minogue (1967); Smith (1986); and, more recently, Brubaker (1996); Calhoun (1997); Greenfeld (1992); and Hechter (2000). Extracts of many of these texts are collected in Hutchinson and Smith (1994).

4   This paradox is captured by the philosopher Slavoj Žižek in a comment he makes (paraphrasing Karl Marx) about bourgeois ideology: it 'loves to historicize: every social, religious and cultural form is historical, contingent, relative – every form except its own. There *was* history once, but now there is no longer any history' (Žižek, 2009: 21).

5   As an alternative to the approaches to nations and nationalism that this chapter takes to be unhelpful, Behnke (1997) offers a useful discussion of the relationship between citizenship, nationhood and political space and the way in which a particular model of political space as a territorial unit is assumed in Roger Brubaker's analysis of nationalism. Yiftachel (2002) offers a critique of the 'spatial blindness' of many theories of nationalism and the analytical fusion assumed between nation and state. This chapter draws on their insights as well as on the works of Bhabha (2004); Chatterjee (1993); Hage (1998); Manzo (1996).

6   This argument follows critiques of the foundational starting points of the discipline of International Relations made by Agnew (2007); Ashley and Walker (1990a, 1990b); Bartelson (2001); Hutchings (2008); Shaw (2004); and Walker (1993), the critiques of the starting points of Women's and Gender Studies offered by Butler (1999) and Hemmings (2011) and the critique of the foundational assumptions of the discipline of History offered by Fasolt (2004).

7   The interrelationship between this idea of time and how it supports a particular understanding of things around us is developed further by Edkins (2003: 34).

8   This is made possible by what Michel Foucault (2002) describes as the shift from a classical to a modern episteme, which he argues took place in the last years of the eighteenth century, when concepts became historicized. This point is also unpacked by Bartelson when he describes that: 'The nation forms a particular concept of political community that is notable for the way in which it is grafted on to a plane of historicity' (2001: 39).

9   For a more critical understanding of this formulation, which reveals the necessarily exclusionary origins of nationalism, see Marx (2003).

10   Although no firm statistics exist, the United Nations Guide for Minorities estimates that

> between 10 and 20 per cent of the world's population belong to minorities. This means that between 600 million and 1.2 billion people are in need of special measures for the protection of their rights, given that minorities are often among the most disadvantaged groups in society, their members often subject to discrimination and injustice and excluded from meaningful participation in public and political life.

See *The United Nations Guide for Minorities*. Available at http://www.ohchr.org/EN/issues/minorities/pages/minoritiesguide.aspx.

Although the work of defending minority cultures that are marginalized by the homogenizing practices of nationalist-statist machines is of course important, it is also worth remembering that 'minorities are a recent social and demographic category' (Appadurai, 2006: 42) and that, only a century ago, the idea that someone formed part of a 'minority identity' made very little sense (Behnke, 1997: 252). The trouble in speaking on behalf of 'minority cultures' is that we join the argument on Gellner's terms and accept his framework of political life as a starting point rather than as a historically contingent form of organizing. For example, in defending minority cultures that were pushed to the edges (or out) of statist territorial units as not going 'meekly to their doom', we risk allowing Gellner to get away with the feat of establishing a world based on the principle of state sovereignty. In defending the case of minority cultures, the task is to find a way of contesting this broader framework of political life – a framework that makes possible the idea of both minority and majority cultures.

11 Marxist theorists of nationalism including Tom Nairn (1997) and Michael Hechter (1975, 2000) have paid significantly more attention to the question of minority nationalism. Specifically, they have sought to explain the politics of peripheral Celtic nationalisms by developing an argument about the 'uneven development of capitalism'. Although Nairn (1997) criticizes Gellner for paying more attention to the machines and instruments of modernization rather than the people affected and cast aside by the process, he nevertheless follows Gellner's central assumption that nationalism forms the 'essence' of an unstoppable modernizing dynamic (1997: 194). Different nationalisms can therefore be explained according to their position on the scale of modern capitalism, and 'minority' and 'majority' nationalisms can be distinguished (and compared) according to their place on this common universal journey. In Michael Hechter's case, his more recent work attempts to take seriously the exclusions created by nationalism in order to develop a case for what he calls 'minority cultural protectionism' (2000). But the problem with Hechter's analysis is that it also assumes Gellner's central formulation that 'Self-determination is a universal good' (Hechter, 2000: 16). In contrast to Nairn and Hechter, we need to find ways of arguing against the broader nationalist imaginary that Gellner sets up and defends: the principle that cultures and polities must match and be anchored within a statist territorial unit. Recalling Appadurai, minorities do not only struggle to find their place within this imaginary; they are *produced* by this political imaginary: 'minorities do not come preformed. They are produced in the specific circumstances of every nation and every nationalism' (2006: 42).

12 Similarly, when Anthony D. Smith discusses the case of minority nationalisms that are without a state, he claims that the Québécois, Basques, Corsicans, Welsh, Kurdish and Tamils can all be understood as nations that have 'retained into the modern epoch a sense of their own cultural distinctiveness' (1995: 62). The problem is that it takes a nationalist imaginary to understand these national formations as having *inherited* their culture, suggesting that each has a distinctive prepolitical identity that eventually 'emerges' into the modern world.

13 The classic statement on this question is of course Ernst Renan's 'Qu'est-ce qu'une nation?' Available in Hutchinson and Smith (1994).

14 In contrast, Partha Chatterjee describes the problem in political terms, when he argues that it's necessary to question this 'supposedly rational and scientific thought' as part of a 'discourse of *power*' and 'to question the very universality, the 'givenness', the sovereignty of that thought, to go to its roots and thus radically to criticize it' (Chatterjee, 1993: 11). This 'is to raise the possibility that it is not just military might or industrial strength, but thought itself, which can dominate and subjugate. It is to appreciate the field of discourse, historical, philosophical and scientific, as a battleground of political power.' (Chatterjee, 1993: 11) For an argument about the residual nationalism in post-colonial critiques of nationalism, see Zachariah (2008).

15 This critique of modernization theory has been further developed in the context of International Relations literatures by Inayatullah and Blaney (2004).

2 Weberian tales: disenchantment, mastery and meaning

1 For an extended critique of Weber's reliance on an orientalist imaginary, see Isin (2002).

2 Weber's concept of rationality (and rationalization) is complex and multifaceted, as is the relationship he draws between rationality and calculability. As Brubaker explains,

for Weber 'a thing is never irrational in itself, but only from a particular…point of view. For the unbeliever every religious way of life is irrational, for the hedonist every ascetic standard' (quoted in Brubaker, 1984: 35). Rationality forms a central essence of modern capitalism because market transactions are not determined by traditional or familial ties but involve the 'deliberate and calculating pursuit of self-interest' (Brubaker, 1984: 10). Monetary calculation is rational because it assigns a numerical value to every good, service and asset, and, whilst self-interest and monetary calculation may have formed part of other economic orders, capitalism's uniqueness lies in its emphasis on calculability. This calculating ethos is also identifiable in the fact that the performance of human and non-human means of production can be calculated, and that the legal and administrative environment that establishes the conditions for economic conduct can be reliably predicted (Brubaker, 1984: 12). For more on the dialectics of Max Weber's social theories, see Lash and Whimster (eds) (1987); Scaff (1989). For more on the experiences of time and space that accompanied the turn of the twentieth century, see Kern (1983).

3   Many of the debates in studies of Weber's political writings revolve around the question of whether Weber is more of a nationalist or a liberal, and whether he places more emphasis on the category of the nation or on the individual. We can read Weber as an arch-nationalist who proclaims that national values should form the ultimate criterion for deciding all social and economic questions; we can also understand him as a 'proto-existentialist', who places his faith in a charismatic individual who can find meaning in a meaningless world (Walker, 1993). I present Weber as someone who captures both positions, and that both are intimately intertwined.

4   For an innovative attempt to take stillness seriously in social theory, see Harrison (2010).

5   See, for example, Weber's essay on 'Between Two Laws' (1916: 1994b), which argues that greater nations face different historical obligations from smaller nations. The responsibilities facing a German nation are different from those confronting Switzerland, Norway, the Netherlands or Denmark. Germany's obligations, for example, lie with building a *Machtstaat* and offsetting the dominance of other great powers such as Russia and England. In contrast, smaller nations have the 'luxury' of focusing on other issues, such as cultural virtues, or a pacifist foreign policy: they can enjoy 'soft politics' that is not considered to be as important or as serious. Political life nevertheless still ultimately involves an interminable power struggle between great and heavily armed nations. For a wide-ranging critique of scalar accounts of politics, see Isin (2007).

6   A similar theme runs throughout Weber's essay on *The Protestant Ethic and the Spirit of Capitalism*, in which he offers a grim evaluation of individual lives as caught within the throes of the technical conditions of machine production. Our only hope for some disruption to the tedium of the rationalizing ethic of industrial organization is for 'new prophets' to come along. Until then, the search for some sense of meaning 'prowls about in our lives like the ghost of dead religious beliefs' (2001: 124).

7   This analysis of political leadership carries distinct echoes of Tony Blair's justification of the decision to follow George W. Bush, President of the United States, to war with Iraq in 2003. This is how the former UK Prime Minister Tony Blair accounted for his decision in his resignation speech in Sedgefield, County Durham on 10 May 2007:

> I was, and remain, as a person and as a prime minister, an optimist. Politics may be the art of the possible; but at least in life, give the impossible a go. Hand on heart, I did what I thought was right. I may have been wrong, that's your call. But believe one thing, if nothing else. I did what I thought was right for our country.

The note of optimism is not Weberian, but the way in which he sought to carry this decision on the basis of his 'passion, a sense of responsibility [and] judgement' is uncannily Weberian.

8 For more on the history of the idea of tragedy, see Steiner (1961).

9 This understanding is further affirmed by George Steiner, who says 'Human life is profoundly tragic, and it cannot be atoned through reason, order, justice or progress through science' (1961: 8).

10 Deleuze goes on to call Heraclitus 'the tragic thinker', which might explain what draws William Connolly to this figure. Heraclitus 'makes existence an *aesthetic phenomenon* rather than a moral or religious one. . . Moreover *he made an affirmation of becoming*' (1983: 23, emphasis in the original).

11 Nevertheless, we might question whether Michael Dillon's reworking of tragedy ultimately offers enough critical tools for contesting a nationalist imaginary. Although the tragic hero is notably different from Weber's heroic individual, perhaps the very notion of individuals 'taking up their freedom' might still sit too comfortably with nationalist thought. Whilst this reworking of the tragic is effective in revealing the contingency of Weber's way of seeing the world, perhaps it fails to offer enough resources for contesting the romantic masculinist idea of a wilful, heroic individual who can leave his mark on the world.

3 Rousseau's legacies: the politics of time, community and loss

1 Rousseau's ideal community, outlined in *Of The Social Contract* (1997), represents a leap from the world of time and change and not an account of what might lie at the end of time or at the peak of humanity's development, such as we find in the idea of a nation. His understanding of political community lies closer to Machiavelli's or Plato's, for whom time represents the *antithesis* of order. Similarly,

> The social pact is not an evolutionary development that follows naturally from the second Discourse; it belongs, rather, to another dimension, a purely normative dimension, outside historical time. We begin *ex nihilio*, without asking what conditions must be met in order for the political ideal to be realized.
>
> (Starobinski, 1988: 30)

It was left to the Abbé Sieyès 'to redefine the identity of the community in such a way that it could serve as the ultimate source and locus of sovereignty' (Bartelson, 2001: 40). For a further discussion of how Rousseau's ideas were taken up and transformed by the modern project of a nation-state, see Wokler (1998, 2000).

2 It also animates several other contemporary political debates, on both the right and the left of politics – in claims about the loss of national sovereignty, of empire, as well as in claims about the loss of a simpler account of identity, or even a coherent political enemy. For more on how narratives that mourn the loss of empire continue to infuse public debate in British politics, see Gilroy (2004).

3 The First Discourse refers to *Discours sur les sciences et les arts* (1751).

4 In this, Rousseau's political thought represents a combination of the classical and the modern, first because he aims to capture a classical notion of the concrete political society that can withstand the inevitable curses of fortune, degradation, collapse and death (Gunnell, 1968: 250) and, second, because he affirms very modern ideas, as expressed by Hobbes and Locke, that the discovery of the proper methods for organizing human society can lead to the conquest of nature and the virtually unlimited improvement of man's estate (Masters, 1976: 197).

5 Although it is of course impossible to speak of the Enlightenment as a single, coherent body of ideas, some key aspects which we may identify with it include the idea that truth is 'one single, harmonious body of knowledge'; the idea that the laws that govern inanimate nature can also be applied to plants, animals and human beings; and that reason forms the means of attaining an authoritative foundation to knowledge (Berlin, 1956). Thus, although thinkers of the Enlightenment vary in the extent of their belief in God, the possibility of progress and the nature of man as good or bad,

they are united in the conviction that 'all problems were soluble by the discovery of objective answers, which, once found...would be clear for all to see and valid eternally' (Berlin, 1956: 28). The idea that the world is fully describable and comprehensible, and orderable by categories, is perhaps most stunningly represented in Diderot and d'Alembert's *Encyclopédie* (1751–1777).

6 His portrait of the ideal society is said to be constructed in the image of his childhood in Geneva, which he remembered as a period of innocence, when life was uniform, in harmony, and when he felt that 'the break between the demands of the world and the demands of the self had not yet taken place' (Cassirer, 1954: 40).

7 This is in marked contrast to Thomas Hobbes's analysis of the state of nature. In remarks directed at Hobbes, Rousseau claims that, although other writers have sought to describe the foundations of society by returning to the state of nature, none of them have reached it (1992: 17). He argues that 'others' have mistakenly attributed to the state of nature qualities such as need, avarice and oppression, but that these qualities only appear with society. For a detailed reading of Hobbes' account of the state of nature and its relationship to his account of politics, see Neal, 2010; Shaw, 2008; Walker, 1993.

8 Rousseau's ideal state was envisioned for his treasured city of Geneva, which at the time had a population of roughly 25,000. In order to maintain the state's uniformity, Rousseau tells us that the best state must be a small state: 'The more the social bond stretches, the looser it grows, and in general a small State is proportionately stronger than a large one...A thousand reasons prove this maxim' (1997: 74). The question of *scale* is thus all important. The drawbacks of a larger state are listed, and they include the difficulty of administrating over a larger territory; the difficulty of feeling affection for chiefs that people never see; the difficulty of enforcing laws and correcting abuse; and, finally, that as the state expands, the possibility for freedom, experienced in the enactment of law, is diminished. Thus, in an enlarged state, more force will be required to maintain unity and to secure the freedom of its citizens: 'in order for the government to be good, it ought to be relatively stronger in proportion as the people is more numerous' (1997: 84). Interestingly, then, Rousseau makes clear that extending the polity will involve extending the use of force.

9 Indeed, this story of progress towards a civilized, enlightened society underpins Modernization Theories (Chakrabarty, 2008; Chow, 1993; Harootunian, 2000; Mignolo, 2000; Seth, 2007), as well as several canonical texts in the discipline of International Relations (Inayatullah and Blaney, 2004), Development (Escobar, 1995), Anthropology (Clifford, 1986; Fabian, 1983; Girard, 1986; Gupta and Ferguson, 1992; Waswo, 1997) and Geography (Gregory, 1994; Livingstone, 1992).

10 For example, as Richard Waswo has shown, the very possibility of being able to embrace 'development' depends in the first instance on the condition of holding citizenship in a nation-state or, at the very least, participating at some level in statist economic, political and social systems that can record someone as a valid claimant and as a political subject (1997). As he outlines, none of these conditions apply to many indigenous peoples throughout the world. Those who refuse, evade or simply live a life outside of the count of statist institutions remain invisible. Such communities are therefore not able to be recognized within the statist terms for being political.

4 Urban cosmopolitanism: the return of the nation in times of terror

1 As part of the visual economy of this particular political climate, *certain kinds* of bodies were understood 'as [more] inclined to commit violence or having tendencies of violence essential to them' (Grewal, 2005: 201) and images of danger, risk and threat 'stuck' to *particular* bodies more easily than others (Ahmed cited in Puar, 2007: 184–187). I return to the politics of 'mistaken identities' in the context of the 'War on Terror' in the next chapter.

2 This point is reinforced by Pheng Cheah who points out that nationalism and cosmopolitanism emerged together in the history of political thought (1998: 22).

3 This framing of the argument draws upon Bartelson's work on political community (2009).

4 This approach fits closely with Inderpal Grewal's, who argues that:

> While some assume that nationalism is linked to a more settled subject and that mobile subjectivity could be resistant to nationalism, it is clear that nationalism itself has proved to be protean and mobile, providing identities and affiliations to mobile as well as settled subjects, and indeed to what have come to be called 'global' and 'cosmopolitan' subjectivities as well as to specific and local ones.
>
> (2005: 35)

5 The '7 Million Londoners, One London' poster campaign was sponsored by London-based advertising and media groups and launched on 1 August 2005; it was replaced in Autumn 2006 by the 'We are Londoners, We are One' campaign, funded by British Gas and Capital Radio.

6 Indeed, the Blitz formed the immediate reference point for almost all the British national newspapers in the aftermath of the bombings, together with reference to the IRA bombings, as proof of the enduring 'calm and courage' of Londoners. *The Guardian* newspaper's editorial on 8 July 2005, the day following the London bombings, opened by quoting George Orwell writing at the time of the Blitz: 'As I write, highly civilized human beings are flying overhead, trying to kill me'. The tabloid newspapers were more excited in their comparisons: 'Adolf Hitler's Blitz and his doodlebug rockets never once broke London's spirit'; 'We survived the Blitz. We lived through 30 years of IRA outrages... Once again the British people will triumph over evil.' (The first quotation is from the *The Sun*; the second is from *The Daily Mirror*. Both are from 'What the Papers Say', *The Guardian*, 8 July 2005.)

7 Samuel Huntington was a member of faculty at the Department of Government at Harvard University and later advisor on national security to the White House in the late 1970s. His book on the *Clash of Civilizations* became a global bestseller. Written following the fall of the Berlin wall and the 'triumph' of neoliberal capitalism, Huntington replaced the map of the world as divided according to First World, Second World and Third World with a new map, which ordered people according to their culture or civilization, rather than according to ideology or rate of economic development. In his new map, he speculated that the world contained seven or eight major civilizations (Western, Confucian, Japanese, Islamic, Hindu, Slavic-Orthodox, Latin American and 'possibly' an African civilization) and declared that the most important fault lines in global politics will become these separating one civilization from another. The book found renewed currency in the aftermath of the attacks on the World Trade Center in New York and in the plane crashes in Washington and Pennsylvania. For a critique of Huntington's original thesis, see Toal (2006).

8 In practice the Games were not necessarily an 'open' event, however. For a critical reading of the Olympic Games as a security event, see Stephen Graham's article in *The Guardian* (2012).

9 Initial signatories included Mayor of London Ken Livingstone; Director of the pressure group, Liberty, Shami Chakrabarti; Secretary General of the Muslim Council of Britain, Sir Iqbal Sacranie; the Muslim Association of Britain; politicians from Labour, Liberal Democrats, Green and Scottish National parties; various writers and journalists; the general secretaries of four national trade unions; representatives of a range of community organizations and faith groups; civil liberties lawyers; and student leaders (London Assembly press release, 26 August 2005, available from www.london.gov.uk/view_press_release.jsp?releaseid=5795).

10 The poster campaign, titled 'It's up to all of us', was supported by the Mayor of

London, the British Transport Police (BTP), the Metropolitan Police Service (Met) and the City of London Police.

11   It is worth noting that the project also attempts to reach out beyond the familiar audiences of academic scholarship. The films are posted on the *Open Democracy* website and on *youtube*, and have been shown in various galleries, museums and film festivals across the US, UK and Mexico, giving participants and viewers an opportunity to offer their own voices to the project.

12   This is drawn from Simmel's seminal article, 'The Metropolis and Mental Life', originally published in 1903, which is again discussed briefly in Chapter 6.

13   For a critical reworking of the tension between 'home' and 'away' see Ahmed (2000). For another critique of Nussbaum's cosmopolitanism, see Connolly (2000).

5 Nationalism and its limits: the politics of imagination

1   The novel was also translated into many European languages and into Arabic, Brazilian Portuguese, Chinese, Hebrew, Hindi and Indonesian.

2   Michael J. Shapiro (2010: 90) draws attention to a similar idea deployed in Hanif Kureishi's film, *Sammy and Rosie get Laid*, when Sammy says to Rosie, 'We're not British, we're Londoners.'

3   For a further critique of an account of modern, Western knowledge as a process of 'unveiling', see Seth (2009). Chakrabarty (2008: 172–179) offers an interesting discussion of Rabindranath Tagore's use of the phrase 'piercing the veil of the real' as involving another form of perception, which we can juxtapose with Hamid's metaphor of the veil.

4   Similarly, Gregory states that his aim is not to adjudicate on questions such as 'Why do they hate us?' (a question which, he points out, was also asked in Iraq) but that 'it is the dichotomy reproduced through [the question] that I want to contest' (2004: 24).

5   Gregory tells us: 'We might think of imaginative geographies as *fabrications*, a word that usefully combines 'something *fictionalized*' and 'something *made real*', because they are imaginations given substance' (2004: 17, my emphasis). Similarly, Said in *Orientalism* explains

> this universal practice of designating in one's mind a familiar space which is 'ours' and an unfamiliar space beyond 'ours' which is 'theirs' is a way of making geographical distinctions that can be entirely *arbitrary*...I use the word 'arbitrary' here because imaginative geography of the 'our land–barbarian land' variety does not require that the barbarians acknowledge the distinction...often the sense in which someone feels himself to be not-foreign is based on a very *unrigorous* idea of what is 'out there', beyond one's own territory. All kinds of *suppositions*, and *fictions* appear to crowd the unfamiliar space outside one's own'.
>
> (1995: 54, my emphasis)

6   Chakrabarty (2008: 175) contends that 'imagination' remains a 'mentalist, subject-centered category' in Benedict Anderson's account of nationalism. For more on the concept of imagination and its ambivalent meanings, see Cocking (1991) and Sallis (2000). For another critical attempt to raise the question of imagination in relation to nationalism specifically, see Redfield (1999). The question of the limits of 'imagination' in steering approaches to critical work connects with debates around 'Non-Representational Theories' as involving a study of more-than-representations (see Anderson and Harrison, 2010).

7   *Half of a Yellow Sun* by Chimamanda Ngozi Adichie (2007) follows Biafra's struggle to establish an independent republic in Nigeria; Rohinton Mistry's *A Fine Balance* (1996) traces the changes in India from independence in 1947 to the State of Emergency declared in 1975; and Bapsi Sidhwa's *Ice Candy Man* (1989) is set around the Partition of India and the birth of Pakistan. The point about the way in which such

novels enunciate a critique of nationalism can be gleaned in quotes such as the following in *Ice Candy Man*, when the child narrator says:

> There is much disturbing talk. India is going to be broken. 'Can one break a
> country? And what happens if they break it where our house is?' ...I ask Cousin.
> 'Rubbish', he says, 'no one's going to break India. It's not made of glass!'
>
> (1989: 92).

There is a broader set of interesting questions to ask about how and why *certain* post-
colonial novels travel well, sell or get translated. In that context, Ahmad (1992) argues
that Frederic Jameson shouldn't understand all post-colonial fiction as representing
critiques of decolonizing nationalism. For an interesting discussion of how an
author's marginality can become politicized and commodified in the global literary
market place, see Brouillette (2007). For another discussion of how literary texts
circulated as part of the geopolitical climate of the 'War on Terror', see Ware (2006).

8 Butler is unsure however how far she would go in pinning down this account as a new
   political orientation or even in naming it conclusively as 'relationality' (2006: 24).
9 For example, according to Nancy, the idea that community is something that *follows*
   from self-contained individuals coming together is back-to-front (Coward, 2009b:
   254). Being means being-with-others.

6 Sites of memory and the city as a melee

1 There is of course an enormous literature, as well as a vast archive of novels and films
   that engage with questions of memory in relation to the Holocaust. For interesting and
   innovative approaches to debates around memory in the city of Berlin and Germany
   specifically, see Huyssen (2003); Ladd (1997); Till (2005); Young (1993); Zehfuss
   (2007). On the politics of memory more generally, see Edkins (2003); Halbwachs
   (1992); Nora (1989); Tolia-Kelly (2010); Winter (1995). For an alternative approach
   to war and the history of killing, see Bourke (1999).
2 Henri Lefebvre's work is also useful in this respect, and his work is drawn upon by
   Amin and Thrift (2002). For his writings on cities, see Lefebvre (1996). For his
   related work on rhythmanalysis, see Lefebvre (2004). For attempts at drawing out a
   different experience of time in relation to a post-colonial experience and, in particular, African cities, see Mbembe (2001) and Opondo (2008).
3 Crucially, Simmel emphasizes the confluence of rational and irrational impulses, and
   therefore the ambivalence of the modern city (see Frisby, 1984). Yet that ambivalence
   is largely written out when his work is taken up by the Chicago School theorists. See,
   for example, Park *et al.* (1967).
4 This is a crucial point that doesn't necessarily come through in Benedict Anderson's
   use of 'homogenous empty time' in *Imagined Communities*. Whilst Anderson borrows
   this image of the angel to explain the experience of time that makes nationalism possible, for Benjamin, this 'was precisely the image of history that had to be refused'
   (Kelly, 1998: 846).
5 The 'thought-image' (Richter, 2007) reinforces Benjamin's chosen method of *showing* rather than *telling* a particular story. The Angel of History is one such
   thought-image, which is intended to paradoxically, 'say in words what cannot be said
   in words' (Richter, 2007: 13). In doing so, the thought-images involve the reader 'in
   a serious play and a vexing dance of meaning' (Richter, 2007: 13).
6 This style has also been deployed by writers including Iain Sinclair in *London
   Orbital: A Walk around the M25* (2002) and *London: City of Disappearances* (2006);
   Rachel Lichtenstein in *On Brick Lane* (2007); and Rebecca Solnit in *Wanderlust: A
   History of Walking* (2001) and *A Field Guide to Getting Lost* (2006).
7 There is now a Memorial to the Homosexuals Persecuted under the National Socialist
   Regime, which lies opposite the Memorial to the Murdered Jews of Europe. There is

also a Memorial to the Murdered Roma and Sinti currently under construction, designed by artist Dani Karavan, to be situated between the Brandenburg Gate and the Reichstag (www.stiftung-denkmal.de/en/memorials/sinti-and-roma-memorial. html#c952).

8   For critical readings of the Bosnian conflict specifically, see Campbell, (1998a); Coward, (2009a).

9   In this way, the idea of the city as a melee also poses a challenge to the notion of a 'divided city' – a concept which is of course especially relevant to Berlin, but which suggests there was once two 'pure substances'.

10 Libeskind is well-known as the designer of the Imperial War Museum of the North in Manchester and the new Royal Ontario Museum in Toronto among several other building projects. He initially won the competition to design the new One World Trade Center (or 'Freedom Tower') in New York City, although his original design was eventually dismissed and the new memorial will be built by architect David Childs. For more on Libeskind's work in general, see Libeskind (2001) and http://daniel-libeskind.com. For Jacques Derrida's response to this museum, see Derrida (1992).

11 The literary critic Matei Călinescu draws a distinction between modernity as a stage in the Western history of civilization involving the ascendancy of rational, scientific and objective thought ('bourgeois modernity') and what he describes as an 'aesthetic modernity', which emerges in the nineteenth century and aims to express 'its disgust through the most diverse means, ranging from rebellion, anarchy, and apocalypticism to aristocratic self-exile' (1977: 42).

12 See, for example, Peter Eisenman's dialogues with the philosopher Jacques Derrida in Kipnis and Leeser (1997).

13 This effect is echoed in another building in the city – the Federal Chancellery, where, on either side of this white concrete and glass building, we find almost an exact replica, in two enormous white concrete pillars with green shoots growing from their tops. This building was designed by Berlin architects Axel Schultes and Charlotte Frank.

14 Peter Eisenman is another internationally recognized architect. He is based in New York and in 1967 founded the Institute for Architecture and Urban Studies (IAUS) (www.eisenmanarchitects.com).

15 This site cost €27.6 million, paid for by the German federal government. Eisenman's design wasn't the first to be selected, but formed the preferred choice of a second judging panel assembled in 1996 (Schlusche, 2005: 19). The idea for a Memorial was promoted by the Society for the Promotion of the Memorial for the Murdered Jews of Europe, organized by Leah Rosh.

16 Other sites of memory in Berlin which claim a connection with places of suffering include the memorial commemorating the deportations of Berlin Jews at the Grunewald rapid transit station; the House of the Wannsee conference memorial on the Grosser Wannsee, where the 'Final Solution' was agreed; and the Topography of Terror exhibition at the former site of the Nazi Secret Police (Schlör, 2005). As both Edkins (2003: 149–170) and Lisle (2006b: 844–845) discuss: the idea of 'authenticity' persistently hovers around memory debates and presents a challenge for museum curators as well as a 'selling value' for tourists.

17 Looking north, towards the Tiergarten, there is now a Memorial to the Homosexuals Persecuted under the National Socialist Regime. There is also a Memorial to the Murdered Roma and Sinti currently under construction, designed by artist Dani Karavan, to be situated between the Brandenburg Gate and the Reichstag (www.stiftung-denkmal.de/en/memorials/sinti-and-roma-memorial.html#c952).

18 Of course, this claim is somewhat undermined by the Memorial's aim – to remember the loss of a single community, but this chapter aims to read these building designs in a way that goes beyond their briefs.

19 This is why, in his other works, Eisenman has experimented with spatial forms including the blur and the trace (1992). In this sense, his designs may also be compared with artist Tomás Saraceno's work, who experiments with spatial forms including webs and clouds. For more on the implications for thinking politics using artworks including Saraceno's, see Closs Stephens and Squire (2012) and Latour (2011). For a conversation between Peter Eisenman and Jacques Derrida, see Kipnis and Leeser (eds) (1997).

20 The installation formed the result of the Manchester International Festival's open commission call, submitted by CUBE (Centre for the Urban Built Environment) and Taylor Young (Urban Planners and Architects). The installation has been acquired by the Whitworth Art Gallery, Manchester, for its permanent collection.

21 Metzger was an initiator of the *Destruction in Art Symposium* in 1966 in London.

Conclusion: the aftermath of nationalist imaginaries

1 This formulation of the problem is echoed in Globalization Studies, which tend to revolve around the question of whether we have moved 'beyond the state'. For a critique of this formulation of the problem, see Elden (2005).

2 This is echoed in the title of his book, *Nations Matter: Culture, History and the Cosmopolitan Dream* (2007b).

3 This also involved assuming the experience of relatively affluent white women as the norm (Hill Collins, 1990; Hooks, 1982, 1984, 1989; Moraga and Anzaldúa (eds) 1981).

4 For another example of this politics of 'double entanglement' in relation to gay rights, see Butler (2008).

5 Ahmed draws here upon Jacques Derrida (who in turn draws on Nietsche) and his call for a philosopher who can think the 'perhaps' (1997): 'The happy future is the future of the perhaps' (Ahmed, 2010: 198).

References

Agnew, John (1998) *Geopolitics: Re-visioning World Politics*, London: Routledge.

Agnew, John (2007) 'Know-Where: Geographies of Knowledge of World Politics', *International Political Sociology*, 1: 138–148.

Ahluwalia, Pal (2007) 'Afterlives of Post-colonialism: Reflections on Theory Post 9/11', *Postcolonial Studies*, 10 (3): 257–270.

Ahmad, Aijaz (1992) *In Theory: Classes, Nations, Literatures*, London: Verso.

Ahmed, Sara (2000) *Strange Encounters, Embodied Others in Post-coloniality*, New York: Routledge.

Ahmed, Sara (2010) *The Promise of Happiness*, Durham, NC: Duke University Press.

Ahmed, Sara and Fortier, Anne-Marie (2003) 'Re-imagining Community', *International Journal of Cultural Studies*, 6 (3): 251–259.

Althusser, Louis (1972) *Montesquieu, Rousseau, Marx: Politics and History*, London: Verso.

Amin, Ash (2002) 'Ethnicity and the Multicultural City: Living with Diversity', *Environment and Planning A*, 34: 959–980.

Amin, Ash (2010) 'The Remainders of Race', *Theory, Culture & Society*, 27 (1): 1–23.

Amin, Ash and Thrift, Nigel (2002) *Cities: Reimagining the Urban*, Cambridge, MA: Polity Press.

Amin, Ash (2012) *Land of Strangers*, Cambridge, MA: Polity Press.

Amoore, Louise (2006) 'Biometric Borders: Governing Mobilities in the War on Terror', *Political Geography*, 25: 336–351.

Amoore, Louise (2007) 'Vigilant Visualities: The Watchful Politics of the War on Terror', *Security Dialogue*, 38: 215–232.

Amoore, Louise (2009) 'Response Before the Event: On Forgetting the War on Terror' in Closs Stephens, Angharad and Vaughan-Williams, Nick (eds) *Terrorism and the Politics of Response*, London, New York: Routledge.

Amoore, Louise and De Goede, Marieke (eds) (2008) *Risk and the War on Terror*, London: Routledge.

Anderson, Ben and Adey, Pete (2011) 'Affect and Security: Exercising Emergencies in UK Civil Contingencies' *Environment and Planning D: Society and Space*, 29: 1092–1109.

Anderson, Benedict (1991) *Imagined Communities: Reflections on the Origin and Spread of Nationalism*, revised and extended edn. London: Verso.

Anderson, Ben and Harrison, Paul (eds) (2010) *Taking-Place: Non-Representational Theories and Geography*, Farnham, Surrey: Ashgate.

Appadurai, Arjun (2006) *Fear of Small Numbers*, Durham, NC: Duke University Press.

Ashley, Richard K. and Walker, R. B. J. (1990a) 'Speaking the Language of Exile:

Dissident Thought in International Studies', *International Studies Quarterly*, 34 (3): 259–268.

Ashley, Richard K. and Walker, R. B. J. (1990b) 'Conclusion: Reading Dissidence/Writing the Discipline: Crisis and the Question of Sovereignty in International Studies', *International Studies Quarterly*, 34 (3): 367–416.

Axel, Brian Keith (2002) 'The Diasporic Imaginary', *Public Culture*, 14 (2): 411–428.

Balibar, Étienne (1991) 'The National Form: History and Ideology' in Wallerstein, Immanuel and Balibar, Étienne (eds) *Race, Nation, Class: Ambiguous Identities*, London: Verso, 86–106.

Balibar, Étienne (2004) *We, the people of Europe? Reflections on Transnational Citizenship*, Princeton, NJ: Princeton University Press.

Barnard, F. M. (1988) *Self-Direction and Political Legitimacy: Rousseau and Herder*, Oxford: Clarendon.

Bartelson, Jens (2001) *The Critique of the State*, Cambridge: Cambridge University Press.

Bartelson, Jens (2009) *Visions of World Community*, Cambridge: Cambridge University Press.

Bauman, Zygmunt (1991) *Modernity and Ambivalence*, Cambridge, MA: Polity Press.

Bauman, Zygmunt (2008) *Modernity and the Holocaust*, Cambridge: Malden, MA: Polity Press.

Behnke, Andreas (1997) 'Citizenship, Nationhood and the Production of Political Space', *Citizenship Studies*, 1 (2): 243–265.

Bell, Vikki (1999) *Feminist Imagination: Genealogies in Feminist Theory*, London: Sage.

Bell, Vikki (2007) *Culture and Performance. The Challenge of Ethics, Politics and Feminist Theory*, Oxford, New York: Berg.

Benjamin, Walter (1968) 'Theses on the Philosophy of History' in Arendt, Hannah (ed.) *Illuminations*, New York: Schocken Books, 253–264.

Benjamin, Walter (1978) *Reflections: Essays, Aphorisms, Autobiographical Writing*, New York: Schocken Books. Edited by Peter Demetz.

Benjamin, Walter (1999) *The Arcades Project*, Cambridge, MA: Harvard University Press.

Bennett, Jane (2001) *The Enchantment of Modern Life*, Princeton, NJ and Oxford: Princeton University Press.

Berlant, Lauren (1991) *The Anatomy of National Fantasy: Hawthorn, Utopia and Everyday Life*, Chicago: University of Chicago Press.

Berlant, Lauren (1997) *The Queen of America Goes to Washington City: Essays on Sex and Citizenship*, Durham, NC: Duke University Press.

Berlant, Lauren (2008) *The Female Complaint: The Unfinished Business of Sentimentality in American Culture*, Durham, NC: Duke University Press.

Berlin, Isaiah Sir (1956) *The Age of Enlightenment: The 18th-Century Philosophers*, New American Library: Muller.

Berman, Marshall (1983) *All that is Solid Melts into Air: The Experience of Modernity*, London: Verso.

Bhabha, Homi K (ed.) (1990) *Nation and Narration*, London and New York: Routledge.

Bhabha, Homi K (2004) *The Location of Culture*, London and New York: Routledge.

Billig, Michael (1995) *Banal Nationalism*, London: Sage.

Blair, Tony (2007) 'A Battle for Global Values', *Foreign Affairs*, 86 (1).

Boothe, K. and Dunne, T. (eds) (2002) *Worlds in Collision: Terror and the Future of Global Order*, Basingstoke: Palgrave.

Borradori, Giovanna (ed.) (2003) *Philosophy in a Time of Terror: Dialogues with Jürgen Habermas and Jacques Derrida*, Chicago, IL and London: University of Chicago Press.

Bourke, Joanna (1999) *An Intimate History of Killing*, London: Granta Books.

Bradbury, Malcolm (1976) 'The Cities of Modernism' in Bradbury, Malcolm and McFarlane, James Walter (eds) *Modernism 1890–1930*, London: Penguin Books.

Braidotti, Rosi (1994) *Nomadic Subjects: Embodiment and Sexual Difference in Contemporary Feminist Theory*, New York: Columbia University Press.

Braidotti, Rosi (2002) *Metamorphoses*, Cambridge, MA: Polity Press.

Brouillette, S (2007) *Postcolonial Writers in the Global Literary Marketplace*, Basingstoke, Hampshire and New York: Palgrave Macmillan.

Brown, Wendy (1995) *States of Injury: Power and Freedom in Late Modernity*, Princeton, NJ and Chichester: Princeton University Press.

Brown, Wendy (2001) *Politics out of History*, Princeton, NJ: Princeton University Press.

Brown, Wendy (2005) *Edgework. Critical Essays on Knowledge and Politics*, Princeton, NJ and Oxford: Princeton University Press.

Brubaker, Rogers (1984) *The Limits of Rationality: An Essay on the Social and Moral Thought of Max Weber*, London: George, Allen & Unwin.

Brubaker, Rogers (1996) *Nationalism Reframed: Nationhood and the National Question in the New Europe*, Cambridge: Cambridge University Press.

Brubaker, Rogers (2004a) *Ethnicity without Groups*, Cambridge, MA and London: Harvard University Press.

Brubaker, Rogers (2004b) 'In the Name of the Nation: Reflections on Nationalism and Patriotism', *Citizenship Studies*, 8 (2): 115–127.

Brubaker, Rogers and Cooper, Frederick (2000) 'Beyond "Identity"', *Theory and Society*, 29: 1–47.

Buck-Morss (1991) *The Dialectics of Seeing*, Cambridge, MA: MIT Press.

Bulley, Dan and Lisle, Debbie (2012) 'Welcoming the World: Governing Hospitality in London's 2012 Olympic Bid', *International Political Sociology*.

Bulson, Eric (2007) *Novels, Maps, Modernity. The Spatial Imagination 1850–2000*, New York and London: Routledge.

Butler, Judith (1992) 'Contingent Foundations: Feminism and the Question of "Postmodernism"' in Butler, Judith and Scott, Joan W. (eds) *Feminists Theorize the Political*, New York and London: Routledge, 3–21.

Butler, Judith (1999) *Gender Trouble: Feminism and the Subversion of Identity*. Tenth anniversary edn., New York and London: Routledge.

Butler, Judith (2004) *Undoing Gender*, New York and Oxford: Routledge.

Butler, Judith (2006) *Precarious Life: The Powers of Mourning and Violence*, London: Verso.

Butler, Judith (2008) 'Sexual Politics, Torture, and Secular Time', *British Journal of Sociology*, 59 (1): 1–23.

Butler, Judith and Scott, Joan (eds) (2002) *Feminists Theorize the Political*, New York and London: Routledge.

Butler, Judith and Spivak, Gayatri Chakravorty (2007) *Who Sings the Nation-State? Language, Politics, Belonging*, London, New York and Calcutta: Seagull Books.

Calhoun, Craig J. (1994) 'Nationalism and Civil Society' in Calhoun, C. (ed.) *Social Theory and the Politics of Identity*, Oxford: Blackwell.

Calhoun, Craig J. (1997) *Nationalism*, Buckingham: Open University Press.

Calhoun, Craig J. (2002) 'The Class Consciousness of Frequent Travelers: Toward a Critique of Actually Existing Cosmopolitanism', *The South Atlantic Quarterly*, 101 (4): 869–897

Calhoun, Craig J. (2007a) 'Nationalism and Cultures of Democracy', *Public Culture*, 19 (1): 151–173.

Calhoun, Craig J. (2007b) *Nations Matter: Culture, History and the Cosmopolitan Dream*, New York and Oxford: Routledge.

Calhoun, Craig J. (2008) 'Cosmopolitanism and Nationalism', *Nations and Nationalism*, 14 (3): 427–448.

Călinescu, Matei (1977) *Faces of Modernity: Avant-Garde, Decadence, Kitsch*, Bloomington, IN and London: Indiana University Press.

Campbell, David (1998a) *National Deconstruction: Violence, Identity and Justice in Bosnia*, Minneapolis, MN: University of Minnesota Press.

Campbell, David (1998b) *Writing Security: US Foreign Policy and the Politics of Identity*. Revised edn. Minneapolis: University of Minnesota Press.

Cassirer, Ernst (1954) *The Question of Jean-Jacques Rousseau*. Translated and edited with 'Introduction' and 'Additional Notes' by Peter Gay. New York: Columbia University Press.

Cassirer, Ernst (1970) *Rousseau, Kant, Goethe. Two Essays*. Translated by James Gutmann, Paul Oskar Kristeller and John Herman Randall, Jr., Princeton, NJ: Princeton University Press.

Chakrabarty, Dipesh (2008) *Provincializing Europe*, Princeton, NJ: Princeton University Press.

Chatterjee, Partha (1987) *The Nationalist Resolution of the Women's Question*, Calcutta: Centre for Studies in Social Sciences.

Chatterjee, Partha (1993) *Nationalist Thought and the Colonial World: A Derivative Discourse? Third World Books*, London: Zed for the United Nations University.

Chatterjee, Partha (2004) *The Politics of the Governed*, New York: Columbia University Press.

Cheah, Pheng (1998) 'Introduction Part ii: The Cosmopolitical Today' in Cheah, Pheng and Robbins, Bruce (eds) *Cosmopolitics: Thinking and Feeling Beyond the Nation*, Minneapolis: University of Minnesota Press, 20–44.

Cheah, Pheng (2003) *Spectral Nationality: Passages of Freedom from Kant to Postcolonial Literatures of Liberation*, New York: Columbia University Press.

Chow, Rey (1993) *Writing Diaspora: Tactics of Intervention in Contemporary Cultural Studies*, Bloomington, IN: Indiana University Press.

Clifford, James (1986) 'Introduction: Partial Truths' in Clifford, James and Marcus, George (eds) *Writing Cultures: The Poetics and Politics of Ethnography*, Berkeley, CA: University of California Press.

Closs Stephens, Angharad and Squire, Vicki (2012) 'Politics Through a Web: Citizenship and Community Unbound', *Environment and Planning D: Society and Space*, 30 (3): 551–567.

Closs Stephens, Angharad and Vaughan-Williams, Nick (eds) (2009) *Terrorism and the Politics of Response*, London and New York: Routledge.

Cocking, J. M. (1991) *Imagination: A Study in the History of Ideas*, New York and London: Routledge. Edited and with an introduction by Penelope Murray.

Connolly, William E. (1988) *Political Theory and Modernity*, Oxford: Blackwell.

Connolly, William E. (1991) *Identity/Difference: Democratic Negotiations of Political Paradox*, Ithaca, NY: Cornell University Press.

Connolly, William E. (2000) 'Speed, Concentric Culture and Cosmopolitanism', *Political Theory*, 28(5): 596–618.

Connolly, William E. (2004) 'The Complexity of Sovereignty' in Edkins, J., Pin-Fat, V. and Shapiro, M.J. (eds) *Sovereign Lives: Power in Global Politics*, New York and London: Routledge, 23–40.

Connolly, William E. (2005) *Pluralism*, Durham and London: Duke University Press.

Cooper, Melinda (2008) 'Orientalism in the Mirror: The Sexual Politics of Anti-Westernism', *Theory, Culture & Society*, 26 (6): 25–49.

Corlett, William (1989) *Community without Unity: A Politics of Derridean Extravagance*, Durham, NC and London: Duke University Press.

Coward, Martin (2009a) *Urbicide. The Politics of Urban Destruction*, New York and London: Routledge.

Coward, Martin (2009b) 'Jean-Luc Nancy' in Edkins, Jenny and Vaughan-Williams, Nick, *Critical Theorists and International Relations*, London and New York: Routledge, 251–262.

Cowen, Deborah and Gilbert, Emily (eds) (2008) *War, Citizenship, Territory*, London, New York: Routledge.

Crang, Mike (2001) 'Rhythms of the City: Temporalised Space and Motion' in May, Jon and Thrift, Nigel (eds), *Timespace*, London and New York: Routledge, 187–207.

Davis, Mike (1990) *City of Quartz: Excavating the Future in Los Angeles*, London: Verso.

Davis, Mike (2000) *Magical Urbanism: Latinos Reinvent the US City*, London: Verso.

Davis, Mike (2002) *Dead Cities*, New York: New Press.

Deleuze, Gilles (1983) *Nietzsche and Philosophy*. Translated by Hugh Tomlinson. New York: Columbia University Press.

Deleuze, Gilles (1995) *Negotiations*, New York: Columbia University Press.

Der Derian, J. and Shapiro, M (1989) *International/Intertextual Relations: Postmodern Readings of World Politics*, Lexington, MA: Lexington Books.

Derrida, Jacques (1997) *Politics of Friendship*, Verso, London.

Derrida, Jacques (2005) *Rogues: Two Essays on Reason*. Translated by Pascale-Anne Brault and Michael Naas. Stanford, CA: Stanford University Press.

Derrida, Jacques (2006) *Specters of Marx: The State of the Debt, the Work of Mourning and the New International*, New York and London: Routledge Classics.

Devji, Faisal (2005) *Landscapes of the Jihad: Militancy, Morality, Modernity*, Crises in World Politics, London: Hurst & Company.

Dillon, Michael (1996) *Politics of Security: Towards a Political Philosophy of Continental Thought*, London and New York: Routledge.

Donald, James (1999) *Imagining the Modern City*, London: Athlone.

Edelman, Lee (2004) *No Future: Queer Theory and the Death Drive*, Durham, NC: Duke University Press.

Edkins, Jenny (1999) *Poststructuralism and International Relations: Bringing the Political Back In*, London: Lynne Riener Publishers.

Edkins, Jenny (2000) *Whose Hunger? Concepts of Famine, Practices of Aid*, Minneapolis, MN: University of Minnesota Press.

Edkins, Jenny (2003) *Trauma and the Memory of Politics*, Cambridge: Cambridge University Press.

Eisenstein, Zillah (2002) 'Feminisms in the Aftermath of September 11', *Social Text*, 72, 20 (3): 79–99.

Elden, Stuart (2005) 'Missing the Point: Globalization, Deterritorialization and the Space of the World', *Transactions of the Institute of British Geographers*, 30: 8–19.

Elden, Stuart (2009) *Terror and Territory: The Spatial Extent of Sovereignty*, Minneapolis, MN: University of Minnesota Press.

Escobar, Arturo (1995) *Encountering Development: The Making and Unmaking of the Third World*, Princeton, NJ: Princeton University Press.

Fabian, Johannes (1983) *Time and the Other: How Anthropology Makes Its Object*, New York: Columbia University Press.

Fanon, Franz (1971) *The Wretched of the Earth*, Middlesex: Penguin Books.

Fasolt, Constantin (2004) *The Limits of History*, Chicago, IL and London: University of Chicago Press.

Fortier, Anne-Marie (2008) *Multicultural Horizons: Diversity and the Limits of the Civil Nation*, London and New York: Routledge.

Foucault, Michel (1979) *The History of Sexuality*, London: Penguin.

Foucault, Michel (2002) *The Order of Things: An Archaeology of the Human Sciences*, London: Routledge.

Frankenberg, Ruth and Mani, Lata (1993) 'Crosscurrents, Cross Talk. Race, "Postcoloniality" and the Politics of Location', *Cultural Studies*, 7 (2): 292–310.

Frisby, David (1984) *Georg Simmel, Key Sociologists*, Chichester: Horwood.

Frisby, David (1985) *Fragments of Modernity: Theories of Modernity in the Work of Simmel, Kracauer and Benjamin, Social and Political Theory*, Cambridge, MA: Polity Press.

Frisby, David (1987) 'The Ambiguity of Modernity: Georg Simmel and Max Weber', in Mommsen, Wolfgang J. and Osterhammel, Jürgen (eds) *Max Weber and his Contemporaries*, London: Allen & Unwin.

Frisby, David (2001) *Cityscapes of Modernity: Critical Explorations*, Cambridge, MA: Polity Press.

Gellner, Ernest (1983) *Nations and Nationalism, New Perspectives on the Past*, Oxford: Blackwell.

Gilroy, Paul (2004) *After Empire: Melancholia or Convivial Culture?*, London: Routledge.

Gilroy, Paul (2006) 'Multiculture in Times of War: Inaugural Lecture at the London School of Economics', *Critical Quarterly*, 48 (4): 27–45.

Girard, René (1986) *Violence and the Sacred*, Baltimore, MD and London: John Hopkins University Press.

Gokay, Bulent and Walker, R. B. J. (2003) *11 September 2001: War, Terror, Judgement*, London and Portland, OR: Frank Cass.

Graham, Stephen (ed.) (2004) *Cities, War and Terrorism: Towards an Urban Geopolitics*, Oxford: Blackwell.

Graham, Stephen (2010) *Cities under Siege: The New Military Urbanism*, London and New York: Verso.

Graham, Stephen and Marvin, Simon (2001) *Splintering Urbanism*, London: Routledge.

Greenfeld, Leah (1992) *Nationalism: Five Roads to Modernity*, Cambridge, MA and London: Harvard University Press.

Gregory, Derek (1994) *Geographical Imaginations*, Cambridge, MA and Oxford: Blackwell.

Gregory, Derek (2004) *The Colonial Present*, Malden, MA, Oxford and Victoria: Blackwell.

Gregory, Derek and Pred, Allan (eds) (2007) *Violent Geographies: Fear, Terror and Political Violence*, New York and London: Routledge.

Grewal, Inderpal (1996) *Home and Harem*, London: Leicester University Press.

Grewal, Inderpal (2005) *Transnational America: Feminisms, Diasporas, Neoliberalisms*, Durham, NC and London: Duke University Press.

Grosz, Elizabeth A. (1994) *Volatile Bodies: Toward a Corporeal Feminism*, Bloomington, IN: Indiana University Press.

Grosz, Elizabeth A. (1995) *Space, Time and Perversion: Essays on the Politics of Bodies*, New York and London: Routledge.

Grosz, Elizabeth A. (1999a) 'Becoming... An Introduction in Grosz, E. (ed) *Becomings: Explorations in Time, Memory and Futures*, Ithaca, NY and London: Cornell University Press, 1–12.

Grosz, Elizabeth A. (1999b) 'Thinking the New: Of Futures Yet Unthought' in Grosz, E. (ed.) *Becomings: Explorations in Time, Memory, and Futures*, Ithaca, NY and London: Cornell University Press, 15–28.

Grosz, Elizabeth A. (2005) *Time Travels: Feminism, Nature, Power*, Durham, NC: Duke University Press.

Gunew, Sneja (2004) *Haunted Nations. The Colonial Dimensions of Multiculturalism*, London and New York: Routledge.

Gunnell, John Gilbert (1968) *Political Philosophy and Time*, Middletown, CT: Wesleyan University Press.

Gupta, Akhil and Ferguson, James (1992) 'Beyond "Culture": Space, Identity, and the Politics of Difference', *Cultural Anthropology*, 7 (1): 6–23.

Hacking, Ian (2000) *The Social Construction of What?*, Harvard, MA: Harvard University Press.

Hage, Ghassan (1996) 'The Spatial Imaginaries of National Practices: Dwelling-domesti-cating/Being-exterminating', *Environment and Planning D: Society and Space*, 14: 463–485.

Hage, Ghassan (1998) *White Supremacy: Fantasies of White Supremacy in a Multicultural Society*, Annandale, NSW: Pluto Press.

Halbwachs, Maurice (1992) *On Collective Memory*, Chicago, IL: University of Chicago Press.

Hamid, Mohsin (2007) *The Reluctant Fundamentalist*, London: Hamish Hamilton.

Haraway, Donna Jeanne (1991) *Simians, Cyborgs, and Women: The Re-Invention of Nature*, London: Free Association.

Harootunian, Harry (2000) *Overcome by Modernity: History, Community and Culture in Interwar Japan*, Princeton, NJ: Princeton University Press.

Harrison, Paul (2010) 'The Broken Thread: On Being Still' in Bissell, D. and Fuller, G. (eds), *Stillness in a Mobile World*, London: Routledge.

Harvey, David (1989) *The Urban Experience*, Baltimore: Johns Hopkins University Press.

Harvey, David (2003) *Paris, Capital of Modernity*, New York and London: Routledge.

Hechter, Michael (1975) *Internal Colonialism: The Celtic Fringe in British National Development, 1536–1966*, Berkeley, CA: University of California Press.

Hechter, Michael (2000) *Containing Nationalism*, New York: Oxford University Press.

Helliwell, Christine and Hindess, Barry (2005) 'The temporalizing of difference', *Ethnicities*, 5 (3): 414–418.

Hemmings, Clare (2011) *Why Stories Matter: The Political Grammar of Feminist Theory*, Durham and London: Duke University Press.

Hennis, Wilhelm (1988) *Max Weber: Essays in Reconstruction*, London: Allen & Unwin.

Hill, Andrew (2009) *Re-imagining the War on Terror: Seeing, Waiting, Travelling*, Basing-stoke, Palgrave.

Hill Collins, P. (1990) *Black Feminist Thought: Knowledge, Consciousness, and the Politics of Empowerment*, New York: Routledge.

Hindess, Barry (2007) 'The Past is Another Culture', *International Political Sociology*, 1 (4): 325–338.

Hindess, Barry (2008) 'Been There, Done That...', *Postcolonial Studies*, 11 (2): 201–213.

Hobbes, Thomas (1996) *Leviathan*, Cambridge: Cambridge University Press. Edited by Richard Tuck.

Hobsbawm, Eric J. (1990) *Nations and Nationalism Since 1780. Programme, Myth, Reality*, Cambridge: Cambridge University Press.

Hobsbawm, Eric J. and Ranger, Terence O. (eds) (1992) *The Invention of Tradition*, Cambridge: Cambridge University Press.

Holston, James and Appadurai, Arjun (1999) 'Introduction: Cities and Citizenship' in Holston, J. (ed.) *Cities and Citizenship*, Durham, NC: Duke University Press.

Honig, Bonnie (2001) *Democracy and the Foreigner*, Princeton, NJ: Princeton University Press.

Hooks, B. (1982) *Ain't I a Woman? Black Women and Feminism*, London: Pluto Press.

Hooks, Bell (1984) *Feminist Theory from Margin to Center*, Boston, MA: South End Press.

Hooks, Bell (1989) *Talking Back: Thinking Feminist, Thinking Black*, London: Sheba Feminist.

Horowitz, Asher (1987) *Rousseau, Nature, and History*, Toronto and London: University of Toronto Press.

Huntington, Samuel P. (1993) 'The Clash of Civilizations?', *Foreign Affairs*, Summer, 72 (3).

Hutchings, Kimberly (2008) *Time and World Politics: Thinking the Present*, Manchester: Manchester University Press.

Hutchinson, John and Smith, Anthony D. (1994) *Nationalism*, Oxford: Oxford University Press.

Huysmans, Jef (2006) *The Politics of Insecurity: Fear, Migration and Asylum in the EU*, Oxford: Routledge.

Huyssen, Andreas (2003) *Present Pasts: Urban Palimpsests and the Politics of Memory*, Stanford, CA: Stanford University Press.

Inayatullah, Naeem and Blaney, David L. (2004) *International Relations and the Problem of Difference*, New York and London: Routledge.

Inayatullah, Naeem and Blaney, David L. (2010) *Savage Economics: Wealth, Poverty and the Temporal Walls of Capitalism*, New York and London: Routledge.

Isin, Engin F. (2002) *Being Political*, Minneapolis, MN: University of Minnesota Press.

Isin, Engin F. (2007) 'City. State: Critique of Scalar Thought', *Citizenship Studies*, 11 (2): 211–228.

Jabri, Vivienne (2009) 'Security, Multiculturalism and the Cosmopolis' in Closs Stephens, A. and Vaughan-Williams, N. (eds) *Terrorism and the Politics of Response*, London, New York: Routledge.

Jackson, Richard, Breen Smyth, Marie, Gunning, Jeroen and Jarvis, Lee (eds) (2011) *Terrorism: A Critical Introduction*, Basingstoke: Palgrave Macmillan.

James, Paul (2006) *Globalism, Nationalism, Tribalism: Bringing Theory Back In*, London, Thousand Oaks, CA and New Delhi: Sage.

Jarvis, Lee (2009) *Times of Terror: Discourse, Temporality and the War on Terror*, Basingstoke: Palgrave.

Kedourie, Elie (1993) *Nationalism*, Oxford and Malden, MA: Blackwell. Reprinted with new foreword by Sylvia Kedourie.

Keith, Michael (2005) *After Cosmopolitanism: Multicultural Cities and the Future of Racism*, London: Routledge.

Kelly, John D. (1998) 'Time and the Global: Against the Homogenous, Empty Communities in Contemporary Social Theory', *Development and Change*, 29: 839–871.

Kern, Stephen (1983) *The Culture of Time and Space 1880–1918*, London: Weidenfeld & Nicolson.

Kingsolver, Barbara (2009) *The Lacuna*, London: Faber and Faber.

Ladd, Brian (1997) *The Ghosts of Berlin: Confronting German History in the Urban Landscape*, Chicago, IL and London: University of Chicago Press.

Lash, Scott and Whimster, Sam (eds) (1987) *Max Weber, Rationality and Modernity*, London: Allen & Unwin.

Lefebvre, Henri (1995) *Introduction to Modernity: Twelve Preludes, September 1959–May 1961*. Translated by John Moore. London and New York: Verso.

Lefebvre, Henri (1996) *Writings on Cities*. Translated and edited by Eleonore Kofman and Elizabeth Lebas. Oxford: Blackwell.

Lefebvre, Henri (2004) *Rhythmanalysis. Space, Time and Everyday life*. Translated by Stuart Elden and Gerald Moore, with an introduction by Stuart Elden. London and New York: Continuum.

Lichtenstein, Rachel (2007) *On Brick Lane*, London: Hamish Hamilton.

Ling, L. H. M. (2010) 'Who is an American?', *International Political Sociology*, 4 (1): 99–103.

Lisle, Debbie (2006a) *The Global Politics of Contemporary Travel Writing*, Cambridge: Cambridge University Press.

Lisle, Debbie (2006b) 'Sublime Lessons: Education and Ambivalence in War Exhibitions', *Millennium: Journal of International Studies*, 34 (3): 841–862.

Livingstone, David N. (1992) *The Geographical Tradition, Episodes in the History of a Contested Enterprise*, Oxford: Blackwell.

Lloyd, Moya (2008) 'Towards a Cultural Politics of Vulnerability: Precarious Lives and Ungrievable Deaths' in Carver, Tervell and Chambers, Samuel (eds) *Judith Butler's Precarious Politics: Critical Encounters*, London and New York: Routledge, 92–106.

Lorde, Audre (2007) *Sister Outsider: Essays and Speeches by Audre Lorde*, Berkeley, CA: The Crossing Press.

Luke, Timothy (2010) 'From "Am I an American?" to "I Am an American!" Cynthia Weber on Citizenship, Identity, and Security', *International Political Sociology*, 4 (1): 85–89.

McClintock, Anne (1995) *Imperial Leather: Race, Gender and Sexuality in the Colonial Context*, London: Routledge.

McRobbie, Angela (2006) 'Vulnerability, Violence and (Cosmopolitan) Ethics: Butler's Precarious Life', *The British Journal of Sociology*, 57 (1): 69–86.

McRobbie, Angela (2009) *The Aftermath of Feminism: Gender, Culture and Social Change*, Los Angeles, CA and London: Sage.

Magnusson, Warren (2000) 'Hyperspace: A Political Ontology of the Global City' in Ericson, Richard V. and Stehr, Nico (eds) *Governing Modern Societies*, Toronto and London: University of Toronto Press, 80–104.

Magnusson, Warren (2012) *Politics of Urbanism: Seeing like a City*, London and New York: Routledge.

Mamdani Mahmood (2002) 'Good Muslim, Bad Muslim: A Political Perspective on Culture and Terrorism', *American Anthropologist*, 104 (3): 766–775.

Manzo, Kathryn (1996) *Creating Boundaries: The Politics of Race and Nation*, Boulder, CO and London: Lynne Rienner.

Marx, Anthony W. (2003) *Faith in Nation: Exclusionary Origins of Nationalism*, Oxford: Oxford University Press.

Massey, Doreen B. (2005) *For Space*, London: Sage.

Massey, Doreen (2007) *World City*, Cambridge, MA: Polity Press.

Masters, Cristina and Dauphinee, Elizabeth (eds) (2007) *The Logics of Biopower and the War on Terror: Living, Dying, Surviving*, London: Palgrave Macmillan.

Masters, Roger D. (1976) *The Political Philosophy of Rousseau*, Princeton, NJ: Princeton University Press.

Mayer, Jane (2009) *The Dark Side: The Inside Story of How the War on Terror Turned into a War on American Ideals*, New York: Anchor Books.

Mbembe, Achille (2001) *On the Postcolony*, Berkeley, CA, Los Angeles, CA and London: University of California Press.

Mbembe, Achille and Nuttall, Sarah (2004) 'Writing the World from an African Metropolis', *Public Culture* 16 (3): 347–372.

Mignolo, Walter (2000) *Local Histories/Global Designs: Coloniality, Subaltern Knowledge and Border Thinking*, Princeton, NJ: Princeton University Press.

Minogue, Kenneth R. (1967) *Nationalism*, London: B.T. Brasford.

Mistry, Rohinton (1996) *A Fine Balance*, London: Faber and Faber.

Mohanty, Chandra Talpade (1991) 'Under Western Eyes: Feminist Scholarship and Colonial Discourse', in Mohanty, Chandra Talpade, Russo, Ann and Torres, Lourdes (eds) *Third World Women and the Politics of Feminism*, Bloomington, IN: Indiana University Press, 51–80.

Mommsen, Wolfgang J. (1984) *Max Weber and German Politics, 1890–1920*, Chicago: University of Chicago Press.

Moraga, Cherrie and Anzaldúa, Gloria (1981) *This Bridge Called My Back: Writings by Radical Women of Color*, New York: Kitchen Table.

Morgenstern, Mira (2009) 'Politics in/of the City: Love, Modernity, and Strangeness in the City of Jean-Jacques Rousseau' in Blackell, Mark, Duncan, John and Kow, Simon (eds) *Rousseau and Desire*, Toronto: University of Toronto Press, 165–186.

Mumford, Lewis (1973) *The City in History: Its Origins, Its Transformations, and Its Prospects*, Harmondsworth: Penguin.

Nairn, Tom (1997) *Faces of Nationalism: Janus Revisited*, London: Verso.

Nancy, Jean-Luc (1991) *The Inoperative Community*. Translated by Peter Connor, Lisa Garbus, Michael Holland and Simona Sawhney. Foreword by Christopher Fynsk. Minneapolis, MN: University of Minnesota Press. Edited by Peter Connor.

Nancy, Jean-Luc (2000) *Being Singular Plural*. Translated by Robert D. Richardson and Anne E. O'Byrne. Stanford, CA: Stanford University Press.

Nancy, Jean-Luc (2003) 'In Praise of the Melee', in *A Finite Thinking*, Stanford, CA: Stanford University Press. Edited by Simon Sparks.

Nandy, Ashis (1987) *Traditions, Tyranny and Utopias: Essays in the Politics of Awareness*, Delhi and Oxford: Oxford University Press.

Nandy, Ashis (1988) *The Intimate Enemy: Loss and Recovery of Self under Colonialism*, Delhi and Oxford: Oxford University Press.

Nandy, Ashis (1994) *The Illegitimacy of Nationalism: Rabindranath Tagore and the Politics of Self*, Delhi and Oxford: Oxford University Press.

Neal, Andrew (2008) 'Goodbye War on Terror' in Dillon, Michael and Neal, Andrew (eds) *Foucault on Politics, Security and War*, Basingstoke, Hampshire: Palgrave Macmillan.

Neal, Andrew (2010) *Exceptionalism and the Politics of Counter-terrorism*, New York and London: Routledge.

Nietzsche, Friedrich (2003) *Beyond Good and Evil*. Introduction by Michael Tanner. Translated by R. J. Hollingdale. London: Penguin Classics.

Nora, Pierre (1989) 'Between Memory and History' in Nora, PIerre and Kritzman, Lawrence D. (eds) *Realms of Memory: Rethinking the French Past*, New York: Columbia University Press, 1–20.

Nussbaum, Martha C. and Cohen, Joshua (2002) *For Love of Country: Debating the Limits of Patriotism*, Boston, MA: Beacon Press.

Opondo, Samson O (2008) 'Genre and the African City: The Politics and Poetics of Urban Rhythms', *Journal for Cultural Research*, 12 (1): 59–79.

Oza, Rupal (2007) 'Contrapuntal Geographies of Threat and Security: US, India, and Israel', *Environment and Planning D: Society and Space*, 25 (1): 9–32.

Özkirimli, Umut (2003) 'The Nation as an Artichoke? A Critique of Ethnosymbolist Interpretations of Nationalism', *Nations and Nationalism*, 9 (3): 339–55.

Pain, Rachel and Smith, Susan J. (eds), Fear, Critical Geopolities and Everyday Life, Aldershot: Ashgate.

Painter, Joe (2012) 'The Politics of the Neighbour', *Environment and Planning D: Society and Space*, 30 (3): 515–533.

Park, Robert Ezra, Burgess, Ernest Watson and Mackenzie, Roderick Duncan (1967) *The City*, Chicago, IL and London: University of Chicago Press.

Pedwell, Carolyn (2010) *Feminism, Culture and Embodied Practice: The Rhetorics of Comparison*, London: Routledge.

Pile, Steve and Thrift, Nigel (eds) (2000) *City A–Z*, London: Routledge.

Pollock, Sheldon, Bhabha, Homi K., Breckenridge, Carol A. and Chakrabarty, Dipesh (2000) 'Cosmopolitanisms', *Public Culture*, 12 (3): 577–589.

Puar, Jasbir (2007) *Terrorist Assemblages: Homonationalism in Queer Times*, Durham, NC and London: Duke University Press.

Rajaram, Prem Kumar and Grundy-Warr, Carl (2007) *Borderscapes: Hidden Geographies and Politics at Territory's Edge*, Minneapolis, MN: University of Minnesota Press.

Rancière, Jacques (1999) *Disagreement. Politics and Philosophy*. Translated by Julie Rose. Minneapolis, MN: University of Minnesota Press.

Razack, 2008 *Casting Out: The Eviction of Muslims from Western Law and Politics*, Toronto: University of Toronto Press.

Redfield, Marc (1999) 'Imagi-Nation: The Imagined Community and the Aesthetics of Mourning', *Diacritics*, 29 (4): 58–83.

Reid, Julian (2009) *The Biopolitics of the War on Terror: Life Struggles, Liberal Modernity and the Defence of Logistical Societies*, Manchester: Manchester University Press.

Richie, Alexandra (1998) *Faust's Metropolis: A History of Berlin*, London: HarperCollins.

Richter, Gerhard (2007) *Thought-Images: Frankfurt School Writers' Reflections from Damaged Life*, Stanford, CA: Stanford University Press.

Riley, Denise (1988) *'Am I That Name?' Feminism and the Category of 'Women' in History*, Basingstoke: Macmillan.

Robbins, Bruce (1998) 'Introduction Part i: Actually Existing Cosmopolitanism' in Cheah, Pheng and Robbins, Bruce (eds) *Cosmopolitics: Thinking and Feeling Beyond the Nation*, Minneapolis, MN: University of Minnesota Press, 1–19.

Rousseau, Jean Jacques (1992) *Discourse on the Origin of Inequality*. Translated by Donald A. Cress. Indianapolis, IN: Hackett.

Rousseau, Jean-Jacques (1997) *Rousseau: The Social Contract and Other Later Political Writings*, Cambridge: Cambridge University Press. Edited by Victor Gourevitch.

Said, Edward W. (1990) 'American Intellectuals and Middle East Politics' in Robbins, B. (ed.) *Intellectuals: Aesthetics, Politics, Academics*, Minneapolis, MN: University of Minnesota Press, 135–52.

Said, Edward W. (2005) *Orientalism*, London: Penguin.

Sallis, John (2000) *Force of Imagination: The Sense of the Elemental*, Bloomington and Indianapolis, IN: Indiana University Press.

Sandercock, Leonie (1998) *Towards Cosmopolis: Planning for Multicultural Cities*, London: Wiley and Sons.

Scaff, Lawrence A. (1989) *Fleeing the Iron Cage: Culture, Politics and Modernity in the Thought of Max Weber*, Berkeley, CA and London: University of California Press.

Scholem, G. G. (2001) *Walter Benjamin: The Story of a Friendship*, New York: New York Review Books.

Sedgwick, Eve Kosofsky (1990) *Epistemology of the Closet*, Berkeley, CA: University of California Press.

Sennett, Richard (1971) *The Uses of Disorder*, New York: Vintage Books.

Seth, Sanjay (2001) 'Liberalism and the Politics of (Multi)culture: Or, Plurality Is Not Difference', *Postcolonial Studies*, 4 (1): 65–77.

Seth, Sanjay (2007) *Subject Lessons: The Western Education of Colonial India*, Durham, NC: Duke University Press.

Seth Sanjay (2009) 'Reason Unhinged: The Non-Western World and Modern, Western Knowledge'. Inaugural address, 13 January; copy available from Professor Sanjay Seth, Department of Politics, Goldsmiths College, University of London.

Shapiro, Michael J. (2000) 'National Times and Other Times: Rethinking Citizenship', *Cultural Studies*, 14 (1): 79–98.

Shapiro, Michael J. (2004) *Methods and Nations: Cultural Governance and the Indigenous Subject*, London and New York: Routledge.

Shapiro, Michael J. (2010) *The Time of the City: Politics, Philosophy and Genre*, New York and London: Routledge.

Shohat, Ella (2002) 'Area Studies, Gender Studies and the Cartographies of Knowledge', *Social Text*, 72, 20 (3): 67–78.

Shaw, Karena (2004) 'Knowledge, Foundations, Politics', *International Studies Review*, 6: 7–20.

Shaw, Karena (2008) *Indigeneity and Political Theory: Sovereignty and the Limits of the Political*, New York and London: Routledge.

Sidhwa, Bapsi (1989) *Ice-Candy Man*, Penguin.

Simmel, Georg (1971) 'The Metropolis and Mental Life' in Levine, Donald N. (ed.) *On Individuality and Social Forms: Selected Writings*, Chicago and London: University of Chicago Press, 324–39.

Simone, AbdouMaliq (2004) *For the City Yet to Come: Changing African Life in Four Cities*, Durham, NC: Duke University Press.

Simone, AbdouMaliq (2011) 'The Surfacing of Urban Life, *City*, 15 (3–4): 355–364.

Sinclair, Iain (2002) *London Orbital: A Walk Around the M25*, London: Granta.

Sinclair, Iain (2006) *London: City of Disappearances*, London: Hamish Hamilton.

Slaughter, James (2007) *Human Rights Inc.*, New York: Fordham University Press.

Smith, Anthony D. (1986) *The Ethnic Origins of Nations*, Oxford: Basil Blackwell.

Smith, Anthony D. (1991) 'The Nation: Invented, Imagined, Reconstructed?', *Millennium: Journal of International Studies*, 20: 353–368.

Smith, Anthony D. (1995) *Nations and Nationalism in a Global Era*, Cambridge: Polity Press.

Smith, Anthony D. (1998) *Nationalism and Modernism: A Critical Survey of Recent Theories of Nations and Nationalism*, London: Routledge.

Smith, Anthony D. (2001) *Nationalism: Theory, Ideology, History, Key Concepts*, Cambridge, MA: Polity Press.

Smith, Gary (ed.) (1989) *Benjamin: Philosophy, Aesthetics, History*, Chicago, IL: University of Chicago Press.

Soja, Edward W. (1996) *Thirdspace: Journeys to Los Angeles and Other Real-and-Imagined Places*, Oxford: Blackwell.

Solnit, Rebecca (2001) *Wanderlust: A History of Walking*, London: Verso.

Solnit, Rebecca (2006) *A Field Guide to Getting Lost*, Edinburgh: Canongate.

Sparke, Matthew (2005) *In the Space of Theory: Postfoundational Geographies of the Nation State*, Minneapolis, MN: University of Minnesota Press.

Spelman, Elizabeth V. (1988) *Inessential Woman: Problems of Exclusion in Feminist Thought*, Boston, MA: Beacon Press.

Spivak, Gayatri Chakravorty (1988) 'Can The Subaltern Speak?' in Nelson, C. and Grossberg, L. (eds) *Marxism and the Interpretation of Culture*, Urbana, IL: University of Illinois Press, 271–313.

Spivak, Gayatri Chakravorty (1996) in Landry, Donna and MacLean, Gerald M. (eds) *The Spivak Reader: Selected Works of Gayatri Chakravorty Spivak*, New York and London: Routledge.

Spivak, Gayatri Chakravorty (1999) *A Critique of Postcolonial Reason*, Cambridge, MA and London: Harvard University Press.

Starobinski, Jean (1988) *Jean-Jacques Rousseau, Transparency and Obstruction*, Chicago and London: University of Chicago Press.

Steger, Manfred (2008) *The Rise of the Global Imaginary*, Oxford: Oxford University Press.

Steiner, George (1961) *The Death of Tragedy*, London: Faber and Faber.

Steiner, George (2001) *Grammars of Creation*, London: Faber and Faber.

Swanton, Dan (2010) 'Sorting Bodies: Race, Affect, and Everyday Multiculture in a Mill Town in Northern England', *Environment and Planning A*, 42: 2332–2350.

Sylvester, Christine (1994) *Feminist Theory and International Relations in a Postmodern Era*, Cambridge: Cambridge University Press.

Thrift, Nigel (2000) '"Not a Straight Line But a Curve", or, Cities Are Not Mirrors of Modernity', in Bell, David and Haddour, Azzedine (eds) *City Visions*, London: Longman, 233–263.

Till, Karen E (2005) *The New Berlin: Memory, Politics, Place*, Minneapolis, MN: University of Minnesota Press.

Toal, Gerard (2006) 'Samuel Huntington and the "Civilising" of Global Space' in O'Toal, G., Dalby, S. and Routledge, P. (eds) *The Geopolitics Reader*, London: Routledge.

Tolia-Kelly, Divya (2010) *Landscape, Race and Memory: Material Ecologies of Citizenship*, Farnham: Ashgate.

Tolstoy, Leo (2003) *Anna Karenina: A Novel in Eight Parts*, London: Penguin.

Tonkiss, Fran (2005) *Space, the City and Social Theory: Social Relations and Urban Forms*, Cambridge, MA: Polity Press.

Tulloch, John (2006) *One Day in July: Experiencing 7/7*, London: Little, Brown.

Valentine, Gill (2008) 'Living with Difference: Reflections on Geographies of Encounter', *Progress in Human Geography*, 32: 323–337.

Vaughan-Williams, Nick (2009a) 'The Shooting of Jean Charles de Menezes: New Border Politics?', in Closs Stephens, A. and Vaughan-Williams, N. (eds) *Terrorism and the Politics of Response*, London and New York: Routledge.

Vaughan-Williams, Nick (2009b) *Border Politics: The Limits of Sovereign Power*, Edinburgh: Edinburgh University Press.

Viroli, Maurizio (1995) *For Love of Country: An Essay on Patriotism and Nationalism*, Oxford, Clarendon Press.

Volpp, Leti (2002) 'The Citizen and the Terrorist', *UCLA Law Review*, 49: 1575.

Walker, R. B. J. (1993) *Inside/Outside: International Relations as Political Theory*, Cambridge: Cambridge University Press.

Walker, R. B. J. (2009) *After the Globe, Before the World*, London and New York: Routledge.

Walker, R. B. J. (2011) 'World, Politics', *Contemporary Political Theory*, 10 (2): 303–310.

Ware, Vron (1992) *Beyond the Pale: White Women, Racism and History*, London and New York: Verso.

Ware, Vron (2006) 'Info-War and the Politics of Feminist Curiosity', *Cultural Studies*, 20 (6): 526–551.

Waswo, Richard (1997) *The Founding Legend of Western Civilization: From Virgil to Vietnam*, Hanover, NH and London: University Press of New England.

Weber, Cynthia (1995) *Simulating Sovereignty: Intervention, the State and Symbolic Exchange*, Cambridge: Cambridge University Press.

Weber, Cynthia (2010) 'Citizenship, Security, Humanity', *International Political Sociology*, 4 (1): 80–85.

Weber, Max (1994a) 'The Nation State and Economic Policy' in Lassman, Peter and Speirs, Ronald (eds) *Weber: Political Writings*, Cambridge and New York: Cambridge University Press, 1–28.

Weber, Max (1994b) 'Between Two Laws' in Lassman, Peter and Speirs, Ronald (eds) *Weber: Political Writings*, Cambridge and New York: Cambridge University Press, 75–79.

Weber, Max (1994c) 'The Profession and Vocation of Politics' in Lassman, Peter and Speirs, Ronald (eds) *Weber: Political Writings*, Cambridge and New York: Cambridge University Press, 309–369.

Weber, Max (2001) *The Protestant Ethic and the Spirit of Capitalism*. Translated by Talcott Parsons with an Introduction by Anthony Giddens. London: Routledge.

Webster's Third New International Dictionary (1971) Massachusetts, USA: G & C Merriam Company. Editor in Chief: Philip Babcock Gove.

Williams, Daniel (ed.) (2003) *Who Speaks for Wales?: Nation, Culture, Identity, Raymond Williams*, Cardiff: University of Wales Press.

Williams, Raymond (1985) *The Country and the City*, London: Hogarth Press.

Williams, Raymond (2009) 'The Tenses of Imagination' in Milner, A (ed.) *Tenses of Imagination: Raymond Williams on Science Fiction, Utopia and Dystopia*, Bern: Peter Lang.

Wilson, Helen F (2011) 'Passing Propinquities in the Multicultural City: The Everyday Encounters of Bus Passengering', *Environment and Planning A*, 43: 634–649.

Winter, Jay (1995) *Sites of Memory, Sites of Mourning: The Great War in European Cultural History*, Cambridge: Cambridge University Press.

Wokler, Robert (1978) 'Perfectible Apes in Decadent Cultures: Rousseau's Anthropology Revisited', *Daedalus*, 107 (3): 107–134.

Wokler, Robert (1987) *Social Thought of J. J. Rousseau, Political Theory and Political Philosophy*, New York and London: Garland.

Wokler, Robert (1998) 'The Enlightenment and the French Revolutionary Birth Pangs of Modernity', in Heilbron, Johan, Magnusson, Lars and Wittrock, Bjorn (eds) *The Rise of the Social Sciences and the Formation of Modernity: Conceptual Change in Context, 1750–1850*, Dordrecht and London: Kluwer Academic, 35–76.

Wokler, Robert (2000) 'The Enlightenment, the Nation-State and the Primal Patricide of Modernity', in Geras, Norman and Wokler, Robert (eds) *The Enlightenment and Modernity*, Basingstoke: MacMillan Press and New York: St Martin's Press: 161–183.

Wokler, Robert (2001) *Rousseau: A Very Short Introduction*, Oxford: Oxford University Press, 2001. Second edn.

Xenos, Nicholas (1996) 'Civic Nationalism: Oxymoron?', *Critical Review*, 10 (2): 213–231.

Yiftachel, Oren (2002) 'Territory as the Kernel of the Nation: Space, Time and Nationalism in Israel/Palestine', *Geopolitics*, 7 (2): 215–248.

Young, Iris Marion (1990) *Justice and the Politics of Difference*, Princeton, NJ: Princeton University Press.

Young, James E. (1993) *The Texture of Memory: Holocaust Memorials and Meaning*, New Haven, CT: Yale University Press.

Young, Robert (2004) *White Mythologies: Writing History and the West*, Abingdon, Oxford: Routledge.

Zachariah, Benjamin (2008) 'Residual Nationalism and the Indian (Radical?) Intellectual: On Indigenism, Authenticity and the Coloniser's Presents', in Bhattacharya, Debraj (ed.) *Of Matters Modern*, Calcutta: Seagull Books.

Zehfuss, Maja ((2002a) *Constructivism in International Relations: The Politics of Reality*, Cambridge: Cambridge University Press.

Zehfuss, Maja ((2002b) 'Forget September 11', *Third World Quarterly: Journal of Emerging Areas*, 24 (3): 513–528.

Zehfuss, Maja ((2009) 'Hierarchies of Grief and the Possibility of War: Remembering UK Fatalities in Iraq', *Millennium* 38 (2): 1–22.

Zehfuss, Maja ((2007) *Wounds of Memory: The Politics of War in Germany*, Cambridge: Cambridge University Press.

Žižek, S (2009) *First as Tragedy, Then as Farce*, London: Verso.

Government reports

'Government Response to the Intelligence and Security Committee's Report into the London Terrorist Attacks on 7 July 2005' (2006) London: The Stationery Office.

'Report of the Official Account of the Bombings in London on 7th July 2005' (2006) London: The Stationery Office.

'Report into the London Terrorist Attacks on 7 July 2005' (2006) London: The Stationery Office, Chaired by Rt Hon Paul Murphy MP.

'Report of the 7 July Review Committee to the London Assembly' (2006) Greater London Authority, Chaired by Richard Barnes MP.

Newspaper articles and political speeches

Blair, Tony (2005) 'We Will Hold True to the British Way of Life'. Press Release 7 July. Available at www.guardian.co.uk/print/0,,5233964-111274,00.html.

Blair, Tony (2006) 'Not a Clash of Civilisations, but Rather a Clash About Civilisation'. Press Release 21 March. Available at www.number10.gov.uk/output/Page9222.asp.

Freedland, Jonathan (2006) 'How London Carried On', *The Guardian*, 7 July.

Graham, Stephen (2012) 'Olympics 2012 Security: Welcome to Lockdown London', *The Guardian*, 12 March.

Halaby, Laila (2007) 'Return of the Native', *The Washington Post*, 22 April. Available at www.washingtonpost.com/wp-dyn/content/article/2007/04/19/AR2007041903000.html.

Hussein, Aamer (2007) 'A Jester Among the Jihadis', *The Independent*, 23 March.

Livingstone, Ken (2005) 'London Will Not Be Divided'. Press release 7 July. Available at www.london.gov.uk/londoner/05aug/mayors-message.jsp.

London Assembly (2006a) 'Only United Communities Will Defeat Terrorism and Protect

Civil Liberties'. Press release 26 August. Available at www.london.gov.uk/view_press_release.jsp?releaseid=5795.

London Assembly (2006b) 'One London'. Press release 6 December. Available at www.london.gov.uk/onelondon.

Manthorpe, Rowland (2006) 'Spirit of the Brits', *The Guardian*, 1 July: 21–22.

Obama, Barack (2008) 'Full Text: Obama's Victory Speech', *BBC News Online*, 4 November. Available at http://news.bbc.co.uk/1/hi/world/americas/us_elections_2008/7710038.stm.

Obama, Barack (2009) 'Text: Obama's Speech in Cairo', *The New York Times*, 4 June. Available at www.nytimes.com/2009/06/04/us/politics/04obama.text.html?_r=1&pagewanted=all.

Olsson, Karen (2007) 'I Pledge Allegiance', *New York Times*, 22 April.

Roy, Arundhati (2002) 'Not Again', *The Guardian*, 30 September. Available at www.guardian.co.uk/world/2002/sep/30/usa.iraq.

Tomasky, Michael (2010) 'We Miss You, George Bush', *The Guardian*, 11 August. Available at www.guardian.co.uk/commentisfree/michaeltomasky/2010/aug/11/congress-usimmigration-how-bush-moderated-gop-extremism.

Transport for London, Mayor of London, British Transport Police, Metropolitan Police Service, City of London Police (2005) 'It's Up To All of Us'. Press release 28 November. Available at www.tfl.gov.uk/tfl/press-centre/press-releases/press-releases-content.asp?prID=603.

'In the Face of Danger' (2005) *The Guardian* (Editorial), 8 July.

'A Dark Day from Which We Will Emerge Stronger' (2005) *The Telegraph* (Editorial), 8 July.

'Muslims Told Not to Travel as Retaliation Fears Grow' (2005) *The Independent*, 8 July.

'What the Papers Say' (2005) *The Guardian*, 8 July.

Films

Ken Loach (2002) *11'09"01: Segment, UK*.

Ken Loach (2006) *The Wind That Shakes The Barley*.

Mira Nair (2002) *11'09"01: Segment, India*.

Cynthia Weber (2007) *I Am an American: Portraits of Post-9/11 US Citizens*.

Films available at www.opendemocracy.net/article/democracy_power/america_power_world/citizen_identity.

Architectural designs and art installations

'Flailing Trees' by Gustav Metzger. First exhibited at the Manchester International Festival, 3–19 July 2009. Available at http://mif.co.uk/event/flailing-garden.

Historic Photographs No 1: Hitler Addressing the Reichstag after the Fall of France, July 1940 (1995) and *Historic Photographs No 1: Liquidation of the Warsaw Ghetto, April 19–28 days, 1943* (1995), both by Gustav Metzger. First exhibited at *Damaged Nature: Two New Works and Documents*, solo exhibition work for the eye to do, Hamilton Street, London (Breitwieser, 1995).

The Jewish Museum, Lindenstraße 9–14, 10969 Berlin. Designed by Daniel Libeskind. First opened as an empty building in 1999; opened as a museum in 2001. Avilable at www.jmberlin.de/main/EN/homepage-EN.php.

The 'Missing House', 15/16 Grosse Hamburgerstrasse, Berlin. Designed by Christian Boltanski. Produced 1990.

The Memorial to the Murdered Jews of Europe, Cora-Berliner-Straße 1, 10117 Berlin. Designed by Peter Eisenman. Field of columns and exhibition centre opened to the public 12 May 2005. Available at www.stiftung-denkmal.de/en/memorials/the-memorial-to-the-murdered-jews-of-europe/history.html#c957.

Exhibition materials, interviews and responses to architectural designs and installations

Breitwieser, Sabine (ed.) (1995) *Gustav Metzger, History History*, Vienna: Generali Foundation, 67–82.

Derrida, Jacques (1992) 'Response to Daniel Libeskind', *Research in Phenomenology*, 22: 88–94.

Eisenman, Peter (1992) Interview prepared by S. Kwinter and F. Levrat, *Architecture d'aujourd hui*, 279: 98–115.

Eisenman, Peter (2005) 'Holocaust Memorial, Berlin', *Architecture and Urbanism*, 8 (419): 52–53.

Jewish Museum Berlin (2001) *Stories of an Exhibition: Two Millennia of German Jewish History*, Berlin: Jüdisches Museum im Berlin Museum.

Kipnis, Jeffrey and Leeser, Thomas, (eds) (1997) *Chora L. Works: Jacques Derrida and Peter Eisenman*, New York: Monacelli Press.

Latour, Bruno (2011) 'Some Experiments in Art and Politics', *e-flux journal*, 23: 1–7 July 2007.

Libeskind, Daniel (1992) 'Between the Lines: The Jewish Museum, Berlin', *Research in Phenomenology*, 22, 82–87.

Libeskind, Daniel (2001) *The Space of Encounter*, London: Thames & Hudson.

Libeskind, Daniel (2007) *Jewish Museum Berlin*, Munich: Prestel Verlag. Fifth edn.

Metzger, Gustav (2007) 'Protest and Survive'. Interview by Mark Godfrey. *Frieze*, June–August, 196–203.

Metzger, Gustav (2009a) Programme Notes, Manchester International Festival, 2–19 July.

Metzger, Gustav (2009b) Podcast from the Manchester International Festival website. Available at www.mif.co.uk [accessed 3 July 2009].

Page, Max, (2005) 'Memory Field', *Architecture*, 94 (6): 38–45.

Schlör, Joachim (2005) *Denkmal für die ermordeten Juden Europas/Memorial to the Murdered Jews in Europe*. Translated by Paul Aston. Munich: Prestel Verlag.

Schlusche, Gunter (2005) *Materials on the Memorial to the Murdered Jews of Europe*. Berlin: Foundation for the Memorial to the Murdered Jews of Europe.

Solomon-Godeau, Abigail (1998), 'Mourning or Melancholia: Christian Boltanski's "Missing House"', *Oxford Art Journal*, 21 (2): 3–20.

Wilson, A (2005) 'Each Visible Fact Absolutely Expresses Reality' in Breitwieser, Sabine (ed.) *Gustav Metzger: History*, Vienna: Generali Foundation, 67–82.

Index